SACREs
Standing Advisory Councils on Religious Education

Their Formation, Composition, Operation and Role on RE and Worship

Monica J. Taylor

NATIONAL FOUNDATION FOR EDUCATIONAL RESEARCH

A Report of Research Sponsored by the National Curriculum Council
in 1990

Published in 1991
By the National Foundation for Educational Research, The Mere,
Upton Park, Slough, Berkshire, SL1 2DQ.

Registered Charity No. 313392

ISBN 0 7005 1288 8

The cartoon by Gillies originally appeared in The Times Educational Supplement,
29.6.90 (p.62), and is gratefully reproduced by permission of the artist.

Contents

Acknowledgements

The author is indebted to:

the LEA advisers and inspectors with responsibility for RE who responded to the circular and especially to those who generously gave of their hard-pressed time in interview;

Brian Gates (REC), Alan Loosemore, Nick Tate and Barbara Wintersgill (NCC) and Sheila Stoney (NFER) for their interest and advice;

Pauline Benefield for library support, Lesley Kendal for data presentation, Tim Wright for cover design and Enver Carim for publication and publicity; and above all to Jocelyn Simmons and Sue Murphy who cheerfully and patiently typed and painstakingly corrected the report and Mary Hargreaves and Rose James who produced the final DTP version.

Abbreviations in the Text

AA	Assessment arrangement
ACT	Association of Christian Teachers
AEO	Assistant Education Officer
AO	Administrative Officer
AMMA	Assistant Masters and Mistresses Association
AR	Annual Report (SACRE)
AREAI	Association of Religious Education Advisers and Inspectors
ARET	Association of Religious Education Teachers
AS	Agreed Syllabus
ASC	Agreed Syllabus Committee
AT	Attainment target
ATRE	Advisory Teacher for Religious Education
ATREL	Association of Teachers of Religious Education in London
BHA	British Humanist Association
CEM	Christian Education Movement
CEO	Chief Education Officer
CLEA	Council of Local Education Authorities
COTO	Council of Teachers Organizations
CRC	Community Relations Council
CRE	Commission for Racial Equality
CRO	Community Relations Officer
CW	Collective Worship
DCEO	Deputy Chief Education Officer
DES	Department of Education and Science
DoE	Director of Education
ERA	Education Reform Act
ESG	Education Support Grant
FARE	The Forms of Assessment in RE Project
FCFC	Free Church Federal Council
FE	Further Education
GRIST	Grant-related In-service Training
HE	Higher Education
HoD	Head of Department
INSET	In-service training
ITT	Initial teacher training

JCC	Joint Consultative Council
KS	Key Stage
LEA	Local Education Authority
LEATGS	LEA Training Grants Scheme
LMS	Local Management Services
MCE	Multicultural Education
NAHT	National Association of Head Teachers
NAS/ UWT	National Association of Schoolmasters/Union of Women Teachers
NATFHE	National Association of Teachers in Further and Higher Education
NCC	National Curriculum Council
NFER	National Foundation for Educational Research
NUT	National Union of Teachers
PACE	Parental Alliance for Choice in Education
PAT	Professional Association of Teachers
PCFRE	Professional Council for Religious Education
PEO	Principal Education Officer
PoS	Programmes of Study
PSE	Personal and Social Education
RC	Roman Catholic
RE	Religious Education
REC	Religious Education Council
SACRE	Standing Advisory Council on Religious Education
SEO	Senior Education Officer
SHA	Secondary Heads' Association
TCC	Teachers' Consultative Committee

Tables and Figures in the Text

The National Context of the Study

SACREs in the National Context for RE

The 1988 Education Reform Act (ERA) placed a statutory duty on every Local Education Authority (LEA) to constitute a Standing Advisory Council on Religious Education (SACRE). For most LEAs this meant drawing together and inaugurating a new body with responsibility to oversee and influence local provision and practice on Religious Education (RE) and Collective Worship (CW). The principal function of the SACRE is:

> *'to advise the authority upon such matters connected with religious worship in county schools and the religious education to be given in accordance with an agreed syllabus as the authority might refer to the council or as the council may see fit.'* (G.B. Statutes. 1988. S.11 (1) (a))

ERA further lays down particular roles for SACRE:

- to require a review of the local Agreed Syllabus (AS) for RE by an Agreed Syllabus Committee (ASC) to be set up by the LEA;

- to consider applications by the headteacher and governing body of any county school as to *'whether it is appropriate for the requirement for Christian collective worship to apply in the case of that school or .... any class or description of pupils at that school'*;

- to consider and advise on particular methods of teaching, the choice of materials and the provision of training for teachers; and

- to publish an annual report on its functions and action particularly specifying any advice, its nature and reasons for giving the advice to the LEA.

ERA also outlined the membership and constituent groups of SACRE which for the first time required the LEA to include

> *'such Christian and other religious denominations as, in the opinion of the authority, will appropriately reflect the principal religious traditions in the area.'* (G.B. Statutes. 1988. S.11 (4) (a))

DES Circular 3/89 (GB.DES. 1989a) gave further advice on the SACRE's functions, composition and proceedings.

SACREs have a specific and wide-ranging curricular remit since they are concerned with statutory provision and practice in education in beliefs and values for all pupils. ERA requires that:

- *'all pupils in attendance at a maintained school shall on each school day take part in an act of collective worship'*; and in a county school collective worship *'shall be wholly or mainly of a broadly Christian character'*, that is, *'if it reflects the broad traditions of Christian belief without being distinctive of any particular Christian denomination'* taken over any school term as a whole (G.B. Statutes. 1988. S.6, S.7 (1),(2),(3));

- every maintained school (county and voluntary including sixth-form colleges and pupils) has to provide a basic curriculum which includes *'provision for religious education for all registered pupils at the school'* alongside the National Curriculum;

- RE is to be in accordance with the local Agreed Syllabus and any AS adopted after ERA *'shall reflect the fact that the religious traditions in Great Britain are in the main Christian whilst taking account of the teaching and practices of the other principal religions represented in Great Britain'* (GB. Statutes. 1988. S.2 (1)(a), S.8 (3)).

With such concerns SACREs occupy a distinctive national (and possibly unique international) position in that they have *local* oversight of RE which has *'special status'* as part of the basic curriculum entitlement of all pupils but not as part of the National Curriculum. According to DES Circular 3/89 (Para 20):

'RE has equal standing in relation to the core and other foundation subjects within a school's curriculum but is not subject to nationally prescribed attainment targets, programmes of study and assessment arrangements.'

However, when drawing up an AS a local ASC *'should assume that there will be a reasonable time available for the study of RE'* and could include attainment targets (ATs), programmes of study (PoS) and assessment arrangements (AAs) in locally determined form. The role of the SACRE in advising on the local implementation and delivery of the AS in relation to RE and of CW is in this respect similar to the national role of the National Curriculum Council (NCC) in relation to the core and other foundation subjects in the National Curriculum. However, the NCC also has recognized responsibilities with respect to RE (but not CW) — to give advice to LEAs on locally determined PoS and ATs, on request.

Whilst for complex interconnected reasons of history, school management, curriculum delivery and monitoring ERA placed RE firmly in the local purlieu of the SACRE, it nevertheless acknowledged the changing religious and cultural background of society as a whole. ERA specifically recognized Christianity as the main religious tradition of the nation and, as such, the need for Christianity to be reflected in RE and in the character of CW. For the first time it also recognized that *'the teaching and practices of the other principal religions represented in Great Britain'* should also form a part of good education for all pupils. Moreover, in prescribing that one of the four constituent groups of SACRE should be composed of representatives of denominations of Christianity other than Church of England and of principal religions *'in the area'* other than Christianity, ERA gave a potential voice to representatives of religious and thereby ethnic minorities on the local management of RE and CW. In so doing, it made statutory provision for local dialogue on education in beliefs and values in a body composed of representatives of different races, cultures and creeds. This study considers, through the perspective of LEA RE advisers and inspectors, how the national framework for RE and CW and the common role and function laid down for SACREs by ERA has been interpreted in the local context of the SACREs' first year of operation.

Aims of the Study

Previous research, undertaken under the auspices of the National Foundation for Education Research/Religious Education Council (NFER/REC) in the autumn of 1988, when RE advisers and inspectors were assimilating the implications of ERA and attempting to implement its requirements, indicated that RE advisers perceived SACREs as a key emerging issue. Since relatively few LEAs had pre-existing SACREs in operation, advisers were centrally involved in their establishment and servicing (Taylor, 1989). The questionnaire survey also revealed both a diversity of interpretation of ERA on RE and CW and a lack of clarity about LEAs' responsibility and schools' provision and practices.

The present study aimed to build on previous work to investigate the role and function of SACREs at a critical initial stage in their operation and to examine their influence on the local profile of RE and CW in the light of recent legislation. Through the perspectives of RE advisers and inspectors, emerging issues in SACRE formation, composition, operation, policy and concerns, in LEA resourcing for SACRE and, in turn, its support to the LEA and schools, could be highlighted. It was also an opportunity to monitor advisers' perceptions of change in RE at a time of considerable national innovation in education as a whole. A further intention was that the study would serve as a complementary context — of breadth and depth — for an analysis of the first annual SACRE reports due to be received by NCC (NCC, 1991). The research report which follows therefore represents the first national evaluation of SACREs and may form a baseline against which to monitor future developments in their role and functioning.

Research Methodology

The research comprised two main aspects: a circular to RE advisers/inspectors in all English LEAs; and in-depth interviews with RE advisers/inspectors and other LEA officers involved with the functioning of their local SACRE in a representative sample of LEAs.

The Circular

In view of the previous lengthy questionnaire survey and in recognition of the wide responsibilities of RE advisers and inspectors in relation to RE and often to other curricular, pastoral, INSET and assessment matters (see Taylor, 1989, pp. 8-12 and p.190) it was decided, in the first instance, to send a brief circular requesting certain basic factual information and relevant documentation which could be easily provided. Accordingly, early in April 1990, a covering letter explaining the background and purpose of the study was sent to Chief Education Officers (CEOs) and Directors of Education (DoEs) in 107 English LEAs, covered by the NCC, with a request to pass on a letter and the circular to the RE adviser/inspector named in the Association for Religious Education Advisers and Inspectors' (AREAI) *Directory of LEA Religious Education Advisers and Inspectors 1989-90,* with encouragement to respond using the enclosed reply paid address label.

The initial circular proforma requested:
- date of the formation of the SACRE;
- dates of meetings of SACRE in 1989-90;
- list(s) of the composition of the local SACRE (marked with the affiliations of the representatives);

- a copy of any local statement about the role and function of SACRE;
- a copy of the Agreed Syllabus;
- a copy of local guidelines;
- and whether the respondent would be prepared to be interviewed about the local SACRE.

Towards the end of May a reminder letter was despatched to non-responding RE advisers/inspectors, informing them of the generally encouraging response, reassuring them of an awareness that SACREs were at different stages of development and operation, and requesting their co-operation. In mid-July further attempts were made by telephone to contact the remaining minority of non-respondents. This provided some relevant background information: that, in addition to appointments of RE advisers/inspectors still being made in the newly constituted Inner London Boroughs, several LEAs appeared to have no adviser/inspector with specific responsibility for RE or were in the process of changing personnel with such responsibility. As a final attempt to maximize the response rate, at the end of August a further request for response by 10.9.90 was sent to the remaining few non-respondents with a slightly modified circular proforma, revised in the light of earlier responses. This additionally requested minutes of meetings of SACRE since its inception in 1988/9, a copy of its Annual Report if available, and specified local statements and guidelines on CW. The majority of responses to the circular were received by the end of June, a few arrived during the summer period and one or two by the deadline of mid-September. During the autumn one or two additional circular responses were received, but were too late to be included in the analysis.

Table 1 indicates the number and percentage of respondents to the circular by LEA type, according to the AREAI directory classification. **Overall there was a response to the circular from 88 out of 107 English LEAs, a response rate of 82 per cent.** This is a good response rate and tends to justify the initial approach of requesting basic factual data which could be easily supplied. There was little difference in the percentage response between the three main LEA types (Counties 85 per cent, Metropolitan Districts 83 per cent and London Boroughs 78 per cent). Within the London Boroughs the lower response of 67 per cent of Inner London Boroughs was due to recent reorganization and lack of RE advisers/ inspectors in post. Within the Metropolitan Districts there was again a much lower response rate from Merseyside. Interestingly, the majority of non-respondents were Labour-led LEAs (63 per cent, 12/19) (see Table 10).

Table 1   LEAs responding to the circular and where interviews were conducted

LEA Type	Respondents to Circular			Interviews		
	N	N by 10.9.90	% of Total LEAs	N 10.5 - 30.7.90	% of Total Response	% of Total LEAs
Counties	39	33	85	12	36	31
London Boroughs	32	25	78	6	24	19
Inner	12	8	67	2	25	17
Outer	20	17	85	4	24	20
Metropolitan Districts	36	30	83	10	33	28
Greater Manchester	10	9	90	3	33	30
Merseyside	5	2	40	1	50	20
S. & W. Yorkshire	9	9	100	3	33	33
Tyne and Wear	5	4	80	1	25	20
W. Midlands	7	6	86	2	33	29
Total	107	88	82	28	32	26

In the overwhelming majority of cases respondents were RE advisers and inspectors, but a few responses came from the clerk to SACRE, a (senior) education or administrative officer in the LEA, or occasionally via the DoE or CEO. Respondents did not appear to have particular problems about supplying information requested. However, subsequent analysis revealed less clarity about, for example, affiliations of representatives in the SACRE group and local statements about the SACRE. In addition, by the deadline three LEAs sent their SACRE's first Annual Report (AR), instead of responding to the circular, and from these it was possible to gain some data for analysis, for example, on SACRE membership. Thus the maximum number of SACREs for which data are available is 91; but, because a full breakdown of membership affiliation or status was not always given, the available N is variable.

The Interview

The second phase of the research involved in-depth interviews with RE advisers and inspectors. The sample selected was an opportunity sample which was influenced by several pragmatic considerations as well as certain pre-established selection criteria. In the first instance sampling was limited by the number and flow of responses to the circular which, as indicated, continued over a period of six months and were lacking in some LEA types and geographical areas. Secondly, respondents needed to have indicated a willingness to be interviewed; fortunately this was not a constraint as before the end of June fewer than ten respondents (half from County LEAs) indicated that they were not willing to be interviewed. A third factor was the need to undertake interviews between May and the end of the summer term.

The main **selection criteria** included factors relating to:

LEA: a proportionate spread of LEA type; geographical distribution; largely urban, rural and mixed LEAs; local religious and ethnic composition; RE profile (e.g. advisory support, influential AS, current complaints);

SACRE: pre-existing or new SACRE; start time; size; membership (especially composition of Group A and D); indications from meeting minutes or AR of nature of meeting and issues under consideration (e.g.: AS, CW determinations, INSET);

**RE Adviser/
Inspector:** status, responsibilities, length of service; previous response to research questionnaire.

The aim was to achieve a sample with a range of indications on the above factors, especially proportionate spread of LEA type and range of status of respondents. Weighting was given to LEAs with pre-existing SACREs in order to allow comparison of present and previous SACRE operation.

Despite the fact that the overwhelming majority of respondents had indicated a willingness to be interviewed, actually fixing and undertaking the interviews proved slightly more problematic. Advisers/inspectors were sometimes repeatedly difficult to contact by telephone; their time pressures and the time constraints of fieldwork were sometimes difficult to reconcile; and two or three, despite having initially indicated they would be interviewed subsequently declined (due to pressure of work, lack of advisory experience in the LEA and with the SACRE) or were absent when contacted for a telephone interview at an agreed time. Nevertheless most respondents contacted with a request for interview agreed to co-operate.

The achieved sample of interviews is detailed in Table 1. **Interviews in a total of 28 LEAs were undertaken, almost one-third of the LEAs from which circular responses were received and just over one-quarter of the total number of English LEAs.** These proportions were well reflected in LEA type — slightly higher for Counties and lower for London Boroughs. Twelve interviews were undertaken in Counties, six in London Boroughs and ten in Metropolitan Boroughs. LEAs were geographically spread (as indicated in Table 1) and representative of the range of other LEA criteria outlined above. Further details on the local contexts of the study are given in Appendix 1.

A total of 31 people were involved in the interviews; in three LEAs there were two interviewees: in one case where both primary and secondary education advisers had responsibility for RE; in another where both the county general adviser for RE and assistant education officer had responsibility for the SACRE; and in a third with both the inspector with responsibility for RE and the clerk to SACRE (also RE centre co-ordinator). Indeed interviewees' status ranged from advisory teacher for RE (ATRE) to senior county inspector and also included a principal education officer with SACRE responsibilities (see p.183 for further details).

Interviews took place between early May and the end of July. By this time SACREs had received a certain profile of attention in professional circles, nationally, regionally and locally (AREAI, REC, Christian Education Movement/Council for Local Education Authorities (CEM/CLEA) and Saltley Trust conferences). In the LEAs, after the initial phase of setting up and getting SACRE underway, interviewees were in a position to take stock of achievements, needs and likely direction of future work for the SACRE and its role re RE and the LEA. Three-quarters (21) of the interviews were undertaken in person and the remainder (seven — six in Metropolitan LEAs and one in a County) by telephone. In-depth interviews lasted for a least one hour and a quarter and up to four hours; the average interview was over two hours in duration.

The fact that in most cases some, if not a considerable amount of documentation had been acquired in advance enabled the interview to check and build on existing information and perceptions. Additionally, where relevant, the interviewer was able to draw on previous responses to the NFER/REC questionnaire as background information to monitor changes over time, particularly, for example, with respect to expected as opposed to actual applications for determinations.

The interview schedule covered:

1. **Local Background**
(a) the respondents (responsibilities, length of time as adviser, ATREs in relation to SACRE);
(b) LEA background in RE (AS, ASC, pre-existing SACRE, RE monitoring and evaluation);
(c) local religious and ethnic composition; significance of the voluntary sector.

2. **SACRE Composition and Formation**
(a) composition of SACRE and affiliation of members;
(b) selection criteria;
(c) determining representation of 'principal religious traditions in the area';
(d) selection of chairperson and group membership;
(e) representation of RE specialists; Humanists;
(f) duration of membership.

3. **SACRE Operation**
(a) actual working procedures of SACRE (attendance, voting);
(b) meetings (frequency, public?);
(c) LEA communication with SACRE — matters referred;
(d) SACRE communication with LEA — requesting information, giving advice;
(e) SACRE communication with schools about its role and function; obtaining evidence on provision and resources;
(f) consultation with others.

4. **LEA Support to SACRE**
(a) resourcing;
(b) role of RE adviser/inspector in relation to SACRE; time; responding to range of interests;
(c) advisers' perceptions of local status and influence of SACRE.

5. **Policy and Concerns of SACRE**

(a)   policy framework and SACRE's involvement in CW determinations and complaints procedures;

(b)   issues raised by schools, parents, member organizations;

(c)   issues in organization and teaching RE (e.g. hourage, staffing, INSET);

(d)   RE in relation to cross-curricular themes and CW.

6. **SACRE's Annual Report**

(a)   audience;

(b)   who writes?;

(c)   nature and structure;

(d)   use;

(e)   likely recommendations;

(f)   likely time of availability of Report.

7. **SACRE's Future Role**

(a)   current constraints;

(b)   promising lines of development.

8. **Other Matters**

(a)   any other issues identified by interviewee;

(b)   collection of local documents.

Interviewees appeared to be open, frank and to enjoy the opportunity for reflection about their SACRE in relation to RE and the LEA. There was little perceptible difference in interviews conducted in person or by telephone; if anything the latter seemed to liberate more disclosures. Many spontaneously welcomed the NCC's demonstration of interest in RE by sponsoring the research and also revealed an interest in knowing more about other SACREs and their operation. However, some interviewees' co-operation was tinged with caution and circumspection which might be taken to indicate a certain insecurity with respect to their role vis à vis SACRE. Several interviews were characterized by 'off the record' remarks which had 'political' connotations; one or two felt that the Chair of SACRE would not have approved the interview and that the Chair's perspective would have been quite different. Some wished to emphasize that the research came at a very early stage in the evolution of SACRE. One or two interviewees expressed concern that the timing of the previous NFER/REC research report, which indicated lack of clarity and diversity of initial interpretation of ERA in relation to RE and CW, may have been to the detriment of RE's status. Due to a certain underlying concern about confidentiality and the ease of identification of interviewees, LEAs where interviews were conducted are not therefore listed.

Available Documentation

A considerable amount of additional documentation, as requested in the circular and in interview, was received.

It was clear from circular responses that the amount of available local documentation varied considerably; for example, advisers fairly frequently indicated that the AS was under review (see p.78) or out of print and that guidelines on CW were in production (see p.138). Interestingly, some circular respondents sent unsolicited copes of SACRE meeting agenda or minutes which provided helpful insights. By comparison, a few interviewees who were otherwise co-operative, felt unable or were subsequently unable to obtain permission (from other LEA officers or the SACRE) to send supporting documentation requested; in one case local sensitivity had been raised due to apparent leakage of information about current work on revisions to the AS. However, many other interviewees kindly sent useful further documentation post-interview.

SACRE ARs and ASs in particular continued to arrive during the writing period. Documents received from each LEA could include: circular response, AS, list of SACRE members, SACRE meeting minutes, statements on the role and function of SACRE, standing orders, terms of reference or constitution, AR, guidelines on RE and CW, letters to schools from the LEA, newspaper cuttings on the SACRE. The main documents are listed in Table 2.

The following analysis thus draws on three main research sources: circular responses, in-depth interviews and supportive documentation used to amplify and check certain data. This initial study did not permit an analysis of the actual operation of SACRE meetings or of perspectives of a cross-section of SACRE members. Indeed, the kind invitation to observe one SACRE meeting, which occurred on the day of interview in one LEA, served to confirm how illuminating such research could be. A case study of models of SACRE operation and related LEA processes could prove revealing of the emerging issues, constraints and decision making on provision and practice in CW and RE and of developments over time.

Table 2   Main additional documentation

LEA Type	Available N	Agreed Syllabus	AS	Collective Worship Guidelines Handbooks	SACRE Annual Reports	SACRE Meeting Minutes	SACRE Inform-ation
Counties	33	24	11	14	11	17	13 R & F 2 TR 8 C
London Boroughs							
Inner	8	+	-	2	2	6	3 R & F 1 SO 3 C
Outer	17	14	4	6	9	6	3 R & F 9 C
Metro-politan Boroughs	30	18	8	10	15	11	5 R & F 1 SO 3 TR 16 C
Total	88	56	23	32	37	40	24 R & F 2 SO 5 TR 36 C

R & F = Role and Function
SO   = Standing Orders
TR   = Terms of Reference
C   = Constitution
+   Due to recent local reorganization new Inner London Boroughs were currently considering whether to adopt the old ILEA AS or produce their own.

SACRE Formation

Pre-existing SACREs

In a previous NFER/REC survey of RE advisers and inspectors in the autumn of 1988 (Taylor, 1989) one-third of respondents (20/61 LEAs; 104 LEAs in England and Wales) claimed that their LEA had a SACRE. It appeared that these SACREs already undertook many of the activities now required of the mandatory SACREs by ERA (see p.1). SACREs most often oversaw the implementation of the AS, production of handbooks and materials and INSET provision, though they were less likely to be involved in giving advice on worship or producing an annual report. Some RE advisers predicted more frequent meetings of the SACRE post-ERA, that they themselves would be more closely involved in advising and servicing it and that applications for determinations on school worship were likely to be a time-consuming concern. Many advisers envisaged the SACRE changing from a discussion group to a decision-making body and that its role and influence would be increased.

In the 1990 survey of English LEAs 18 out of 88 (20 per cent) respondents to the circular indicated that their LEA had had a SACRE (or equivalent body with broad, not exclusively professional membership, such as a Standing Consultative Committee) prior to 1988. The oldest SACRE dated from 1940 and the most recent, established pre-ERA, dated from 1986. One-third had been in existence since the 1970s. The Counties (10) were more likely to have had a pre-existing SACRE than either the Metropolitan Boroughs (5) or the Outer London Boroughs (3).

Of the sample of LEAs where RE advisers/inspectors were interviewed nine out of 28 (32 per cent) had pre-existing SACREs (six Counties, one Outer London Borough, two Metropolitan Boroughs). Indeed, this was a criterion for interview, in order to compare perceptions of previous and current SACREs, their roles, functioning, concerns and influence. Most of the pre-existing SACREs were set up after the completion of the work of a local ASC. Half of these SACREs had been in continuous existence since the 1970s, and, in one or two cases, under the regulations of ERA, they were being reconstituted for the third time. Most RE advisers/inspectors in LEAs with pre-existing SACREs spoke of their usefulness and support to RE.

A ten-year-old SACRE in one County was seen as in partnership with the LEA, elected members, advisers and officers. Originally a continuation of the ASC, it had overseen the production of a three-volume handbook of guidance on age-related themes for the AS. On each unit there had been considerable debate within SACRE, both between denominational representatives and concerning equal opportunity issues. This had been enjoyed as a learning experience.

Another County SACRE had, since 1974, supported working groups to develop thinking and produce papers on provision and class practice for primary, secondary and post-16 RE and collective worship. It had also sponsored a Mode 3 O-level and a Mode 2 A-level in RE.

A Metropolitan SACRE of ten years standing and 28 meetings had been effective in promoting good and lasting community relationships. It held a series of public meetings with speakers from the LEA, HMI and local teacher training institutions which promoted questions and open discussion.

In many of the LEAs with pre-existing SACREs ERA was seen as giving the SACRE a *'new lease of life'*. Although one or two LEAs regarded it as an opportunity to set up a new structure, **in most cases at least some continuity of membership was considered important**. Where previous and current SACRE membership lists were available it was clear that in some cases relatively minor changes had been made, for example, that LEA officers were no longer **members** of SACRE. In the newly constituted Inner London Boroughs there was not necessarily any prospect of continuity of membership and experience with the erstwhile ILEA SACRE. But in LEAs which had relatively recently hosted an ASC there was evidence of the transfer of many members to the new SACRE and instances where an influential Chair of ASC subsequently became Chair of SACRE. Similarly, some advisers reported considerable continuity in the constitution and operation of the previous and new SACREs. Generally the perceived value of the erstwhile SACREs contrasted with the view expressed by two or three advisers that in their LEAs the statutory requirement by ERA to constitute a SACRE had *'come as a shock, and had not previously been thought necessary'* or, indeed, *'was not wished'*.

New SACREs: Approaches to their Formation, Size and Representation

Neither ERA (GB. Statutes, 1988) nor the DES Circular 3/89 (GB.DES, 1989a) gave guidance as to the formation of the now statutory SACREs, even though for the majority of LEAs this meant bringing together such a body for the first time. The DES Circular only indicated that LEAs should *consult locally* before appointments to the four component groups were made and that *'the LEA must take all reasonable steps to assure itself that the persons so appointed are representative, as the case may be, of the denominations or associations in question'*. It therefore seemed appropriate in interviews with RE advisers/inspectors to review the local processes of formation of the SACRE as a whole and the overall criteria for selection of representatives. Moreover, given the innovative nature of Group A, *'such Christian and other religious denominations as, in the opinion of the authority, will appropriately reflect the principal religious traditions of the area'*, which was likely to prove controversial in its formation and composition, the process of determining and the criteria for reflecting the principal religious traditions of the area were aspects for particular focus.

Several interviewees reported that an AREAI conference, which had included discussion of how to set up a SACRE and draft a constitution, had proved helpful. The REC Handbook (REC, 1989a) also offered an *aide memoire* and suggestions regarding consultation. Otherwise, in the absence of more specific national or professional guidelines, it was open to individual LEAs to set in motion their own procedures for the SACRE's formation. Not surprisingly, LEAs differed in their approaches which depended on the combination of several factors. Several LEAs in the sample started from the drafting of a constitution which detailed membership to be approved by the Education Committee. Elsewhere such a document was produced 'after the event' as a codification of practice. Some RE advisers/inspectors saw the actual process of setting up the SACRE as crucial to its credibility; others reported a more pragmatic approach: *'we've got to do it, so let's get on and do it'*. In several LEAs with a current SACRE or recent ASC there was an opportunity to rethink the SACRE composition. Sometimes this resulted in disbanding the original SACRE and deliberately setting out afresh to form a certain group. Elsewhere there was a concern to ensure continuity, especially of committed attendees and those with an understanding of RE, and in these cases it was more a matter of members choosing to opt out and not continue.

Thus there were two main criteria implicit in the formation of SACREs after the 1988 Act: first, the extent to which the overall composition was predetermined by the LEA or whether it was responsive and flexible in relation to emerging interests and nominations; and, secondly, the degree of emphasis on and balance between the size of the SACRE and its representativeness. These considerations were generally seen as particularly pertinent to Group A.

In several LEAs sampled the RE Adviser/Inspector, sometimes in conjunction with an advisory/inspectorial colleague or administrative or executive officer, was responsible for drafting an initial paper on SACRE composition and formation, for discussion by LEA officers or the Education Committee. However, this did not always result in the RE adviser's advice being taken. For example:

- in one LEA the adviser wrote a paper on membership and numbers for discussion with the DCEO. It was decided to wind up the existing SACRE and reconstitute one with a wider range of members. Even so the adviser would have liked more representatives of the other Christian denominations in Group A, to include a Quaker and a Humanist. However, under the Act the SACRE was perceived to have become more political, with the inclusion, in Group D, of LEA officers and elected members, and this in itself affected perceptions of appropriate SACRE composition;

- elsewhere a senior assistant DoE wrote a paper on SACRE formation but without any consultation with the RE adviser to whom it appeared as an administrative exercise, undertaken without forward planning and without involving educational criteria.

A particular characteristic of SACREs in some sample LEAs which operated by a predetermined view of the composition and size of the SACRE was that of the mathematical model or formula. (Analysis of circular returns confirmed a relatively high proportion of SACREs had equal numbers of members in two, if not three, of the four constituent groups and that this was especially likely in the County SACREs (see p.28). Interviews revealed that parity of numbers across groups could be used as part of an equal opportunities philosophy — being perceived as psychologically important that one group was not seen to outnumber another. However, it was much more likely that the mathematical model was used for 'administrative neatness' without any justificatory rationale and without realization of the inbuilt inequality in the representation of the groups. Interviews suggested that mathematical models were most likely to have been implemented where a senior LEA officer, the Education Committee or the SACRE Chair who was an elected member, had a decisive role. The point of interest was to what extent such predetermined numbers were subsequently open to modification as a result of applications from interested parties, whether they were dealt with by co-option, or resisted.

This issue related to the view taken locally of the desirable size of the SACRE overall. Interviews also revealed a general awareness of the need to balance size against representativeness, especially in relation to the extent of membership of Group A. **In the sample of 28 LEAs there was a fairly even trend towards size or size and representativeness as the main criterion for formation of the SACRE. A few LEAs favoured representativeness above all. Metropolitan LEAs tended to use size as the criterion, Counties either size or size and representativeness and London Boroughs favoured representativeness.**

Size — a smaller SACRE was often perceived as likely to be more co-operative and manageable. In practice, the overall size of the SACRE, especially where a mathematical model was followed, was sometimes determined by the number in Group C (teachers) or D (LEA), which were usually perceived as less problematic. In some cases SACRE size seemed related to local issues of control: for example, senior education officers and elected members were sometimes said to want a small inactive SACRE and to limit the representation of religions other than Christianity where the LEA was 'wary' about (the absence of) its multicultural/antiracist policy or its attitude to minority ethnic communities. Indeed, SACRE size could be sensitive to political change. For example, numbers in one of the largest SACREs were originally approved by the Education Committee, which also subsequently decided to increase the LEA group. With a change in local political control LEA membership was reduced and there was a proposal to cut the group overall and particularly the numbers of Group A, which currently allowed for representation of denominations within religions other than Christianity — thus countering the local equal opportunities tradition.

Size and Representativeness — this approach attempted to balance these two factors so as to arrive at a group which was more or less representative but of a size to form a working group, rather than a formal body. Unlike the mathematical model, there was no explicit formula by which such an equation could be achieved — it was essentially one of qualitative judgement based on knowledge of the locality and relative aspects of representativeness. For example, one adviser reported criteria such as weighting according to numbers of members in a diocese or religious group, bodies which expressed an interest, and those having a philosophy in accordance with the aims and objectives of the LEA curriculum policy, such as breadth and a valuing of critical openness, thus excluding representation of evangelical groups. Another LEA which requested information on the size of congregation, effectively excluded Humanists and also Quakers because of small meeting numbers.

Representativeness — was based on an overriding principle to be fair to all local associations and communities and was sometimes related to a strong local equal opportunities tradition. In some cases there was a deliberate attempt, occasionally enshrined in the constitution, to ensure that the non-Christian membership of Group A outnumbered that of the members of Christian denominations other than Church of England (see p.36). Sometimes this required persistence to achieve: for example, in one LEA the then ruling political group initially directed that the SACRE should be as small as practicable; but through the persistence of the RE inspector, the consultation process itself, a previous large ASC and perceived needs and interests of the local communities, a body of double the size, with most of the increase in Group A, was eventually allowed on the basis of the established tradition of good relations and trust. In LEAs where representativeness was the overriding criterion there was often sensitivity to minorities, whether they were members of religions other than Christianity or denominations within Christianity other than Church of England. Thus places on SACRE were offered not in relation to the extent of membership of principal religious traditions of the area or other Christian denominations, but on the basis of the existence of these communities and associations locally.

Another aspect of representativeness was that of knowledge and experience of education; in setting up SACREs some had regarded it as important to have strong educational representation or even experience of RE in all SACRE's constituent groups (not just in Group C, as suggested by the DES Circular); whereas in others this, if achieved, had been incidental.

Determining the Principal Religious Traditions of the Area

Determining Group A *'such Christian and other religious denominations* [which].... *reflect the principal religious traditions in the area'* has been in many LEAs a major concern of RE advisers/inspectors and a cause of initial, and sometimes continuing, controversy. The REC Handbook (9.2.1) suggested channels for consultation and the need to contact representative bodies, if necessary at their own locations and in languages other than English, to obtain nominations from within the faith community. Interviews revealed a wide variation in approach and state of preparedness for such a task by LEAs. In several cases local religious groups were already well known to long-serving RE advisers/inspectors. But elsewhere there was an absence of local knowledge. Some *'looked around and saw'*; others enlisted the help of the multicultural education (MCE) adviser or Community Relations Officer (CRO); but any existing local surveys were usually in relation to minority ethnic group membership and not specifically religious affiliation. A few RE advisers/inspectors interviewed were unaware of the processes of consultation as this had occurred before taking up their appointment; but one or two had themselves found determining representation of the principal religious traditions of the area a mysterious process. Some, however, had made impressive and extensive efforts at democratic consultation.

The nature and extent of local consultation with bodies representing Christian denominations other than Church of England and faiths other than Christianity varied considerably:

- occasionally interviewees reported there had been no serious attempt at local consultation;

- a few acknowledged that consultation had been selective; the religions or denominations to be represented had been predetermined. Where the religious groups were already known sometimes the individual representative was hand-picked; interestingly, in cases where consultation or checking with local religious bodies occurred this was most likely to be mentioned in connection with Jewish groups who, although often acknowledged not to be numerous, were seen to be deserving of representation;

- in some cases where there was ignorance of local groups advertisements were placed in the press inviting nominations; soundings were also taken amongst local community groups; although these were '*not crisply systematic*' a consensus emerged;

- **in the majority of cases in the interview sample wide consultation occurred, the process depending on existing local knowledge of relevant bodies or whether this was in itself a prior research activity;** subsequently nominations were invited and either selected or ratified, depending on whether the LEA wanted the religious groups to be represented on SACRE and if it saw the religious body as responsible for delegating its own representative.

The following examples illustrate interesting types of consultation.

First, in relation to **establishing the principal local religions as a basis for consultation:**

- occasionally advisers went to local headteachers to discover the religious backgrounds of children in school;

- sometimes in co-operation with MCE advisers or a CRO who undertook local surveys of faith groups or made direct contact with local religious or community leaders and obtained nominees. This could result in the nomination of '*worthy citizens*' with a '*high political profile*' and occasionally their religious credentials were queried; or the RE adviser could subsequently write to or visit the faith groups requesting nominations and a paragraph of personal information.

Secondly, **where there was existing information on or channels of communication** with the range of local religious bodies there was direct contact by the RE adviser by writing, personal visits or through meetings.

For example:

- in one LEA a letter was sent to all local religious organizations listed in a community action group in each of the four borough areas, informing them of and asking about their interest in the SACRE. The organizations (recently represented on the ASC) were automatically put on the SACRE, so it was a question of opting out rather than in. This resulted in a large SACRE, although some organizations failed to send a representative to meetings;

- in at least three cases, where there were already strong local contacts with local religious groups through a recent ASC or the RE adviser/inspector and a deeply held view that religious bodies which wished to be represented should be enabled to do so, such organizations were invited by letter or visit to a pre-meeting or RE developmental conference at which the nature and function of SACRE was explained. In these cases the LEA outlined ideas about the size of and representation on SACRE and the bodies present were invited to comment and make their own nominations. This indicated responsive flexibility. It tended to generate a larger representation than originally intended, but allowed for representation by denominations of Christianity and other world religions as requested, and representatives who were the responsibility of the nominating body. Even so, it appears that in many cases proposed names of SACRE members went to Education Committee for approval.

The process of consultation to determine the principal religious traditions of the area and their representation on SACRE gave rise to several **conceptual and practical issues.**

What counts as a religious group?

It is important to note that this is not the same kind of question as 'Is this a religious group which we want to be represented on the SACRE?' Rather it raises the question as to how a religious group is to be defined — at least for the purposes of a SACRE. For example, should national associations (e.g. Indian, Bangladeshi) or cultural and welfare associations (e.g. Sikh or Pakistani welfare associations) count as religious groups for the purpose of membership of Group A, as in a few SACREs?

What does it mean to represent a religion?

In certain cases, due to factionalism within a religious group or the existence of a few similar denominational groups within the area, it was sometimes difficult to obtain a nominee who enjoyed the support of the religious group as a whole. In these cases it was all the more important that the nomination should emanate from the faith community. However, even though ERA enjoined upon an LEA the obligation to '*take all reasonable steps to assure itself that the persons so appointed are representative ... of the denominations or associations in question*' it is by no means clear how LEAs did in fact establish the *bona fides* of nominees. Moreover, what did '*representative*' mean in practice in terms of the deliberations of the SACRE? At least it would seem reasonable for such a representative to be careful of the interests of the faith community in respect of RE. There could be a fine boundary between such a position and promoting a particular religious viewpoint. Interviewees reported that some representatives of certain evangelical and traditional Christian viewpoints and of some other world religions experienced difficulty in confining themselves to an application to religious education. Others, however, noted a growing understanding of their role.

Which religious bodies should be contacted/represented?
In some cases there was lack of knowledge of the local existence of some religious groups. Conversely, in some localities the existence of several denominational groups of a religion other than Christianity but without an overarching federation or council was perceived as problematic if allowance was only made for one representative of the religion on SACRE. Only a few SACREs allowed for representation of denominations within a world religion other than Christianity (see pp.39-40). In the absence of a local or regional Free Church Federal Council (FCFC) LEAs often went directly to member churches. By comparison, in the case of some groups, e.g. Hindus and Sikhs, it was more likely to be reported that they did not know where to establish contact. Moreover, even though some religious groups (e.g. Jews) were not recognized as numerous locally and did not apply for representation on SACRE contacts were nevertheless pursued. Thus a related issue for some SACREs was how to accommodate 'late' applications and demonstrations of interest if the numerical and religious composition of Group A of SACRE had been predetermined. Across SACREs there were thus certain anomalies: some religious groups were active in promoting and increasing their representation, whereas the claims of other groups to be represented were not recognized, even to the extent of a co-option, though vacancies for a prescribed group could still exist.

What is meant by reflecting the principal religious traditions in the area?
The issue in this case was what counted as the area and whether representation of what were seen as major world religions could be justified in a local SACRE even if their members were not locally numerous. To an extent this paralleled the process of establishing contact with groups, which in some cases was local, metropolitan or regional, whereas in others contact with nationally representative agencies preceded local consultation. Occasionally this became the catalyst for the formation of a local federation which could negotiate with the LEA. In some LEAs equal representation was allowed to world faiths whose affiliates were not locally numerous though they could be nationally. Some advisers felt strongly that the SACRE should comprise representatives of the major religions of the country. Moreover, some representatives (especially Muslims and Humanists) lived out of the LEA area (see p.30 and p. 38).

Commencement of New SACREs

With the exception of SACREs in Inner London Boroughs, whose
starting date was correspondingly later (1.9.89), the legal duty to constitute
a SACRE in all other LEAs commenced from 29.9.88, two months after
ERA received Royal Assent. However, such a short time scale, occurring
at that time of year, did not allow for LEAs to engage in a wide
consultative process and bring together what, for most, was a new and
potentially controversial and influential body. **Available data from 88
LEAs responding to the circular show that overall the start dates ranged
from 9/88 to 2/90, a period of 18** months (irrespective of the later start of
Inner London authorities) (Figure 1). Metropolitan authorities had both
the earliest start date (9/88) and the widest range of start dates (9/88 - 2/
90). By comparison, start dates for SACREs in both Outer London
Boroughs and Counties ranged across one calendar year. The earliest
County SACRE (1/89) was set up some four months after the first
Metropolitan SACRE. Interestingly, the most common commencement
month for SACREs (excluding those in Inner London) was February
1989 — 16 SACREs (18 per cent) — almost six months after the due date.

Figure 1   Range of commencement dates of SACREs

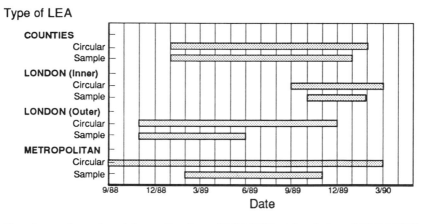

Results are based on information from 88 SACREs (circular) and 28 SACREs
(sample)

22

From the perspective of the research it is thus important to note that, notwithstanding the fact that one-third of the 28 LEAs where interviews took place had had SACREs prior to 1988, in terms of the reconstitution of SACREs under ERA (and irrespective of Inner London authorities) the actual formation, and hence length of time in operation of SACREs ranged over the period of one year (11/88 - 12/89, again most commonly 2/89 in six SACREs (21 per cent)). Thus the experience of SACRE of RE advisers/inspectors interviewed varied correspondingly.

SACRE Composition

SACRE Size and Groups

ERA (S.11(4)) defined the composition of SACREs in terms of four constituent groups:

'(a) *such Christian and other religious denominations as, in the opinion of the authority, will appropriately reflect the religious traditions in the area;*

(b) *.....the Church of England;*

(c) *such associations representing teachers as, in the opinion of the authority, ought, having regard to the circumstances of the area, to be represented; and*

(d) *the authority.'*

In addition (ERA (S.11(3))

'where any agreed syllabus for the time being adopted by the authority is in use at one or more grant-maintained schools, [SACRE should include] a person appointed by the governing body or (as the case may be) by the governing bodies of the school or schools concerned.'

and SACRE may also include co-opted members.

The members of the groups are appointed by the LEA after appropriate consultation and ensuring that persons appointed are representative of the denominations or association (ERA S. 11(4), 13(1)) (see pp.20-21). ERA made no stipulations as to the size of SACRE, but indicated the need for adequate representation given local circumstances. However, although the structure of the composition of SACRE largely reflects that of ASCs, the injunction to include representatives of religions of the area other than Christianity in Group A is a significant departure, officially recognizing the existence of a multifaith Britain. Even though the four constituent groups each have only one vote, the range of membership, in terms of numbers, religious, educational, ethnic, political and other interests within and between groups could be considerable. Depending on the working procedures and climate of the SACRE meeting (see p.63ff) and to what extent individual members were in practice perceived as representing their organization/association, Group or idiosyncratic interests the defined composition of SACRE had the potential to give voice to various perspectives in discussion of the nature of and provision for RE and CW in the locality.

Figure 2   Size of SACREs by type of LEA

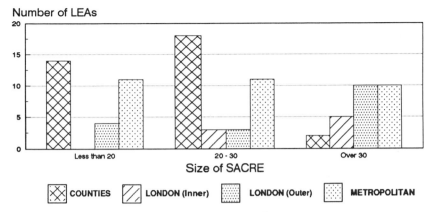

Results are based on information from 91 SACREs

Figure 2 shows that **from available information for 91 SACRES (34 Counties, eight Inner London, 17 Outer London, 32 Metropolitan Boroughs) (85 per cent of 107 English SACREs) the total size of SACREs varied between 12 and 50 members.** Overall SACREs were fairly evenly divided between those with fewer than 20, 20-30 or 30 plus members, although a slightly higher proportion (38 per cent) had 20-30 members. Four SACREs, all in LEAs with a relatively high multiethnic population, had 40 or more members. There was however, some **variation by LEA type:**

Counties had an overall range of 12-37 members and were mainly divided between those with 20-30 members — the majority (52 per cent) — and those with fewer than 20 members (41 per cent);

London Boroughs: although the range of members varied between Inner (20-38) and Outer London Boroughs (17-50) overall they were more likely than other LEA types to have more than 30 members (in 60 per cent of all cases);

Metropolitan Boroughs showed the greatest range in membership (13 - 48) and were evenly divided between those with fewer than 20 members, 20-30 and 30 plus members.

Alternatively, the **range in membership** varied as follows:

fewer than 20 members in 24 per cent of Outer London Boroughs compared with 41 per cent of Counties;

20-30 members: in 18 per cent of Outer London Boroughs compared with 34 per cent of Metropolitan Boroughs and 52 per cent of Counties;

30 plus members: in only six per cent of Counties compared with 31 per cent of Metropolitan Boroughs and 60 per cent of London Boroughs.

The range of SACRE composition may be illustrated by the following examples.

The smallest SACRE, in a County authority, had 12 members, comprising:

Group A (3)	-	one Roman Catholic, one local Council of Churches, one *'representative of non-Christian religions'*;
Group B (3)	-	Church of England (from three dioceses);
Group C (3)	-	teachers nominated by the local teachers' council;
Group D (3)	-	LEA representatives;

Two co-options, one to Group A and one to Group C.

By comparison, **the largest SACRE**, in an Outer London Borough, with 50 members, comprised:

Group A (23)	-	one Roman Catholic, one Greek Orthodox, one Free Church representative, one Afro-West Indian United Council of Churches, one Armenian Community Church, one Baha'i, one Buddhist, four Hindus (two denominations), one Jew, four Muslims, six Sikhs (three denominations), one Humanist;
Group B (6)	-	Church of England;
Group C (12)	-	two NUT, three NAS/UWT, two AMMA, three NAHT, one SHA, one PAT;
Group D (9)	-	local councillors.

A **more typical SACRE**, with 26 members, in a Metropolitan authority comprised:

Group A (9)	-	two Roman Catholics, one Baptist, one Methodist, one United Reformed Church, one New Testament Church of God, one Jew, one Muslim, one Sikh;
Group B (5)	-	Church of England (two from each diocese, one vacancy);
Group C (5)	-	NUT, NAS/UWT, AMA, NAHT, SHA, one representative each (selected by JCC);
Group D (7)	-	seven councillors (four Conservative, two Labour, one Liberal Democrat)

Three observers (two Muslims, one Christadelphian)

Plus officers in attendance - DCEO, specialist adviser Humanities, senior general primary adviser, community relations officer, SACRE clerk - an advisory teacher.

Table 3   Size of constituent SACRE groups by LEA type

LEA Type	Available N	Group A	Group B	Group C	Group D	Overall Total
Counties	34	259	137	173	163	732
London Boroughs						
Inner	8	106	41	47	52	246
Outer	17	177	83	110	103	473
Metropolitan Boroughs	32	313	137	195	160	805
Total	91	855	398	525	478	2256

Table 3 gives a breakdown by constituent groups of SACREs within different types of LEAs. The overall number of members in 91 SACREs for which information was available in mid-September 1990 was 2256. SACREs in London Boroughs, taken as a whole, had the largest average membership (29 members) compared with those in Metropolitan authorities (25) and Counties (22). **Of the four constituent groups, Group A had the largest number of members overall (855) and in each of the LEA types. Group C was the second most numerous overall (525) and Group B had the lowest membership (398).**

As interviews revealed (see p.17) in setting up SACREs LEAs often attempted to bring together a body which was representative and which would not be too unwieldy and unable to work as a whole. The view was expressed that a constituent group membership of three was too small, that five or six would be better. In some LEAs the number suggested or agreed for one of the constituent groups (e.g. Group D, LEA, four, or Group C, teachers, five) could be taken as the base number for the other constituent groups. With the exception of Group A, which was usually more numerous, some LEAs seem deliberately to have worked to a mathematical model and irrespective of other considerations to have decided on equal numbers in all or two of Group B, C and D. The REC Handbook (9.2.2) suggested that representativeness of various interests should be paramount to ensure that different constituencies can have a voice and thus *'many later complaints may be avoided'*.

Indeed, **analysis of 91 SACREs revealed that as many as 59 (65 per cent) had at least two of Group B, C or D with the same number.** The common number of the groups ranged from three to seven, the most popular being five or four (Counties four, London Boroughs six, Metropolitan Boroughs five). **Overall, 20 SACREs had Group B, C and D each with the same number of members.** Interestingly, this was much more likely to apply in Counties (almost one-third, 12) than in London (two) or Metropolitan Boroughs (six). Counties were also more likely to have two constituent groups (of B, C or D) with the same number (almost half, 16) compared with London (11) and Metropolitan Boroughs (12). Thus, overall, as many as four-fifths of SACREs in County authorities, compared with just over half in Metropolitan and London Boroughs, had at least two constituent groups which were numerically equivalent. Four LEAs (two Counties, two Metropolitan Boroughs) seemed to have placed particular weight on numerical parity for the four constituent SACRE groups; ironically, each chose a different number — three, four, five and six — as their base.

This also needs to be seen in the light of the generally greater representation in Group A. **Overall 70 per cent of SACREs** (64/91; 23 Counties, 20 London, 21 Metropolitan Boroughs) **had a Group A membership which was more numerous than that of each of Group B, C or D.** No SACRE had a Group A which was less numerous than any of Group B, C or D. Indeed **seven SACREs** (two Counties, one Inner London Borough, four Metropolitan Boroughs) **had a Group A membership which was equal to (one case) or greater than the sum total of Group B, C and D.** Whilst this would not be significant with respect to voting outcomes it might well influence the working of meetings and perceptions about representation.

A more numerous Group A membership, and to a greater extent a dominant Group A, appeared to be a statement of positive action in favour of securing a representation reflecting the religious traditions of the area. By comparison, it was interesting that some SACRE membership lists received in response to the circular started with Group D, councillors, frequently followed by Group B, Church of England, Group C, Teachers and lastly Group A — which may also be taken as a statement of interest or status. Some interviewees, moreover, expressed some concern and disquiet about SACRE composition:

- one whose SACRE of 19 had no representation of religions other than Christianity felt that the SACRE was teacher- dominated and should be more representative of the community;

28

- one with a SACRE of 14 (Group A, three) also wanted a wider representation on SACRE;
- another was alarmed at the reappraisal and possible reduction in SACRE membership as a result of a change in political control in recent local elections;
- two or three interviewees indicated that due to staffing difficulties in the LEA at the time of SACRE formation its composition did not receive due attention.

In what follows it is convenient to analyse the four constituent groups of SACRE independently, but a number of **overlaps** occurred: of interest and background within SACRE; of membership between SACRE and ASC in the LEA; and of membership with other SACREs in adjacent LEAs.

Within a SACRE

Overlaps of religious affiliation and educational experience in various sectors of education; for example, several SACREs had Group A or B members who were also teachers; one Group A included an LEA advisory teacher in a discipline related to RE, and two HE lecturers, one Hindu, one Muslim.

Overlaps of educational experience and religious affiliation — members of Group C and D in addition to being professional or political representatives could also have firm religious beliefs; for example, one SACRE chair was a well known Roman Catholic and augmented the RC representation.

Overlaps of ethnic background and educational experience — some SACREs included (usually in Group A) members of minority ethnic groups (Muslim, Hindu, Sikh) who were also teachers, sometimes of RE.

Overlaps of political interest and religious affiliation or educational experience — for example, a Group A member who was also a member of Education Committee; a Group C member who was also Chair of Education Committee.

Thus representatives could often have more than one dimension of interest.

Between SACRE and ASC

Membership was often automatically transferred (unless the representatives opted out) from SACRE to ASC where a local ASC was constituted in parallel to the SACRE to revise the AS. This could make heavy expectations and demands on members. Often the ASC was augmented by additional teacher members.

Between SACRE and SACRE

There were overlaps of membership, with for example: one prominent Muslim academic serving on two neighbouring LEA SACREs; one Church of England diocesan representative on at least three SACREs in the diocese; one Jain on two contiguous SACREs; one Humanist appearing on several SACRE lists in the London area. These overlaps suggested factors other than local representation came into play in SACRE composition.

Group A

Group A was usually both the largest and most diverse group. Neither ERA nor DES Circular 3/89 gave specific guidance as to how LEAs should set about determining *'the Christian and other religious denominations, as ...... will appropriately reflect the principal religious traditions in the area'.* However, the REC Handbook made some practical suggestions about channels of communication whilst emphasizing that nominees should be knowledgeable about education, representative of a denomination and not of a council (as such an organization might cover several Christian or other denominations), and sufficiently numerous to be representative of interests (ordained and lay) of the various churches and other religious *'denominations'.* The statutory rubric for Group A did, however, offer pause for thought both to LEAs setting up new SACREs from the beginning and to those with pre-existing SACREs. For the latter it could occasionally mean a continuation of its earlier wider-ranging membership or, more often, especially in less multiethnic areas, an opportunity to rethink and extend its membership to include representatives of world religions other than Christianity or denominations of Christianity.

Table 4 shows that **Group A varied widely between as few as three and as many as 24 members.** This was by far the widest variation in membership of the four constituent groups of SACRE and the group over which there was least uniformity. However, almost half (43/91) SACREs had from five to nine members in Group A. Five or eight members were the most frequent numbers for Group A, especially in County and Outer London SACREs. Metropolitan authorities tended towards six members. As already mentioned (see p.28), in each LEA type there was a strong trend (in over two-thirds of SACREs) for Group A membership to be more numerous than that of each of Group B, C or D. Moreover, in a few SACREs Group A outnumbered the total membership of Group B, C and D (see p.28). The total number of Group A members across 91 SACREs was 855 — 38 per cent of total SACRE members.

Table 4   Group A: total other Christian denominations and other religions represented on SACREs

LEA Type	Available N	Total Group A	Range	Most Frequent
Counties	34	259	3-18	5 or 8
London Boroughs				
Inner	8	106	9-18	equal
Outer	17	177	5-23	8
Metropolitan Boroughs	32	313	4-24	6
Total	91	855	3-24	5 or 8

Further analysis of available information on Group A composition for 86 SACREs (33 Counties, eight Inner London, 16 Outer London and 29 Metropolitan Boroughs) in Figure 3 shows that **overall the number of representatives of the Free Churches** (e.g. Baptist Union, Methodist Churches) (276) **and other Christian denominations** (e.g. Roman Catholic, Orthodox Churches) (187) **was greater than that of representatives of religions other than Christianity** (370). This overall dominance of representatives of Christian denominations in Group A however is largely due to their proportionately greater presence in County (62 per cent) and to a lesser extent Metropolitan authorities (54 per cent).

By contrast, in London Boroughs the number of representatives of Christian denominations and religions other than Christianity in Group A was very similar. **Counties and Metropolitan Boroughs showed the greatest contrasts in Group A:** whereas Counties overall had more representatives of the Free Churches than of other Christian denominations or religions other than Christianity, Metropolitan authorities overall had more representatives of religions other than Christianity than of other Christian denominations or the Free Churches. Nine SACREs had more representatives of Christian denominations other than those from the Free Churches and 18 SACREs had an equal number.

Figure 3   Constituent groups of Group A membership

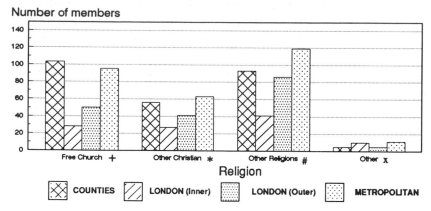

Results are based on information from 86 SACREs

+   Free Church includes: African and Afro-Caribbean Churches, Baptist Union, Free Church of England, Methodist Churches, Salvation Army, United Reformed Church

*   Other Christian Denominations include: Orthodox Church, Pentecostal Churches, Roman Catholic Church

Other religions include: Baha'i, Buddhism, Hinduism, Islam, Judaism, Sikhism

x   Other includes: Humanists, CRC, welfare and cultural groups

The Free Church representation was calculated on the basis of Free Church Federal Council (FCFC) membership formally listed in its 1988-9 Annual Report. Free Church representatives ranged from one to eight (in Metropolitan Boroughs) although they more usually numbered up to five (Counties) or six (London Boroughs). **The majority of SACREs (50/86, 58 per cent) had either three or four Free Church representatives.** But 27 (31 per cent) of SACREs (nine Counties, seven London and 11 Metropolitan Boroughs) had only one or two Free Church representatives. There seemed some variation at local level as to which representatives were formally counted as within the FCFC, for example some of the 'evangelical' or 'black' churches. But further analysis of Free Church membership which was possible for 62 SACREs (23 Counties, eight Inner London, 14 Outer London and 17 Metropolitan Boroughs) showed that the Methodist Church, Baptist Union and United Reformed Church were most likely to have representatives (see Figure 4). There was an appropriate and proportionately high, but nevertheless small, representation of African and Afro-Caribbean Churches in SACREs in Inner London Boroughs. With the exception of the Methodists (up to three), the range of members of a particular Free Church denomination never exceeded two, but membership was usually only one. Occasionally representatives were listed as belonging to a Council rather than a specific denomination.

An earlier analysis of SACRE membership undertaken for the FCFC Education Committee (Marratt, 1990) which indicated a slightly lower representation of the Free Churches, expressed concern that *'there is ignorance of the variety of Free Church denominations or the commitment of their adherents to the county school system'*. Moreover, it suggested that *'there is no logical reason why LEAs should not similarly extend the numbers on Committee A of SACRE to ensure that it is an appropriate reflection of the area, whether this be of the Free Churches or of other religions'*. Later interviews with RE advisers/inspectors suggested that there had been *'some lobbying nationally and locally'* to increase the Free Church representation.

Figure 4   Free Church representatives on SACREs

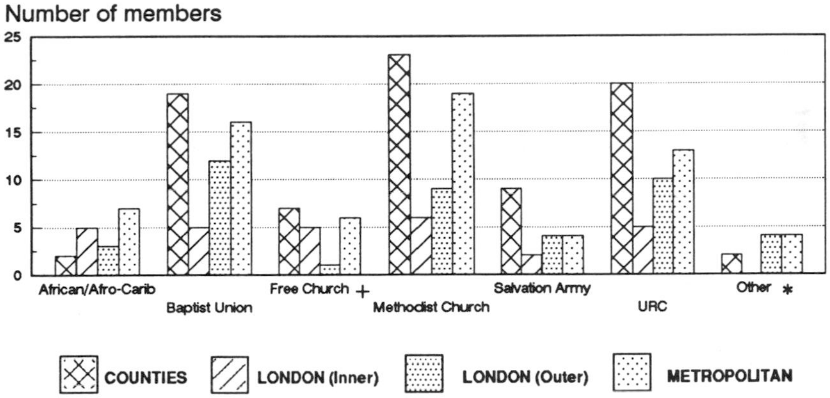

Results are based on information from 62 SACREs

+   Free Church used in the specific sense of Free Church of England, not generically Free Church Federal Council

*   Other includes, for example, Congregational Federation

The REC Handbook had noted that *'since denominational regions are rarely coterminous with LEAs'*, the national FCFC office might be approached to co-ordinate nominations. Advisers interviewed indicated that local co-ordination of FC nomination varied and occasionally concern was expressed that nominees did not appear to represent the principal Free Churches of the area. This remained an issue even if they had backgrounds in religious education. Unfortunately, this initial study of SACREs did not extend to exploring the criteria for nomination with the various nominating bodies.

Figure 5   Christian denominations other than within the Free Church Federal Council

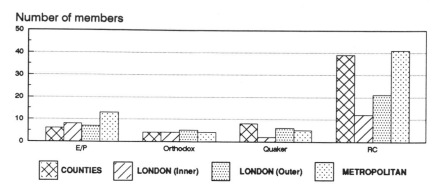

Results are based on information from 83 SACREs

E/P Evangelical/Pentecostal

An analysis of representatives of Christian denominations other than those affiliated to the FCFC for a total of 83 SACREs (30 Counties, eight Inner London, 16 Outer London and 29 Metropolitan Boroughs) with available information is given in Figure 5. **Roman Catholicism was most likely to be represented: each of these 83 SACREs had at least one RC representative;** this was the usual number, although RC representation ranged from one to three and Inner London SACREs were as likely to have two representatives as one RC representative.   Roman Catholic representatives (113) outnumbered those of any of the constitutive denominations of the FCFC, although the overall representation of the Free Churches as a whole was greater (276). Thirteen SACREs had the same number of Roman Catholic representatives as those of the Free Churches. The relatively high representation of Roman Catholicism on SACREs probably reflects the representation of Roman Catholicism as a local religion rather than the relationship between Roman Catholic schools and their adoption of the local AS. Indeed, some advisers argued against proportionately greater representation of Roman Catholicism as RC schools were not involved in implementing the AS. Interview data also indicated that the representation of more than one RC in well over one-quarter of SACREs (24/83 cases) may have been related to the fact that an LEA could be in more than one diocese. Occasionally it was said RC representatives showed little interest in SACRE. Yet in a few cases the Catholic Church was reported to have disputed its numerical allocation in relation to the number of representatives of other Christian denominations or of other world religions, especially if the latter were increased.

In one such case the adviser argued for deliberate positive action and that Hinduism, Islam and Sikhism should each have two representatives, who could lend mutual support and help develop confident participatory skills. Although the RC representative agreed, the diocese, failing to appreciate the positive action argument, dissented and made direct representation to the CEO for an increase in its representation.

Overall, representatives of Evangelical and Pentecostalist Churches (34) outnumbered those of Quakerism (21) or the Orthodox Churches (17). There was usually only one Evangelical or Pentecostal representative on a SACRE, but seven SACREs had two such representatives. Interviews indicated this was an area of controversy and polarised views: in some cases 'black' churches and/or house church groups were perceived as problematic; elsewhere they were positively welcomed or at least allowed. Quakers were sometimes said to be disproportionately influential locally and also represented among teachers. **Both Evangelical groups and Quakers featured with more than usual frequency among those religious groups which had applied to SACRE for representation but had been refused.** As might be expected, the Orthodox churches were more likely to be represented in London Boroughs.

A total of 81 out of 91 SACREs which responded to the circular had at least one representative of a religion other than Christianity. Conversely, however, as many as ten SACREs (six 'white highlands' Counties; one Outer London Borough and three Metropolitan Boroughs) had no religion other than Christianity represented. Interviews which occurred in relation to a SACRE in each LEA type revealed different approaches to this issue:

One County SACRE of 21 members, in an LEA which claimed only two or three schools with significant numbers of children from religious backgrounds other than Christianity, had included a Community Relations Council (CRC) representative who also happened to have a religious background other than in Christianity.

One Outer London LEA with a SACRE of 18 members had made some attempt to contact local Jewish and Muslim groups when setting up SACRE, but apparently none saw SACRE as significant until about three months after it had started working. By then the SACRE's constitution was agreed and elected members were not prepared to extend Group A — the key criterion for the SACRE being size. As a result a Jewish and Muslim representative were both co-opted.

At the first meeting of a Metropolitan SACRE with 19 members some concern was expressed at the lack of representatives of religions other than Christianity. After review the SACRE decided to retain its membership (although other co-options were made apropos of Group C) because of the small numbers of members of faiths other than Christianity and uncertainty over representativeness as the bodies had no organized federation. An additional concern was that recognition of such religions could lead to applications from other Christian denominations such as The Salvation Army or Jehovah's Witnesses, whose local membership was also small, and that the SACRE might become too large.

By contrast, there are as many as 31 SACRES (N = 88, 35 per cent) where in Group A the number of representatives of religions other than Christianity are at least equal to those of Christian denominations other than Church of England. These were evenly spread by LEA type: Counties 10, London Boroughs 10, Metropolitan Boroughs 11. Indeed, in 20 of these SACREs (22 per cent) the representatives of other world religions outnumbered those of Christian denominations in Group A. These SACREs were more likely to be in Metropolitan or London Boroughs (eight each) than Counties (four). Interviews revealed that this had generally been the result of deliberate planning, but sometimes on account of changes due to lobbying.

One Metropolitan LEA which set out to give more places to representatives of world religions other than Christianity perceived this as historically necessary for race relations locally, so as to give ethnic minority members confidence and to allow their voices to be heard. Objections from the RC diocese were not upheld by the SACRE itself. Muslims were originally allocated six places (more than any other group in the SACRE overall) and on this basis Hindus and Sikhs lobbied to increase their representation. In all cases fewer are allowed voting rights.

In another Metropolitan authority which allowed representation of all religious groups who wished to be represented, Muslims (of different denominations, mosques, cultural and welfare associations and a women's association) outnumbered representatives of Christian denominations. Some Christian representatives *'raised their eyebrows'* at this but accepted the Muslim dominance in Group A when they realised the representatives in the other groups were predominantly Christian. The inspector felt this was related to the fact that SACRE members had recently worked together on the ASC and knew and respected one another.

Conversely, another Metropolitan authority had been concerned to get the right balance between Christian denominations and religions other than Christianity. Originally the latter group (including cultural groups) outnumbered the former but growing pressure from other Christian denominations was gradually altering the balance.

By comparison, in a County LEA which had intended that the number of Christian denomination representatives and of representatives of other religions should be equal, Muslims lobbied and gained two additional seats (five in total) largely because they argued their adherents locally outnumbered (by four to one) those of Hindus (two seats). The SACRE consultation and local political response to the Muslim Educational Trust (MET, 1989a) pamphlet had influenced local Muslims to form a Council of Mosques which then lobbied the LEA. The adviser saw ERA as enfranchising by allowing Muslims representation on SACRE — a body which oversees a subject about which they have sensitive and strong views.

Figure 6 presents some comparisons by LEA type between the range of representatives of denominations of Christianity other than the Church of England (86 SACREs: 33 Counties, eight Inner London, 16 Outer London, 29 Metropolitan Boroughs) and representatives of other religions (76 SACREs: 26 Counties, eight Inner London, 16 Outer London and 26 Metropolitan Boroughs). For example, the overall range of representatives of other Christian denominations (2 - 12) was roughly half that for other religions (0 - 19). However, overall the most frequent number of representatives of other Christian denominations was seven compared with four representatives of other religions. In relation to LEA type, Counties had the smallest and Metropolitan authorities had the greatest range of representatives of other Christian denominations. Regarding representatives of religions other than Christianity, Inner London Boroughs had the smallest and Outer London Boroughs the greatest range.

Figure 6   Group A: representatives of other Christian denominations compared with representatives of other religions

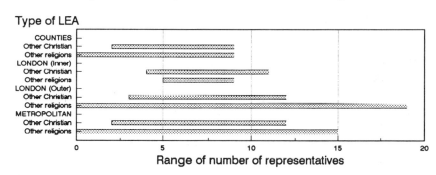

Results are based on information from 86 SACREs (other Christian) and 76 SACREs (other religions)

A total of 11 religions other than Christianity were represented. These comprised: Armenian Church, Baha'i, Buddhism, Confucianism, Hinduism, Islam, Jainism, Judaism, Rastafarianism, Sikhism, Zoroastrianism. The largest number of religions other than Christianity represented were eight in each of two SACREs, one in an Outer London and one in a Metropolitan Borough.

37

One with 11 members in the other religions sub-group comprised: Baha'i, Buddhist, Hindu (2), Jain, Jew, Muslim (2), Sikh and Humanist.

One with nine members in the other religions sub-group comprised: Baha'i, Black Church (not listed as a Christian denomination), Buddhist, Confucianist, Hindu, Jew, Muslim, Sikh and Humanist.

Three SACREs had members from seven religions other than Christianity.

A total of 17 (out of 76, 22 per cent) SACREs (four Counties, four Inner London, six Outer London and three Metropolitan Boroughs) had representatives of the five major world religions other than Christianity (Buddhism, Hinduism, Islam, Judaism, Sikhism). Additionally seven of these SACREs (one Inner London, four Outer London and two Metropolitan Boroughs) had a Baha'i representative. Interviews suggested that this could be a reflection of the intention to include representatives of these religions, even if they were not strictly a *principal religious tradition of the area*, because they were seen as making an important contribution to the study of religion. In such cases Muslim, Jain and Humanist representatives, sometimes of international repute (and acceptable to the relatively few local adherents) were also 'imported' from other, usually adjacent LEAs. County SACREs occasionally included representatives of world religions other than Christianity because an international centre for the religion (Baha'i, Buddhism, Judaism) was located in the area, even though the local faith community was not numerous. At the other end of the spectrum there were eight (six County) SACREs with only one representative of a religion other than Christianity, which in most cases was Islam. A further 11 SACREs had only two representatives of religions other than Christianity, the most popular combination, in almost half of these SACREs, being of Islam and Judaism.

Figure 7 shows that for a total of 76 SACREs (26 Counties, eight Inner London, 16 Outer London and 26 Metropolitan Boroughs), responding to the circular specifying representatives of religions other than Christianity, the most numerous representatives overall were of Islam (106), Hinduism (64), Judaism and Sikhism (62 each). Buddhism (21) and Baha'i (12) were less well represented. The number of representatives of the different religions was similar across different LEA types, with the exception of Islam, **which was better represented in the Metropolitan authorities, as was Judaism in London LEAs. It was usual for a SACRE to have only one representative of each religion other than Christianity. However, 25 SACREs (four Counties, four Inner London, five Outer London and 12 Metropolitan Boroughs) had more than one representative** (usually two) of at least one religion other than Christianity. The greatest number of representatives in any one SACRE were as follows: Judaism 2, Hinduism 5, Islam 6, Sikhism 6.

Figure 7   Representation of the most common religions other than Christianity in Group A

Number of representatives

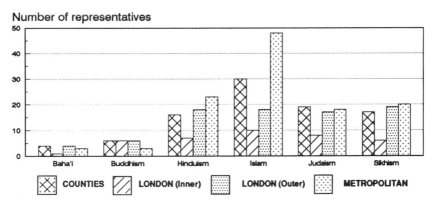

Results are based on information from 76 SACREs

In Group A there was an in-built emphasis on denominations of Christianity other than Church of England but ensuring the representation of denominations of other world religions represented in the area was a greater challenge. Interviews in 28 LEAs (nine with more than one representative of at least one religion other than Christianity) indicated that RE advisers/inspectors at least were aware of such an issue and often regarded it as problematic. In addition to some local political and religious challenges to such representation (see p.17) there was sometimes inadequate LEA knowledge to distinguish denominations or to be able to confirm the representativeness of representatives. Thus although this was usually seen as a matter for the faith groups themselves to determine it could result in local difficulties where there was, for example, no Council of Mosques. In another instance a group of young *'reactionary'* Muslims challenged the representation of Islam on SACRE by traditionalist older men, but when this was referred back to the Council of Mosques itself to decide the *status quo* prevailed. Moreover, in a few SACREs representation on Group A did not necessarily confer a right for all members to vote within Group A (see p.36) and some LEA interviewees regarded this as an issue for Group A to determine. Two examples of denominations being distinguished may be given:

In a SACRE with 12 members in Group A, in addition to representatives of African Evangelical Church of God, Baha'i, [X] Synagogue, FCFC (3), Greek Orthodox Church, and Roman Catholic Church there were representatives of Gujerati Muslim Society and Islamic Brotherhood, Gudwara Nanak Parkesh Sikh Temple and Ramgarhia Sikh Temple, and of Hindu Temple Society and Shree Hindu Satsang Mandel.

39

Another SACRE of 23 members in Group A comprised in addition to RC, Jewish, Armenian, Afro-West Indian Council of Churches, Greek Orthodox, Humanist, Buddhist Society, Baha'i, FCFC and Central Jamia Masjid (Muslim) (4) representatives, those of the Hindu Temple Trust (2) and Vishwa Hindu Kendra (2), and of three Sikh denominations: Sri Guru Singh Sabha (3), Ramgarhia Sabha (2) and Sri Guru Ravi Das Sabha (1).

Indeed, there were **several controversial issues connected with the diversification and numbers of Group A**. These issues comprised:

- the inclusion **of representatives of religions other than Christianity even though these were not principal religious traditions of the locality** (see p.38);

- **vacancies**, which were particularly high in Group A compared with others (see p.57); in some cases religious groups were said to be slow to nominate representatives despite contact by the LEA; in other cases there was evidence that they were only now learning of the SACRE; the Black Churches, Hinduism, Judaism, Quakerism and Sikhism were all named by a few interviewees as principal religions of their areas which had not proposed a nominee. The extent of consultation and its timing appeared critical; LEAs needed to pursue such groups if representatives were to be taken seriously;

- by contrast, there were also those **SACREs which had received requests for inclusion from local groups which had been turned down**; among the sample (in addition to the major issue of Humanists, see pp.41-44) those denied representation included Baha'i, Quakers, Jews and Afro-Caribbean churches, Evangelical Alliance and a Muslim political group. The more liberal SACREs invited such applicants to a meeting to put their case — and some co-options resulted. But often the criteria for rejection were unclear or some mix of political, numerical, religious and educational criteria;

- such decisions in turn contrasted with those five SACREs which included representatives of bodies which, at first sight, might be seen, from a Western perspective, but not necessarily from **within** the bodies themselves, not as religions but rather as having primarily:

    1. a **cultural or welfare orientation**, e.g. Muslim, Community and Welfare Centre or Mosque and Islamic Cultural Society;

    or 2. **a national orientation**, e.g. Indian Association;

    or 3. a combination of 1. and 2., e.g. Bangladeshi Islamic Cultural Association;

    or 4. possibly also with a **specific local or UK orientation**, e.g. X Sikh Association or Y Bengali Association;

    or 5. with **an educational** orientation, e.g. Muslim Educational Trust;

or 6. **a gender emphasis,** e.g. Pakistani Women's Association;

or 7. **a race relations orientation** — two SACREs had a CRC/CRE member and three had such co-options although their representation could be controversial.

However, this may be justifiable given that for the first time ERA (S.2 (a)) mentions that the maintained school curriculum should also promote the *'cultural'* development of pupils at the school and of society.

One of the most highly charged debates about appropriate membership focussed on whether a Humanist should be included in Group A. However, this was again a matter of wide variation in practice, ranging from LEAs and SACREs where it was just not an issue, or where discussion had not been allowed to occur, to those where there was heated debate and controversial outcomes with ongoing repercussions. Out of 76 responses to the circular which could be analysed for Group A membership there were only 17 SACRE members representing Humanism, fewer than the representatives of Buddhism. Humanists were represented by LEA type as follows: Counties four, Inner London Boroughs seven, Outer London Boroughs five and Metropolitan Boroughs one, plus two co-options (one each in a County and Inner London Borough). In the interview sample there were five LEAs whose SACREs had a Humanist representative (two Counties, one Inner London, two Outer London) and one co-option (Inner London).

In three of these SACREs the RE adviser/inspector felt that the representation of Humanism on SACRE was not controversial, either because a previous local SACRE had included a Humanist or because SACRE members were not well known to one another and may not have been aware of one another's backgrounds. In any case, these advisers felt the inclusion of a Humanist was justified since the member represented a lifestance of a locally significant group and of pupils who were not from active faith backgrounds.

In one LEA whether Humanism should be represented on SACRE involved a one-and-a-half hour debate in Education Committee; after deadlock it appeared to have been resolved by the numerical criterion as it was argued that there were more Humanists in the area than Sikhs or Hindus, who were already represented.

Elsewhere, Humanists had initially been excluded on grounds of numbers and as not constituting a religious group. Subsequently the adviser's view had been sought in SACRE and on her recommendation a co-option had been agreed — the Humanist being seen to make an important contribution.

In one case the Humanist who had already been on the ASC continued on SACRE but was later the subject of a removal attempt by SACRE itself. The Humanist did not live locally. It was useful for the LEA to be able to say that it and not the SACRE ratified appointments.

Thus Humanist representatives were not necessarily secure from challenges. RE Advisers/Inspectors reported that there could be advantages to having a Humanist on the SACRE: one was said to be *'articulate'* and to *'challenge the assumptions of the AS'*, another was *'very open'* and *'a healer of divisions'*, and others recognized that Humanists *'were doing good work'*.

Where Humanism was not represented on the SACRE interviewees were asked whether the matter had come up for discussion and, if so, what had been the circumstances and outcome. Respondents were fairly evenly divided, with slightly more (over one-third of the sample) claiming that the issue had not been debated. Those who reported that the issue had not arisen pointed to several reasons:

- one or two observed that no Humanist had been discovered in the local community survey;

- a few noted that Humanists had not approached the LEA/SACRE for membership, even if they were originally represented in local RE or SACRE development conferences;

- in a few cases, where the composition of SACRE had been predetermined by the LEA, officials had interpreted legislation so as to exclude Humanism on the grounds that it did not constitute a religion; in one LEA the matter was politically sensitive: a Humanist was present on the ASC but within SACRE it was said that such a viewpoint was represented by several teachers; elsewhere an application by a Humanist headteacher was not discussed — LEAs preferred applications from the British Humanist Association (BHA) or local groups.

When asked to predict the likely outcome if application for Humanist representation arose for consideration:

- one doubted whether some LEA/SACRE members would understand the issue — the responses would be likely to be *'what would a Humanist be interested in SACRE for?'*;

- two were uncertain of the reaction of the local *'high Church County set'* or *'the Christian Squiring Brigade'*;

- two thought that it would still be too controversial and would be refused;

- a few, however, thought it would be less controversial now and likely to succeed, even if only on the basis of a co-option, provided representativeness could be assured.

Several interviewees expressed their own personal support for the inclusion of a Humanist representative, but were aware that this was a more liberal view than that taken by other LEA officers or SACRE members, and often felt that their own position was not sufficiently secure to *'start stirring'*, whilst wishing that Humanists would apply. Indeed, in the majority of instances in the sample where such applications had been received and had been discussed they were in fact refused. Exclusions had been made on the basis of several, often relatively unclear, reasons:

- an application might *'not be taken seriously'*: **size of the SACRE** — representativeness but with some predetermined perception of a functional size — could be the overwhelming criterion in some cases;

- in others the apparent **lack of numbers of Humanists** locally seems to have been the criterion — jokes that Trotskyists or Marxists would be more common could also be made;

- some rejections were made on the grounds that **Humanism was not a religion** — one adviser suggested that, since the AS emphasized Christianity not just religion, non-religious backgrounds were irrelevant — confirmed by SACRE meeting minutes on consideration of an application by local Humanists:

  '...... it was felt that the Humanist viewpoint, while being valuable for moral education, did not offer any specific assistance to the deliberations of SACRE.'

- some used a **mix of religious and numerical criteria** — one SACRE had twice formally voted upon a Humanist application with a split in the voting (Group C and D in favour, Group A and B against). The LEA clerk advised against membership other than as a co-option on religious grounds. However, all co-options within an apparently set limit had been allocated to teachers early in the SACRE's life. Also some Muslims who were well represented on SACRE apparently objected to a place being allocated to a relatively small group locally. Humanists thus seemed to suffer a double handicap on religious and numerical grounds;

- **strong personal antipathy on the part of the Chairperson** was indicated in two or three cases. This occurred where a prominent Humanist was available locally and when *'it was the mind of the then Chair and members not to include a Humanist on religious grounds'* and the Chair turned down the suggestion of a co-option or observer status for personal reasons;

- in another SACRE an application from the BHA had been considered twice alongside applications from the FCFC; a co-option might be possible, if not the constitution might need to be changed; the adviser suspected the main criterion for exclusion might be **fear**.

In practical terms a yet more concerted approach and backing from the BHA, along the lines for the FCFC, may be needed to secure better representation of Humanism on local SACREs. White (1990a) has pointed to some of the fears and benefits and (1990b) to the politics behind Humanist representation:

> '*I was at first refused membership of .... SACRE, although I have lived and taught in the Borough for many years and they inherited the ILEA Syllabus which includes Humanism. However, the Teachers' Committee, the Other Faiths Committee— and the Church of England Committee!— combined to vote against the Tories to secure my co-option.*'

The depth and diversity of responses to the issue of inclusion of a Humanist prompts the question: to what extent have SACREs and LEAs taken on board the existence of a secular society as a context for their work? Moreover, as yet, no SACRE appears to have recognized, as does DES Circular 16/89 (GB. DES, 1989(b)), that some pupils have no religious background, by including per se an interested parent or member of the local community with no religious or Humanist affiliation.

Group B

Group B membership — representatives of the Church of England — was both more easily resolved and less numerous than that of Group A. As Table 5 shows, Group B varied between one and seven members. Two large Metropolitan SACREs appeared to have only one Church of England member. Two-thirds of SACREs (66/99) had three — five Church of England members and over half (50) four or five members. Five was generally the most frequent number, though the London Boroughs had a tendency to have six members. Not surprisingly, larger SACREs tended to have larger numbers in Group B, though a few had a Group B which seemed intentionally more numerous than other Groups. In only 12 out of 91 SACREs (seven Counties, five Metropolitan Boroughs) was the membership of Group B equal to that of Group A. About half of these SACREs were in 'white highlands' LEAs. In all other cases Group A outnumbered Group B, sometimes considerably, the greatest range being 20 to one. In fact the total membership of Group B across the 91 SACREs which amounted to 398 was the lowest for any of the four constituent groups of SACRE, and was not augmented by co-options or observers. Even so, together with the considerable presence of representatives of other Christian denominations in Group A, and other Christians in Group C and D, the religious background of the majority of representatives on SACRE nevertheless remained in the main Christian. Such an ethos was reflected in the workings of the SACRE.

Table 5   Group B: Church of England representatives on SACREs

LEA Type	Available N	Total Group B	Range	Most Frequent
Counties	34	137	2 - 6	4 or 5
London Boroughs				
Inner	8	41	3 - 6	6
Outer	17	83	3 - 6	6
Metropolitan Boroughs	32	137	1 - 7	5
Total	91	398	1 - 7	5

Interviews in one quarter of LEAs confirmed that the determination of the membership of Group B had, in the overwhelming majority of cases, been least contentious. Members of Group B were usually nominated by the local diocese(s), by the Diocesan Director of Education or Board of Education, sometimes in consultation with voluntary-aided schools. Many of Group B members such as the Diocesan Director of Education, the Diocesan Board's advisory teacher or schools officer and heads or teachers in voluntary-aided schools had professional educational involvement. Others such as governors or clergy had close ties.

In one case the local Bishop was a member of Group B and played a key role as Chair of SACRE.

Elsewhere the local Diocesan Director of Education was not included on SACRE because of his strong objection to the current AS.

In another Metropolitan SACRE Group B included a Methodist who was approached by the Diocese.

Apart from such anomalies, more discussion about Group B nominations was required where the LEA area was not contiguous with that of the diocese and involved two or more dioceses. In one Metropolitan authority the number of diocesan members of Group B was related to the number of schools in each diocese. It was sometimes especially important that both traditionalists and those committed to radical equal opportunities and positive race relations approaches should be represented in Group B. Occasionally, however, one or two members of Group B could be perceived as professionally out of tune. Reconsideration of SACRE members in previously existing SACREs could result in significant changes with what one adviser perceived as a regrettable loss of local clergy and heads. In a few cases there was evidence that the local diocese had requested and been granted an increase in the originally intended membership of Group B. Diocesan Directors of Education could be members of more than one SACRE; one appeared to be a Vice-Chair of one SACRE and a member of two others.

Group C

Group C — teachers' associations — was potentially a group most likely to represent the interests of RE teachers and the needs of subject delivery. ERA indicated that Group C should comprise *'such associations representing teachers as, in the opinion of the authority, ought, having regard to the circumstances of the area, to be represented'*. DES Circular 3/89 elaborated that *'The Secretary of State ..... believes that there would be advantage in ensuring that members representing associations of teachers include teachers of religious education'*. As the REC Handbook observed, it would be important that teacher and headteacher members covered a range of schools in view of the head's responsibilities for ensuring provision of RE and CW and in order to represent diverse school circumstances.

Table 6 Group C: teachers and teachers' association representatives on SACREs

LEA Type	Available N	Total Group C	Range	Most Frequent
Counties	34	173	3- 8	4 or 5
London Boroughs				
Inner	8	47	2-10	5
Outer	17	110	3-12	7
Metropolitan Boroughs	32	195	2-13	5
Total	91	525	2-13	5

Table 6 shows that Group C varied between two and 13 members with the greatest range in the Metropolitan authorities. Three-fifths of SACREs had four — six members and just under half had four or five members in Group C. Despite the trend for at least two of Groups B—D to have similar numbers, as many as 33 SACREs (seven Counties, three Inner, seven Outer London Boroughs and 16 — half — the Metropolitan Boroughs) had a Group C which was more numerous. **Indeed, a few SACREs were teacher dominated.** The total number of Group C members across the 91 SACREs was 525.

In practice in determining the composition of Group C, LEAs took several approaches based, as suggested, on teachers' associations, individual teacher representatives or some combination of both. Further analysis of available information for 78 SACREs (28 Counties, seven Inner London, 15 Outer London, 28 Metropolitan Boroughs) shows that, although in the majority of SACREs (68 per cent, 53/78) Group C was composed of representatives of teachers' associations, in a not insignificant minority (19 per cent, 15/78) Group C was composed of (head)teacher members representing age-related or school-type interests. A further ten SACREs (13 per cent) had both types of membership (Figure 8).

Figure 8   Composition of Group C

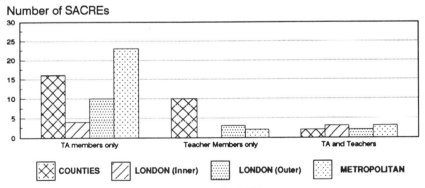

Results are based on information from 78 SACREs
TA - Teachers' Association

Figure 9 gives a breakdown of teachers' association representatives by association and LEA type, based on available information from 63 SACREs (18 Counties, seven Inner London, 12 Outer London, 26 Metropolitan Boroughs) which included at least some teachers' association representatives. It was usual for each association represented to have one representative in Group C but some SACREs (three in Outer London Boroughs, ten in Metropolitan Boroughs) had more than one representative of at least one teachers' association. The largest number was six National Union of Teachers (NUT) members, but three was more usual. Figure 9 shows that four-fifths (81 per cent, 298/368) of teachers' association members were distributed amongst five major unions - NUT, National Union Of Schoolmasters/Union of Women Teachers (NAS/UWT), Assistant Masters and Mistresses Association (AMMA), National Association of Headteachers (NAHT) and Secondary Headteachers' Association (SHA). Heads' associations held 29 per cent of places.

Figure 9 **Teachers' association representatives on SACREs by association**

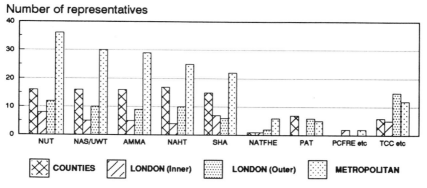

Results are based on information from 63 SACREs
PCFRE includes ARET, ACT and ATREL
TCC includes JCC and COTO

Interview data in 28 LEAs indicated that in at least three-quarters of cases the LEA had approached its local Teachers' Consultative Committee (TCC), Joint Consultative Committee (JCC) or Committee of Teachers' Organizations (COTO) for nominations of teachers' association representatives. As Figure 9 shows, in some cases membership allocation to Group C was given to the local TCC, JCC or COTO as such. However, LEAs did not always explicitly request representatives of different unions or teachers with experience of RE; hence some anomalies occurred. For example, one County SACRE had no representative from the largest teachers' association locally, the NUT. Elsewhere, union representation on SACRE reflected that in the JCC. As Figure 9 also indicates, there were relatively few representatives (18) of the Professional Association of Teachers (PAT). Local recognition of this association in the TCC/JCC seemed variable and sometimes controversial. However, where PAT representation occurred, it appeared that the union had insisted on representation, even if it did not nominate an RE specialist. Occasionally SACRE was the only local education body on which PAT was represented.

Figure 9 also reveals that **the association membership of Group C was overwhelmingly linked to the primary and secondary education sector. Across 63 SACREs there were only ten representatives of further and higher education interests (NATFHE). Moreover, there was very little representation of associations of teachers of RE.**

Indeed, **the extent of representation of teachers with experience of RE or Group C of SACRE was often a matter of concern to RE advisers/ inspectors. It appeared that even where the LEA had requested that teachers' associations nominate (head)teachers with RE experience this did not necessarily occur or to a sufficient degree.** In some cases teachers' associations sent their officials rather than seeking out members who could represent the interests of RE. Occasional insights were gleaned from advisers about local difficulties, although information about how teachers' associations made their nominations was not sought.

> In one London Borough the local teachers' unions were reported to have been beseiged by Heads of RE departments offering to serve on SACRE. But in the event a *'weak'* group resulted. This issued in openly expressed disagreement, with RE teachers claiming that unions were not *'working the system'*. Thus one or two co-options of RE teachers were made.

> Elsewhere, there was disquiet because it was felt that RE teachers on SACRE were there by default and were not necessarily specialists. In this, and several other cases where the AS was under revision, additional teachers were being sought for the ASC.

Similar concerns were expressed about the balance of primary/secondary interests represented by Group C members. RE advisers/inspectors notably failed to evince similar concerns about low representation of college interests. **There was usually an imbalance in favour of secondary education** amongst the representatives of Group C unless teachers' associations consciously opted for nominees with primary education backgrounds. In one or two cases LEA suggestions about the balance of nominees in relation to age of schooling were overridden by political considerations. Elsewhere local TCC/JCC nominees who included more heads and secondary teachers were complemented by co-options.

It was apparently with such initial concerns (despite the ERA wording of *'teacher associations'*), that 15 LEAs had sought teacher members who would *as individuals* directly represent RE interests in primary or secondary education. This occurred more often in County authorities (see Figure 8). Ten other SACREs had a mix of teachers' associations and individual teacher members in Group C. Analysis of the composition of Group C in these 25 SACREs showed that such members were still most likely to be heads but that primary/secondary or first/middle/upper school representation was more evenly balanced.

Nevertheless, there were relatively few infant, special school, sixth-form college, further education (FE) college or higher education (HE) representatives. In a few SACREs it was a deliberate intention that Group C should include representatives of local race or multicultural education units or black teachers. But elsewhere, **even in obviously multiracial areas, the potential contribution of teachers from religious or cultural backgrounds which were not mainstream Christian was not necessarily perceived as a possible criterion for representation on SACRE.**

The notion of representation seems to have been little explored in relation to Group C of SACRE. If the interests of teachers of RE in general and of RE itself were to be well represented by teachers' associations or individuals, setting aside any particular or organizational interest, then channels of communication needed to be established to determine the concerns of teachers of RE and to feed back information on SACRE's deliberation and decision making.

Group D

Group D — the Local Education Authority — could be very controversial in its membership. Neither ERA nor DES Circular 3/89 made suggestions as to the composition of LEA membership, but the REC handbook observed that such nominees should *'represent not only the views of the LEA, but also the interests of parents and the wider community'*. Essentially there were two main categories of membership of Group D on SACRE: that of councillors and of LEA officers. The latter could alternatively, or, in a few cases, in addition, be *in attendance* at SACRE. Thus Group D could consist of: councillors only as members (plus LEA officers in attendance); councillors and LEA officers as members; councillors and LEA officers as members (plus LEA officers in attendance).

Table 7 shows that **Group D varied between three and 14 members.** However, **over two-thirds of SACREs (65/91) had four—six members** and just under half (44/91) had four or five members in Group D. Four was generally the most frequent number, though once again the London Boroughs had a tendency to have six members. Although there was a trend for Group B — D to have similar numbers, 15 SACREs (one County, two Inner, six Outer London and six Metropolitan Boroughs) had a Group D which was more numerous. A higher proportion of Outer London Boroughs thus had a Group D larger than that of Group B or C. The total number of Group D members across the 91 SACREs was 478.

Table 7   Group D: Local Education Authority representatives on SACREs

LEA Type	Available N	Total Group D	Range	Most Frequent
Counties	34	163	3 - 8	4
London Boroughs				
Inner	8	52	4 - 14	6
Outer	17	103	3 - 9	6
Metropolitan Boroughs	32	160	3 - 11	3 - 5
Total	91	478	3 - 14	4

Further analysis of the composition of Group D, on the basis of **available information for 66 SACREs (22 Counties, eight Inner London, 13 Outer London and 23 Metropolitan Boroughs) shows that almost two-thirds (41/ 66) had only councillors as members of Group D** (Figure 10). In this case their numbers ranged from three to eight with Counties having the widest spread. A higher proportion of Counties for which information was available had only councillors in Group D. Interview data in 28 LEAs revealed that in at least one quarter of these cases the councillors were *all* members of the local Education Committee. Moreover, **in about half of the LEAs sampled Group D councillors included senior politicians such as the Chair or Deputy of Education Committee, Chair of Schools Sub-Committee or even Chair of Council (see also pp.117-118).** Such members were likely to be seen as giving status to SACRE, though it was occasionally argued that this was unnecessary because of the claimed local decentralization of educational administration.

LEAs were fairly evenly divided as to whether councillors from two or three political parties were represented in Group D. In some authorities the inclusion of one or more councillors from a second or third party occurred even if one party was locally predominant, but this could be tokenistic and the majority party could still have an in-built advantage. Occasionally only councillors from one political party were represented in Group D. There were local variations as to whether the status of councillors and their political affiliation was marked on the list of Group D members. During the interview period some local authorities experienced local elections which in some cases altered the political and individual representation of councillors. In one such LEA, as a result of change in local council control, there was a proposal to reduce the number of councillors and the overall size of the SACRE. In some cases, due to the initial involvement of the local Education Committee in setting up the SACRE and the dominance of SACRE Chairs from Group D, the number of members of Group D sometimes determined the numerical formula on which the other SACRE groups were based.

Figure 10   Group D composition: Councillors and education officers as members

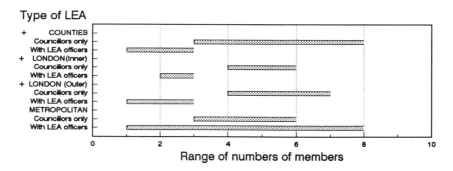

Results are based on information from 66 SACREs

+   One County had an Archdeacon listed in Group D.
     One Inner London Borough had two councillors plus 12 governors.
     One Inner London Borough and two Outer London Boroughs gave no further information about the composition of Group D in addition to councillors.

Twenty out of 66 SACREs for which information was available listed LEA officers as members of SACRE. Over half of these SACREs — a disproportionately high number — were in Metropolitan Boroughs. The number of LEA officers who appeared to be considered as *members* of SACRE ranged from one to eight, with the greatest range in the Metropolitan Boroughs.

One Metropolitan SACRE comprised: three councillors (one Labour, one Liberal Democrat, one Conservative, although the Council is predominantly Labour); eight LEA officers: senior assistant director with responsibility for schools, senior primary adviser, senior secondary adviser, multicultural education adviser, primary and secondary head teachers, a special school representative and an advisory teacher from the multicultural education language service.

Another SACRE comprised: two councillors: the Chair and Vice-Chair of Education Committee; six LEA officers: the Director of Education, principal adviser, general adviser for humanities, assistant director for primary and special education, assistant director of secondary education and the warden of the teachers' centre.

In 26 LEAs lists of SACRE members cited LEA officers as *in attendance* rather than as members. Numbers ranged from one to five with no significant difference across the LEAs. One effect of ERA was that LEA officers were sometimes no longer members but in attendance. There seemed little difference in the type of LEA officer (education officer, administrative officer, adviser/inspector, etc.) considered as a member of SACRE or in attendance. However, in some cases RE advisers/inspectors if not of senior status were listed as in attendance (possibly as SACRE clerks) whereas more senior advisory/inspectorial colleagues were listed as members.

Examples of LEA officers in attendance were:
- in one County SACRE: general inspector for RE, general inspector MCE, SEO, AEO, AO (all policy, planning and review division);
- another County SACRE: deputy director of education, two AEOs, general county adviser RE and curriculum adviser;
- one Metropolitan SACRE: the DCEO, specialist adviser for humanities, senior general primary adviser, community relations officer, advisory teacher (clerk).

Such input might reflect importance accorded to SACRE and the desire to treat it seriously and/or to influence it (see also pp.115-117).

Interestingly, **four SACREs (out of 66) (one County, one Outer London Borough and two Metropolitan Boroughs) had LEA officers as members and in attendance at SACRE.** Only two SACREs — in Inner London Boroughs — appeared to have given any specific attention to allowing representation of the wider educational community (apart from CRC) in Group D. One SACRE had two vacancies reserved for *'black and ethnic minorities group representative and a governor of [local] schools'*. Another, atypical, SACRE had 14 members of Group D of whom only two were councillors and 12 were school governors. The council apparently viewed this as a means of direct contact with schools by which

SACRE could gain information for decision making and feedback advice and had sent out letters of invitation to all governing bodies. As a result governor members included several chairs of governors of schools of different age ranges, an interdenominational schools worker and two or three teachers.

Co-opted Members

ERA (S. 11 (3) and S. 13 (4)) indicates that the SACRE itself (but not the ASC) may appoint co-opted members, and DES Circular 3/89 clarifies that co-opted members do not have a vote. The number of co-options in relation to intended numbers of the SACRE and their perceived function are interesting issues.

Table 8   Co-options on SACREs

LEA Type	Available N	No. of SACREs with Co-options	No. of Co-optees	Range
Counties	34	14	63	1 - 6 (27)[+]
London Boroughs				
Inner	8	2	5	2 - 3
Outer	17	3	7	1 - 4
Metropolitan Boroughs	32	8	17	1 - 8
Total	91	27	92	1 - 8 (27)

+   One County, exceptionally, had 27 co-optees

Table 8 shows that **30 per cent (27/91) of the SACREs had enlarged their membership with co-options. Overall these amounted to 92 members, an additional four per cent of the total SACRE membership (see p.27). The Counties were more likely than other types of LEA to have co-opted members — two-fifths in fact had made co-options.** The numbers of co-options in SACREs ranged from one to eight generally, though the majority of SACREs with co-opted members had

54

only one or two. Exceptionally, one County with a total SACRE membership of 17 (Group A five, Group B four, Group C four, Group D four) had, in addition, appointed 27 co-opted members

'drawn from a wider range of faith groups and denominations than are represented by the constituent members. Their main task is to offer advice to SACRE when necessary or they may be called upon for specific purposes to assist SACRE to carry out its task.'

These co-options were predominantly from Group A: Baha'i one, Free Church four, Hindu one, Humanist three, Jew two, Muslim four, Sikh four, but also more than doubled the teacher representation (plus six teachers' association representatives, one ATRE and one university lecturer).

Further analysis of available information for 20 SACREs shows that co-options were most often in SACREs based on some kind of mathematical model and made in relation to Group A and especially Group C as follows:

Group A: undefined three, Baptist one, Buddhist one, Evangelist one, Hindu one, Humanist two, Jew two, Muslim one, Quaker three.

For example, one Outer London SACRE (Group A five, Group B four, Group C four, Group D five), with no representatives of a religion other than Christianity in Group A and which was not prepared to extend Group A, made four co-options: one Baptist, one Jew, one Muslim and one member of PCFRE.

Group C: undefined one, teachers' associations four, teachers (by school type, age group or status) 11, ATREs four, MCE one, colleges seven.

SACREs made co-options in relation to Group C to augment or compensate for the relative lack of RE teachers at all levels appointed to Group C.

One County SACRE, for example, had decided to co-opt a primary RE co-ordinator, a secondary RE specialist, a local HE Religious Studies lecturer and a college field officer (like a diocesan advisory post) to complement the secondary and head teacher bias of the local JCC nominations.

There were relatively few other co-options: for example, Group B one, School Christian Worker one, LEA officer one, CRE one.

For example, in one Metropolitan SACRE an LEA officer was co-opted in recognition of establishing community links, work on the previous ASC and continuing interest in the local RE Centre.

Whilst one or two RE advisers/inspectors were reluctant that SACRE should admit co-options — *'where would one stop?'*, some did not rule out the possibility that SACRE would make co-options in future. A constitution might allow for co-options, perhaps for a specific time period, partly as a way of ensuring a cycle of membership and availability of specialist contributors. Indeed, **in those SACREs with co-opted members it was evident that they could add significantly to the discussion and work of the SACRE. However, in view of co-optees' lack of voting rights the appointment of co-options could be tokenistic and marginalizing.** If co-optees were influential and made a useful contribution why not appoint them as full members of a particular group?

The issue of co-options seems further compounded by the existence of observers in five SACREs (predominantly in Metropolitan Boroughs). These observers, in some cases at least, appeared to have similar rights to co-optees, namely that they received SACRE papers, might speak through the Chair but not vote. Such observers included CRC representatives, HMI, RE Centre staff, Methodist Education Officer and representatives of Christian denominations (Christadelphians) and world religions other than Christianity (Muslims). Interestingly, two SACREs with no co-options had observers who might otherwise have been additional to Group A and who had applied to the SACRE for membership. If meetings were not otherwise public, observer status and continuing attendance might require review in the light of overall membership numbers and adequate representation of the principal religious traditions of the locality.

ERA also made provision for any **grant maintained schools** to be represented on SACRE (see p.24). Such members do not have a vote (DES Circular 3/89, Para 16). Ten per cent (9/91) of SACREs (five Counties, one Outer London Borough and three Metropolitan Boroughs) had a representative from a grant-maintained school. Two such SACREs were in the interview sample. In one LEA the anticipated inclusion on SACRE of a representative from a grant maintained school was seen as likely to affect the numerical formula and balance of the groups and to bring about further extensions. In another authority there was reported to have been initial hostility to having a grant maintained school representative on SACRE and a questioning of the right to representation because of previous acrimony between the LEA and school over the opting out arrangements. The RE adviser, however, recognized the school's good practice in RE and its involvement in the ASC.

Vacancies

A total of 22 SACREs (ten Counties, four Inner, five Outer London and three Metropolitan Boroughs) had at least one vacancy. The largest number of vacancies (22) occurred in Group A; these were evenly divided between places set aside for representatives of Christian denominations and other world faiths. Other vacancies occurred in Group B (three), C (nine) and D (two). No SACRE, other than in an Inner London Borough, had more than two vacancies. One such SACRE with 33 members had an additional eight vacancies. Some difficulties were encountered in filling places, especially those allocated to representatives of certain denominations or religions other than Christianity. This might result from lack of knowledge of the availability of a place, perhaps due to inadequate local consultation procedures, or relatively small numbers of representatives of a religion locally. Alternatively, in some areas there were reports of reluctance by some religious groups to be represented on and to participate in SACRE, either because of perceptions of institutional authority or because representation on the local CRC was seen to give a more directly influential voice. **Contacts with local religious groups by RE advisers in conjunction with other education and community professionals thus needed to be made and developed in order to generate confidence and valued mutual support.** Such situations might be contrasted with those SACREs where applications from religious groups and others to be represented on SACRE had resulted in co-options, observer status or politely firm rejections. **Whilst in their first year of operation SACREs might be expected to have some initial challenges in determination of membership, vigilance is needed to follow up groups for whom an earmarked place has not been filled. In the longer term the issue for membership would be to keep a balance between a degree of flexibility in response to local changes and turnover of members, according to specified duration and other factors affecting mobility, in view of the implications for SACRE INSET and the local delivery of RE.**

Chair of SACRE

The appointment of Chairperson of SACRE, and from which group, together with the Chair's influence on the conduct and nature of meetings (see pp.72-74) was one of the most controversial and potentially challenging issues for SACRE. DES Circular 3/89 (Para 18) noted that:

> *'The Act does not prescribe how the Chairman of a SACRE should be appointed.... It is open to the authority to appoint the Chairman or to allow the Council to appoint its own Chairman from amongst its members.'*

The very appointment of the Chair could be contentious. Some SACRE constitutions revealed that the authority clearly took the initiative and stipulated that it would appoint the Chair. Interviews confirmed that in the majority of cases the local authority, usually its Education Committee, decided on a Chair for SACRE in advance of its first meeting. In a few cases the nominee was put to SACRE for ratification and there was occasionally some feeling that the Chair was imposed, but that it was difficult to comment. In some instances even the RE adviser/inspector had no foreknowledge about the Chairperson. But when the SACRE itself chose its Chair the adviser could be critically involved. However, in fewer than one-quarter of the interview sample did SACRE have an open and not previously organized choice of Chair; even then, in one or two cases, elected members were quick to have themselves nominated. **Thus the matter of a Chair for SACRE was largely regarded as an aspect over which the authority should demonstrate its control and influence.**

Figure 11   Chairs of SACREs by Group

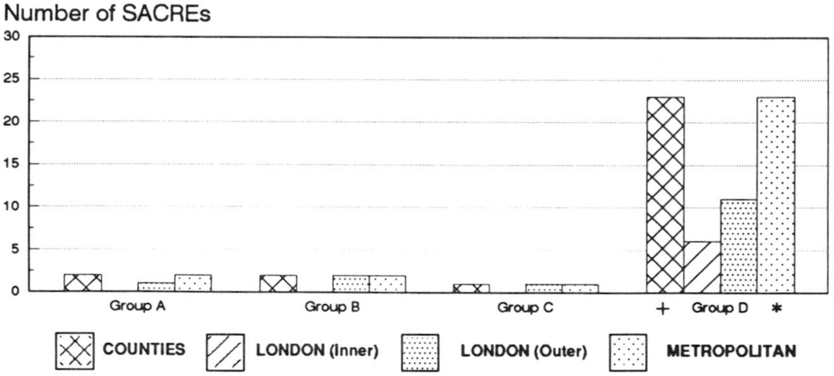

Results are based on information from 81 SACREs

+   plus one Chair ex-groups

*   plus two Chairs ex-groups and one by rotation of group per meeting

Analysis of **available information for 81 SACREs (28 Counties, six Inner London, 16 Outer London and 31 Metropolitan Boroughs) showed that 63 (78 per cent) had Chairpersons from Group D,** the local education authority. There was some variation by LEA type: 82 per cent Counties, 77 per cent of London Boroughs and 74 per cent of Metropolitan Boroughs with Chairs from Group D. Thus **very few SACREs (14) had Chairs from Group A, B or C. Of these Group B was marginally more popular across LEA types** (see Figure 11). Interestingly, in addition, in three SACREs the Chair did not appear to be a member of any constituent group of SACRE and in one SACRE the Chair was held by rotation of group for each meeting. Another SACRE had an arrangement to rotate Chair and Vice-Chair annually, passing through Group A — D. One Outer London Borough is reported to have a Humanist as its Chair (White, 1990a). The SACREs without a Chair from Group D were more likely to be in Labour-led Metropolitan LEAs; but in terms of an overall analysis of political control by LEA type the pattern did not appear atypical (see pp.189-190).

Interviews revealed that in the majority of cases where the SACRE Chair was from Group D he or she was usually a member of the dominant political party, on Education Committee, sometimes its Chair or Vice-Chair, and occasionally even the Chair of the Council. But in one SACRE the Chair was the Director of Education and in another the Assistant Director of one of four LEA divisions. Interviews in such authorities suggested that in what might be a politically sensitive role it was thought important, in the first instance at least, to have a Chair of SACRE who was skilled, influential and understood local systems. Where the SACRE Chair was a member of Education Committee he or she could be a strong mediating link and able to voice the interests of the SACRE and RE in local educational management.

Several RE advisers/inspectors whose SACRE was chaired by an elected member of Council or Education Committee perceived distinct benefits to SACRE and RE of a politically skilled, influential Chair who had a good understanding of broad educational issues and also often found such Chairs personally supportive. For example:

> in one LEA the SACRE Chair, who was also Chair of the Education Committee, was very keen that SACRE members should be those most able to care and communicate about and influence RE in schools and to publicize the SACRE and its role. A speech delivered at SACRE's first meeting emphasizing SACRE as '*a new and exciting partnership between the Authority, the faith communities and the schools*' was issued to the press and schools.

However, there could also be tensions between RE advisers and the SACRE Chair, about: heavy or formal chairing of meetings; the expression of strongly held views running counter to those of professionals; allowing '*potentially dangerous*' issues from SACRE to go forward to Education Committee; and even the lack of enthusiasm of councillors or Chair and Vice-Chair who preferred to attend other Council meetings. Indeed, in two or three SACREs in the interview sample the current Chairperson was a major issue. This was partly because other SACRE members reportedly perceived the Chair's ineffectiveness, but also because, even where there was a slight indication that after the first year SACRE might chose its own Chair, the LEA had still exercised *its* right to select the Chair. In these cases the SACRE was challenging the appointment of Chair and requesting through Education Committee a revision to its constitution and procedures to allow the SACRE to elect its own Chair.

Where it had been given explicit consideration, there were variable limits set on the duration of the Chair, ranging from one to four years. For example:

- after one year a new appointment had to be made or reappointment affirmed by the Education Committee which could effectively operate a system of patronage;

- or the Chair/Vice-Chair of SACRE was linked to the Chair or Vice-Chair of Education Committee and hence changed accordingly;

- a few SACREs were allowed to elect their own Chair annually, or after the first year or two: in one case, a SACRE wanted to change its constitution to allow for the re-election of a Chair beyond a two-year period of office.

The position on a **Vice-Chair** of SACRE was far less clear. Circular and interview responses indicated that **at least ten per cent of SACREs had no provision for a Vice-Chair.** Some RE advisers/inspectors were unsure about whether there was a Vice-Chair locally or suggested that one might be elected in the absence of the Chair. **Indeed, it was more likely for SACRE to elect its Vice-Chair, even where the LEA appointed the Chair.** With one exception, where a misunderstanding had resulted in an embarrassing tie, such elections appeared to have been amicable and a source of satisfaction to the SACRE. **Available information for 38 SACREs (17 Counties, one Inner London, eight Outer London and 12 Metropolitan Boroughs) showed that only 12 (32 per cent) had a Vice Chair from Group D, perhaps reflecting, by contrast with the appointment of Chairperson, the SACRE's increased role in its self-regulation. The majority of Vice-Chairs were thus fairly evenly divided between Group B, C and D with some variation by LEA type** (see Figure 12). County SACREs tended to show a preference for Vice-Chair from Group B, rotation or sharing by Groups; Outer London SACREs tended to prefer Group A; and Metropolitan SACREs Group D.

Further analysis for the 38 SACREs for which information was available on both Chair and Vice-Chair interestingly revealed:

- half (19) had a Chair from Group D plus a Vice-Chair from another Group; over half (10) of these SACREs were in Counties; the most popular combination, in nine SACREs overall, was for Group D (Chair) and Group A (Vice-Chair);

- one-quarter (nine), most likely Metropolitan authorities, had both a Chair and Vice-Chair from Group D;

- one-fifth (seven) — evenly spread across LEA type — had neither a Chair nor Vice-Chair from Group D; various combinations occurred: A/A, A/B, A/C, B/C, C/B, C/C and Ex-group and B;

- only three had a Chair other than from Group D — in fact all from Group B — and a Vice-Chair from Group D.

Figure 12   Vice-Chairs of SACREs by Group

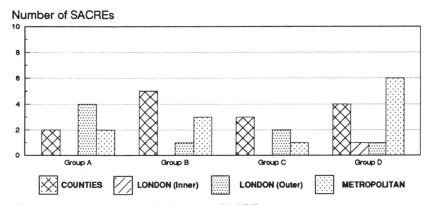

Results are based on information from 81 SACREs

+ plus one Vice-Chair by rotation Group A-C, one shared Group B and A, one shared Group C and B

In some SACREs, especially those where pre-meetings of constituent groups were regularly held, these groups also had their own Chairs and occasionally Vice-Chairs.

Interviews indicated a division of opinion on local authority flexibility or control about appointment of Chair; some saw the appointment by the LEA as a rigid provision in the SACRE's constitution; others perceived some room for manoeuvre and the possibility of change to an election by SACRE sanctioned by Education Committee. There was in some quarters a sense that as SACRE became more self-confident it would be likely to challenge LEA control over the appointment of Chair. Moreover, a question might be raised about the role of Vice-Chair in the absence of the rotation of Chair and Vice-Chair. Even where a SACRE was able to elect its Vice-Chair this might only be a semblance of democracy with no real change of control or influence through the Chair by the LEA.

Duration of Membership

In terms of duration of membership of SACRE LEAs sampled were divided between those where there was a clear specification and those where there were no rules or where the position was unclear. The absence of a defined limit could be associated with a lack of a constitution or terms of reference. A few interviewees noted that membership duration had been overlooked and might require specification but one or two had been advised not to raise the issue. **The most common pattern in over one quarter of the LEAs sampled (especially the Counties) was for SACRE membership to last for a period of four years**, coinciding with local elections. A few other SACREs had a three-year membership period: one of these had suggested a rotation of one-third of the members within this time in order to allow for confidence building, understanding of traditions and an injection of new blood. A few had an indefinite membership: in one SACRE elected members served for one year, other members indefinitely, and co-optees could attend three meetings.

Indefinite membership tended to be associated with the view that since members were representatives they were entitled to stand until they were replaced by their nominating body, unlike the SACREs where the LEA took control by specifying duration. Interpretation of the notion of representation was an issue (see pp.20-21). Once again there was a need for balance: for provision for renewal of membership on the one hand, and some continuity on the other, especially relating to overseeing implementation of the AS and monitoring RE provision. Whilst a certain turnover of membership is inevitable, too frequent changes could make for extra demands in terms of INSET for SACRE members.

SACRE Operation

SACRE's operation needs to be considered in two ways: its procedures and the substance of its deliberations. Its manner of working raised issues about its constitution, the attendance of members and the public, the frequency, dates, times and places of meetings, whole and sub-group meetings, meeting style and atmosphere, voting and minutes of meetings. The substance of SACRE's considerations could be broadly divided into those matters referred by the LEA, requests by SACRE for information, and its communications with schools (see pp.76ff).

Procedure

Terms of Reference, Standing Orders and Constitutions

ERA gave scant guidance on the procedure to be adopted by SACREs, other than in relation to the mannner of voting (see p.75). It was therefore a matter of some interest as to whether attention had been given to defining in writing the terms of reference, standing orders or constitution of SACREs. Although the titles and nature of such documents varied and made categorization difficult, **a SACRE was more likely than not to have some formally elaborated remit and procedures.** In response to the circular's request for local documentation on the role and function of the SACRE, over two-thirds of respondents (62/88, 70 per cent; Counties 23/33, London Boroughs 17/25, Metropolitan Boroughs 22/30) sent examples (see Table 2) of their constitutions, terms of reference, standing orders or statements of their roles and fuctions (see also p.88). By comparison, three-quarters of the SACREs in the 28 LEAs sampled had such written 'constitutions' (Counties 8/12; London Boroughs 5/6; Metropolitan Boroughs 8/10). The slightly higher proportion of Boroughs, especially London Boroughs, in the sample with a written formal remit is related to the fact that, despite the circular's request, it was sometimes only during interview that the existence of such documents became apparent.

Interviews and meeting minutes indicated that where a SACRE constitution or similar document existed the need for or nature of such a constitution had quite often been a matter for discussion at an early, if not the first, meeting of SACRE. But it had not always been raised as an issue even if there were a pre-existing SACRE, reconstituted post-ERA. **Although it appears that RE advisers/inspectors or other LEA officers would usually have outlined to SACRE its role and function at an initial meeting, it was more likely for a member of the LEA's legal or administrative department to draft a constitution. It was rare for a SACRE to develop its own, though**

this could be a valuable experience of learning to work together. Sometimes SACRE was presented with the constitution as a *fait accompli*; in other cases it was able to be discussed and accepted by SACRE as its own. In some authorities the SACRE's constitution had to be ratified by the Education Committee. Although a thorough analysis of available documents has not been possible, variation is evident in tone (legalistic, well defined, democratic, flexible or developmental) and scope (whether, for example, it includes reference to the appointment or election of a Chair and/or Vice-Chair, length of members' service, (named) substitutes and a quorum). In a few SACREs early meeting time was taken up with deliberating the fine wording of the constitution. Indeed, one or two SACREs seemed to have become preoccupied with debating their procedures and self-government as well as their role and function, sometimes to the extent of requesting legal clarification. Elsewhere it was said SACRE liked its constitution and saw it as *'protective'*. Thus the existence, development and nature of a constitution could in itself reflect the attitude of the LEA to the SACRE as a local educational committee and to the extent of its powers and influence.

Attendance

The majority of RE advisers/inspectors interviewed claimed that **overall attendance at SACRE meetings was good** (roughly 80 per cent plus). Generally, and in the cases where it was said to be fair or poor, attendance related to factors such as: dates, times, and place of meetings and travel distance (see pp.66-69), or lack of adherence to recognized meeting procedures. For example, failure to send apologies resulted in a meeting being abandoned as it was inquorate due to lack of a member in each Group. Across the LEAs sampled spontaneous **mention was made of poor attendance of individual representatives of many of the religions and of the LEA**, with two groups receiving most comment. Some elected members' attendance was said to be poor due to perceived lack of commitment because of nomination *ex officio*, meeting times (especially if in the evening, see p.68), and other commitments, particularly nearer local election time — which in some places occurred during the interview period. Attendance of representatives of religions other than Christianity in Group A was also said to be problematic and, in particular within that group, the attendance of Muslim representative(s) (in almost one-fifth of interviews). Interviewees suggested various explanatory hypotheses: difficulty in obtaining leave from work or being less prepared to leave their own business (yet elected members received attendance fees); locally controversial events; travel difficulties (even with variable meeting places); lack of familiarity with meeting procedures or language; inhibition and alienation from meeting atmosphere and hence lack of participation in meetings (see pp.73-75).

Continuous absence necessitated personal follow-up by RE advisers/ inspectors or the SACRE clerk. Vacancies within the various groups (see p.57) according to intended SACRE membership also required persistence to fill, even if the religious affiliation of teacher or LEA representatives compensated to some extent. This was a murky area, bound up with the notion of 'representation', as some saw attendance (or vacancies) as an issue more for the nominating bodies. On the other hand, attendance could have been emphasized by the LEA as a condition of nomination and acceptance and as an earnest of commitment to the development of the SACRE and RE locally. An alternative was to incorporate in the structure of SACRE a system of **(named) deputies or substitutes** for representatives. In a minority of cases this had been allowed from the beginning, sometimes as a way of circumventing problematic meeting times. **There was elsewhere a growing recognition of a need for substitutes even if provision were not mentioned or allowed in the constitution.** Depending on the degree of formality of the meeting it might be important to have named recognized deputies; attendance could admit of cultural variation, as in a case where Muslims sometimes sent cousins as their representatives. Elsewhere SACRE had discussed whether substitutes should be allowed a voice or a vote.

Open to the Public?

A major issue, though not explicitly recognized by SACREs, is whether meetings are open to the public. The LEAs sampled were equally divided between those RE advisers/inspectors who reported that SACRE meetings were open to the public and those who said they were not or were unclear. Even pre-existing SACREs which had previously held open meetings had not necessarily reached this point since reconstitution. A further related issue is whether open meetings are well publicised in advance so that members of the public are aware of them. Indeed, it appeared rare for meetings to have advance publicity even if they were said to be public. Moreover, it was generally reported that in any case there had been no requests and that the public did not attend. Some interviewees questioned whether there would be a sufficient level of interest, but in one or two cases lay observers were present. The issue then became whether or not they should be co-opted. A few constitutions specified when others could be invited: generally heads and deputies or sometimes governors were invited or expected to attend to speak to their school's application for a determination. At least one SACRE specified that in such instances parents should also be present. Other LEA professionals, in addition to those officers listed as members of SACRE or in attendance, occasionally also observed meetings. Some RE advisers/inspectors claimed that members of the public would be welcome as observers even though SACRE meetings were not advertised, though one or two noted that *'the location would not allow for many to be present'*. Few meetings however, would be as open to community participation as the SACRE which comprised eight Muslim representatives (five mosques, three community associations) and allowed for substitutes. On one occasion an unknown Muslim made a particularly spirited contribution and on inquiry was found to have been the taxi driver of one representative who had stayed on for the meeting. Generally however, as with other aspects of wider communication, little encouragement had been given to public attendance at SACRE meetings.

Meeting Frequency

The frequency of meetings was another matter which needed to be decided and in some cases was specified in the SACRE's constitution. Replies to the circular which asked for both the date of formation of the SACRE and the dates of meetings in 1989-90 (and in three additional cases information from respondents who sent Annual Reports) indicated that there was sometimes a gap of two or three months (occasionally several months) between SACRE formation and first meeting. Given that the DES Circular 3/89 *due date* of formation of SACREs in *Inner* London (1.9.89) was almost one year after that in other LEAs (29.9.88) and the fact that most SACREs were actually formed several months after their respective due dates (see p.22) *the numbers of meetings have been calculated for the first full year of meetings of each individual SACRE according to reliable meeting date information up to the end of July 1990.* This cut-off date means that in addition to the eight Inner London SACREs, numbers of meetings are also underestimated for 13 SACREs (six Counties, two Outer London Boroughs, five Metropolitan Boroughs) which had not met for one full year by the end of July 1990 (a total of 23 per cent of those for which information is available). By contrast, five SACREs had met for almost two years.

Analysis reveals a considerable variation by LEA type in the range of the number of meetings held during the first year (see Table 9), from 1—12 across all SACREs (N=91), though the usual number was three or four. Further analysis including meetings up until the end of July 1990 where this exceeded the first full year showed a proportionate increase of one or two meetings for the Counties, and only in the case of Outer London Boroughs a change in the range (two—nine). Information from interviews indicates that at least half of the sample held termly meetings and that this was the normal pattern. However, a few held meetings twice termly and exceptionally,

Table 9   Number of SACRE meetings in their first year up to July 1990

LEA Type	Available N	Range No. Meetings Across Each SACRE's First Year	Usual Number of Meetings in First Year
Counties	34	3-8	3
London Boroughs			
Inner	8	3-4	3
Outer	17	1-7	4 or 5
Metropolitan Boroughs	32	1-12	4
Total	91	1-12	3-5

monthly, as the AR of the SACRE in the Metropolitan Borough with 12 meetings in its first year showed. Frequency of meetings and amount of business to transact might relate to whether the AS were under revision and hence overlap with ASC meetings. Some SACREs made a slow start in meeting date and pattern, increasing the number of meetings latterly. Yet a few others had postponed meetings, cancelled them, because of insufficient business or because of uncertainty as to whether a determination application could be considered if only the deputy head were present, or abandoned the meeting, because it was inquorate.

Meeting Length, Dates and Times

Meeting Length. An ordinary business meeting could vary from half an hour to three and a half hours; around two hours was the average. If some form of INSET were involved meetings could last a half or whole day. Some RE advisers felt their SACRE meetings were too brief; others considered them too long and wanted a recognized closure of 10 p.m.

Meeting Dates. In a multifaith body such as SACRE it was important to be aware of and sensitive to the religious observances and festivals of world religions other than Christianity when setting meeting dates; this could involve consciousness raising of LEA administrative officers acting as SACRE clerks; for example, not setting meetings on Fridays if a Muslim presence were expected. Setting meeting dates ahead could prove difficult if dates of religious festivals, such as Eid, were not fixed or known. Such instances indicated a need for open negotiation and raised a question about the extent to which British institutional life has yet to recognize and incorporate the religious observances of world religions other than Christianity.

Meeting Times. Whether the SACRE should meet in the morning afternoon or evening, was in some cases, clearly a controversial matter. Interview responses indicated no clear pattern overall, though there was a trend towards evening meetings in the Metropolitan Boroughs. The main issues seemed to be whether the LEA provided teacher supply cover for daytime meetings; the view of elected members on meeting times; and the proportion of SACRE members (mostly in Group A) who were in unrelated full-time employment, who were most adversely affected by daytime meetings. Whilst to some extent it was a question of the status of the meeting and whether expenses were available, there were also other relevant considerations of religious and local council practice.

> In two or three cases Muslims and Sikhs were reported to want evening meetings, which usually started at 6.30 p.m., put back to 7.30 or 8.00 p.m. to allow for evening prayer — but this was not always well received by Christian members.

> The majority of members in another SACRE wanted meetings at 4.00 p.m. instead of 6.00 p.m., but elected members claimed this was inconvenient and made the matter a formal complaint.

> Elsewhere elected members in SACREs with daytime meetings were said not to appreciate the difficulties for those in employment : in one case councillors and teachers whose presence was supported by the local authority abandoned a meeting to demonstrate solidarity with ambulance workers who had withdrawn their labour, thus rendering the meeting inquorate — an unfortunate example to the other members who had taken a day's leave from work.

In response to the issue of meeting time a few SACREs were experimenting with alternate daytime and evening meetings.

Meeting Place and Accommodation

Meeting Place. At the outset the nature of the meeting place of SACRE had not necessarily been given much thought in terms of its implications for meeting style, atmosphere and community perceptions, but there was evidence of changing practice. Many SACREs had held initial or early meetings in the formal arena of the Council Chamber in the City, Borough or County Hall, which could prove somewhat overawing for all but elected members. Several, however, had subsequently moved to smaller more conducive rooms in Education Offices or at the Civic Centre. Some had held one or more meetings at different locations across the county or borough, usually in teachers' centres or schools. RE advisers/inspectors were most likely to be instrumental in suggesting alternative venues. Some saw this an an important transition phase, though others felt it was too early for their particular SACRE. Meeting in schools or teachers' centres, especially if there were access to RE exhibitions, could provide an educational framework for SACRE discussions, though members might need encouragement to take advantage of the setting. Given the institutionalization of other aspects of the SACRE it might be important to consider, as a few had done, holding meetings from time to time in locations of minority ethnic settlement to support such SACRE members and reach into the communities they represent.

Accommodation. Within the meeting place the degree of formality of seating was an important contributory factor to meeting atmosphere. Council Chambers were formal environments if discussion were intended. Some SACREs were reportedly LEA-dominated with RE inspector/ adviser, senior education officer, SACRE clerk and sometimes other LEA officers flanking the Chairperson and set apart from the body of the meeting. Seating position could point up role confusions where RE inspectors/ advisers/advisory teachers were members of SACRE as such or in another capacity (see p.53), as distinct from in attendance. Some SACREs had moved to more informal seating patterns so that all members could see one another. Consideration also needed to be given to provision of accommodation for pre-meetings of the constituent groups or for working parties or sub-committees.

Agenda Setting

Agenda setting **appeared to be a highly variable practice which could be inclusive or exclusive of SACRE members as a whole.** There were differences of approach affecting whether members were able to influence the agenda or were aware that they could contribute agenda items, and whether this was facilitated. RE advisers/inspectors were usually concerned in some way with agenda setting and meeting briefings, often with another LEA officer and/or the SACRE Chair. Although it is unclear to what extent SACRE was informally involved, the following examples indicate ways in which agenda setting *involving SACRE* occurred.

One senior adviser in a Metropolitan Borough with a long-standing SACRE wrote to all members for agenda items. He considered this important for the meeting to work satisfactorily, even though it increased his work load. He felt the practice was reinforced by the particular role given to SACRE by ERA. Items were then discussed with the SACRE Chair and an agenda drawn up.

One County authority held a high-powered pre-SACRE briefing for its Chair, the CEO, Head of Schools Division and the County Solicitor, partly because SACRE was the first agenda item on Education Committee meetings. There was also a lot of contact between the RE adviser and SACRE members before meetings to raise concerns.

Another SACRE held a pre-SACRE urgent business group meeting for one morning which comprised: one member of each of SACRE's constituent groups, its Chair and Vice-Chair, the Diocesan Director of Education and one LEA representative (but not the RE adviser) to draw up the agenda and review major issues.

An associated pre-meeting issue was the degree to which SACRE members were duly prepared, with papers circulated in advance, or whether documents were tabled at the meeting. Given the number and complexity of some issues under discussion prior opportunity for reading and reflection was imperative for informed and serious consideration and debate.

Associated SACRE Meetings

A few interviewees claimed that SACRE only met as a whole group, but others indicated that various groupings met for different purposes on a regular basis or according to issues being raised. Such meetings could take various forms.

Working Parties or Sub-committees. Although some local authority legal advisers seem to have queried whether sub-committees involving SACRE members were allowable under the Act, a number of SACREs had set up, or were moving towards, local working parties which included SACRE members, sometimes one from each group. There were working parties on: how the SACRE runs, SACRE's role in complaints procedure, drafting a constitution, a survey of RE provision, CW, assessment and attainment, support to governors and school visits. One SACRE had two standing working parties for primary and secondary RE, each comprised of teachers and diocesan members, which had produced various guidelines. Notwithstanding this level of active involvement by some SACRE members, working parties for the ASC, which sometimes also included SACRE members, tended to take even more time.

Pre-meetings of SACRE's Four Constituent Groups. DES Circular 3/89 (Para 16) indicated that each constituent group of SACRE *'is to regulate its own proceedings'*. Several LEAs in the sample made regular or *ad hoc* provision of accommodation for these pre-meetings for up to one hour prior to full SACRE meetings and, if necessary, during the meeting — usually for discussion of determination applications. Sometimes the RE adviser/ inspector was invited to give guidance. It was again a moot point as to whether such pre-meetings were open to the public. There were some indications that whilst diocesan members of Group B, teachers' association members of Group C, and elected members in Group D might have other opportunities for meeting and brief discussion of SACRE matters, this was less likely to occur for the diverse members of Group A. **Structured opportunities for the separate meeting of Group A might therefore be**

all the more important given their varying perspectives, as in the following examples.

In one SACRE with seven members in Group A the four members of the religions other than Christianity (Baha'i, Buddhist, Jew, Muslim) held a pre-meeting and then sent one representative, by alphabetical order of faith, to the main group meeting.

Each constituent group of another SACRE held regular pre-meetings prior to the full SACRE regarding matters for decision. LEA officers perceived this as important in allowing members a voice given the variable numbers within the groups (18, 5, 7, 7). Full attendance could be important as last-minute arrivals could sway a vote. Interestingly, all except Group A used secretarial facilities of the LEA, thus effectively making Group A's minutes private.

Elsewhere it was open to the four groups to meet in advance and the LEA was prepared to pay travel expenses. The RE inspector encouraged pre-meetings and important preparatory and contextual work, not least in getting to know the perspective of the group spokesperson. Each group had met at least once. Groups were asked to report back to the whole SACRE on issues discussed.

Within SACRE Meetings. These usually comprised separate group discussions on determinations, or, in some cases where the RE adviser/inspector introduced task-related INSET, for example, organizing new groups to consider CW or writing the AR.

SACRE as a Whole: Style and Atmosphere

The nature of the whole SACRE meeting itself was a matter of keen interest to RE advisers/inspectors and raised controversial issues. The degree of formality or informality in the **style of the meeting** was related to several factors, especially the accommodation, the felt presence or orchestration of the LEA, the leadership of the SACRE chair and the kind of meeting procedure followed. The Chairperson was critical and could be contentious by personality or appointment (see pp. 57-59). Tensions could arise if there were not considerate communication between the Chair, RE adviser/inspector and SACRE clerk. Some SACRE members could be alienated by too formal a use of council committee procedures. Interviewees with previous experience of SACREs reported changes in meeting style, both from more debate and informality to an 'Education Committee' style, and in the opposite direction. Generally time was needed to get new members *'tuned in'* and there was usually a feeling in the reconstituted SACREs that they were not yet operating at the same level as previously. Discussion, learning to work together and appreciation

71

of different points of view were enhanced by small group meetings and informal opportunities for communication over refreshments.

The **atmosphere of meetings** was reported to be variable across SACREs and could change between and during SACRE meetings. Some said there was little discussion or argument and meetings were not contentious. On the other hand, **many claimed meetings were harmonious, lively or indeed** *'characterized by good humour, forceful argument and debate'*. In one case a residential which had been held for members of the ASC at a particularly controversial point some years previously, and which had resulted in great solidarity, was still referred to locally and provided a bank of fellow feeling on which the SACRE continued to draw. Other interviewees reported changes in meeting atmosphere: one SACRE had started tensely with members lacking in mutual trust but there had been many demonstrations of goodwill and the inspector was *'impressed by the general will to avoid controversy'*; elsewhere the level of debate was said to be improving and alternative viewpoints were more likely to be advanced. However, the harmony of the meeting could be fragile and easily upset by local political changes or heavy-handed chairing of meetings which could reinforce and alienate the perceptions of minority communities.

Promoting Communication within SACRE

Thus, in addition to the manner of regulation of meetings and the good will in principle of members to work together, participation in, and the efficiency and effectiveness of SACRE also depended on three main factors.

Understanding of RE. SACREs were deliberately comprised of members representing a range of different religious, educational and political perspectives. This was a potent mix of people with strongly held views which could be more or less informed, on the one hand, about religious and community perceptions or, on the other, about RE and actual school and college practice. Whilst some interviewees found some councillors ill-informed about education and RE in particular, or narrow in their perceptions, others levelled similar criticisms at some members of Group A. Generally — though there were individual exceptions — Church of England members of Group B and teacher members of Group C were thought to be more likely to share educational language and to make informed comment — perhaps to some extent because of previous SACRE experience. Given good will, there was further scope for expanding horizons through SACRE INSET.

Understanding Meeting Procedure. Use of local authority committee procedures could be unnecessarily mystifying for SACRE members who were not habituated to such meeting style. Several interviewees observed that, although elected members liked a debating style, others did not know how to respond. This could make for inbalance if the political and LEA officer members were predominant. Although a few felt that minority ethnic group members in their SACRE were well attuned to institutionalized rules and manner of procedure and had learnt to *'operate the system'*, others were more likely to see this as problematic. For example:

> one Hindu repeatedly questioned standard minuting procedure at the beginning of each meeting, dealing with matters arising;

> elsewhere a Sikh repeated objections to alleged bias on a questionnaire to parents, used as evidence in support of determination applications, each time an application was considered, even though there had been a long debate about the point when the first application was reviewed in the meeting. Some members lost patience and the Chair dealt somewhat abruptly with the issue. This resulted in a walkout by the Sikh who was followed by other Sikhs, representing a different, usually opposed denomination, plus Hindu and Muslim members, in response to what they saw as the domination of the white political right;

> one Muslim presented a *'list of demands'* to SACRE on behalf of the community. The RE Inspector spent some time drafting *'a suitable response'* for the next meeting but the Muslim member was absent, thus provoking a critical response from some *'white highlanders'*.

Whilst any SACRE member might demonstrate lack of familiarity with or abuse of meeting procedure, there was a special need to be sensitive to possible cultural differences in style of presentation and to view them in the light of minority perceptions of the local political, ethnic and racial context. An additional general factor was whether tight chairing of a meeting was considered to the authority's short-term advantage to minimize discussion on controversial issues and to pass recommendations 'on the nod' thereby, limiting SACRE's role, or whether the authority gave due weight to SACRE as a deliberating and decision-making body.

Inter- and Intra-group Dialogue. Both understanding RE and understanding meeting procedures were related to the more general issue of promotion of dialogue within and between SACRE groupings which needed to be addressed.

> **Whole SACRE.** Notwithstanding the goodwill of some members some interviewees felt that the meeting was *'an uneasy mix which does not gel'* as members were people who would not usually meet together. Meetings could thus be dominated by the articulate who knew how to *'play the committee game'*. Articulacy could vary from individual to individual and group to group depending on location. For example, in some cases only minority ethnic members with strong views were said to speak, whereas elsewhere there was differentiation between members from Asian backgrounds which were dominant among minority ethnic

communities locally and black members in a minority. In some SACREs pre-meetings were suggested as a strategy for developing articulacy and confidence. Some interviewees reported increasing general participation in meetings over time.

Within Groups. Group A was usually the most diverse and most numerous group and one which needed to allow expression of many viewpoints to reach a decision by vote or consensus. Indeed, in some ways the diversity of Group A mirrored that of SACRE as a whole. Occasional social initiatives to enable Group A to get to know each other better were not always successful. In many SACREs constituent groups reflected SACRE as a whole in appointing a Chair and secretary and again the Chair could be a critical influence. This was a skilful and sensitive role as such a spokesperson in the main SACRE meeting could find him or herself having to put forward a majority decision and reasons to which he or she did not subscribe. Another, but usually more recondite issue, was possible exertion of political pressure in Group D, where this was composed solely of elected members proportionate to local representation and thus sometimes with an in-built party political majority. If this were overt in the SACRE it could however be challenged by other groups.

Between Groups. Some interviewees with previous SACREs reported that the reconstituted body had gained a great deal by the statutory expansion of Group A to include representatives of religious denominations other than Christianity which '*appropriately reflect the principal religious traditions of the area*'. However, in a SACRE where the non-Christian members were effectively marginalized, specifically in terms of voting rights, by only being given co-opted status, there could be direct confrontation with elected members, with the LEA advisers trying to hold the middle ground. Several interviewees considered a key issue was to promote dialogue between Group A, B and C on the one hand and Group D on the other. There were examples of polarization — on CW guidelines in particular. But in multiethnic communities the controversial issues with which SACRE had to contend could unite, divide and cross its constituent groups.

For example, in one SACRE local elections had resulted in an unexpected change of council and new SACRE chair. In a geographically and racially divided area immediate cuts in funding to voluntary community groups and a race unit had coincided with the emergence of a narrow '*defensive*' view of Christianity articulated in SACRE, apparently in reaction to a previous authority policy which positively supported equality of opportunity and multifaith RE. This had compounded issues which had begun to surface in the SACRE of polarization between two groups of Sikhs, one of which saw RE and CW in relation to ERA as a way of inculcating Sikhism in school. This was related to wider community issues and fears about cultural and hence religious preservation on account of a decline in community language speaking by third- and fourth- generation Sikhs. Both the Church of England group, aided by elected members recently appointed to SACRE, and the Sikh group, essentially wanted a particular interpretation of their faiths to be incorporated into the school-based education of their children. Whilst other SACRE members could themselves hold views of equal strength, they recognized the mainstream *educational remit of SACRE and were attempting to accommodate diversity rather than toe a confessional line.* In such contexts the structural provision of an on-going opportunity for interfaith and intercommunity dialogue in SACRE could in itself be a strength.

Voting

ERA and DES Circular 3/89 were more explicit about the form of voting which SACRE was to follow:

- each constituent group has one vote (S. 11 (6));
- a vote by Group A-C may require a review of the AS (S.11 (7));
- grant maintained school representatives and co-opted members have no vote (Para 16);
- decisions within a group about how a vote is to be cast do not require unanimity (Para 16).

Many SACREs had reiterated or elaborated on these rules in the SACRE's terms of reference, standing orders or constitution. Even so, it was surprising that not every SACRE appeared to have a statement about what constituted a quorum. Where specified, a quorum admitted of variable interpretation across SACREs.

It was thus interesting to find that at least three-quarters of interviewees in each LEA type claimed that their SACRE operated or aimed to operate mostly by consensus. Only one or two, where meetings in the first year were dominated by determinations, reported votes were usually taken. However *'consensus'* could mask a range of meanings and procedures. Advisers had sometimes explained to SACRE *'that it was important to act by consensus'*. In other cases there had been careful prior negotiation about controversial matters. *'Consensus'* could be a passive acquiescence *'on the nod'* or an active expression of common will and intent. One senior adviser with a previous longstanding SACRE claimed that *'it would be a sad day if it came to a vote'*. The aim was to develop consensus in the new SACRE but *'this is not achieved over night. In the early stages there has been blood on the carpet whilst we have been sorting out our ideas. The only way to consensus is through honest debate.'*

Furthermore, even if the aim was towards consensus, many of the SACREs sampled had taken one or two votes in addition to those on the AS and determinations. Matters which drew a vote included (most frequently): CW guidelines, SACRE constitution, involvement in complaints procedure, election of Chair, co-options, survey of RE provision, teaching time, INSET, funding of an RE centre and voluntary-aided schools.

Minutes of Meetings

A final issue about meeting procedure concerned minutes of meetings. Minutes of meetings for 40 SACREs (17 Counties, 12 London Boroughs, 11 Metropolitan Boroughs) were received during the research period. A methodological feature of interest was that some RE advisers/inspectors who were prepared to be interviewed at length nevertheless were not empowered or felt unable to supply meeting minutes, whilst some circular respondents returned such documents without such a direct request. This is in itself indicates a variation in the degree of openness surrounding SACREs, reinforced by a scrutiny of the minutes. Whereas a few did indicate a level of debate, discussion, suggestion, dissent, the majority were fairly tightly written formal records which gave little indication of the feeling of meetings. A few were mere records of decisions taken. Exceptionally, an interviewee commented that SACRE was *'a talking shop'* with little formally agreed to record. Elsewhere, however, it was more the case that some contentious meetings *'were not reflected in clever minute writing'*. In some authorities the nature of minutes of meetings as an agreed record was given heightened significance if meetings or minutes were open and available to the public. Such availability was likely to be an issue of local controversy and a matter of reference in some SACRE Annual Reports.

SACRE's Agenda: Referrals, Requests and Communication

ERA prescribes the duty of every local SACRE as:
> *'to advise the authority upon such matters connected with religious worship in county schools and the religious education to be given in accordance with an agreed syllabus as the authority may refer to the council or as the council may see fit.'*

(GB. Statutes, S. 11 (1) (a))

Further DES Circular 3/89 specifies:

> 'The SACRE has two particular functions: it can require its LEA to review its current agreed syllabus; and secondly, it may determine, on application by the head teacher, that the requirement for collective worship in county schools to be wholly or mainly of a broadly Christian character shall not apply to the collective worship provided for some or all of the pupils in a particular school.' (Para 11).

In carrying out these functions the DES Circular elaborates:

> 'It is for an LEA to decide what matters it wishes to refer to its SACRE; but the Act says that these should include in particular methods of teaching, choice of teaching materials and the provision of teacher training. The SACRE is not confined to advising on matters referred to it by the LEA; it may offer advice on any matters related to its functions as it sees fit.' (Para 12).

Subsequently, the REC Handbook suggested that, in addition to its statutory duties, the SACRE would need to consider how it might provide information about its own role and function for governors, headteachers and parents.

The interview attempted to explore these aspects of the SACRE's operation: matters referred by the LEA to SACRE; information requested by the SACRE (and advice given — see p.174ff); communication with schools and colleges about SACRE's role and function; and communication with other professionals such as HMI, the press and the wider public. Whilst two or three interviewees claimed that it was sometimes difficult to distinguish the respective input of the LEA, SACRE and educational institutions, because of a working partnership, it was clear from other accounts that there was often an attempt to define these boundaries or keep them clearly defined and to forestall or limit the raising of issues which were, in the LEA's perception, locally controversial.

Matters Referred to SACRE by the LEA

It was perhaps surprising to find that **as many as one-third of interviewees claimed that their LEA had not referred any matter to SACRE for its attention.** Of the remainder, a very few indicated that the input had all been from the LEA (see p.119) **but in the majority of SACREs matters for consideration on the agenda seemed to derive both from LEA referrals and requests from SACREs for information.** There appeared to be several reasons why LEAs may not have referred any matters to SACRE. In a few cases RE was low profile and not necessarily controversial: one interviewee suggested the SACRE was only working because legally required — otherwise some work would be done on the curriculum and probably the AS, but SACRE meetings would not have occurred. In other cases it appeared to be a matter of the LEA trying to keep professional control over RE: it might be thought important to be seen to have a nominal discussion in SACRE — even though members might be perceived as ill-informed, they were seen to be concerned and supportive; or it might be a question of failing to raise consciousness, limiting their access to information. Alternatively, there was a sense of not wanting SACRE to make decisions until it was perceived to have a better understanding through consistently good practice. In a few other cases however, the SACREs themselves were active and tended to keep the LEA 'on its toes'.

Despite SACRE's particular remit over the AS, and the fact that ERA's requirements for RE and the bringing into existence of the SACRE itself had given greater prominence to this area of the curriculum, it is not unremarkable that **over one-third of LEAs (10/28) where interviews were conducted had brought the AS to the attention of the SACRE in its first year of operation.** Indeed, in interviews and in responding to the circular, as many as 23 LEAs (half Metropolitan Boroughs) indicated that the local AS was currently undergoing revision. **The AS, and its need of revision was thus often one of the first matters to be referred by the LEA to the SACRE - sometimes at its very first meeting. Its revision was, in turn, one of the first recommendations SACRE made to the LEA.**

In three LEAs (one where the AS dated from the early 1950s and two from the mid-60s) where there had previously been a lack of interest in developing a new one, a change of DoE in one LEA, and, in the others, a local feeling of need for a clear statement of what RE stands for and its unique contribution to the curriculum had, together with the stimulus of ERA, brought about the establishment of ASCs which apparently marginally predated, or were only ratified by, SACRE.

In one LEA with an AS dating from the early 80s specifying a framework of aims and objectives and suggesting teaching approaches, the adviser brought to SACRE's attention the fact that it gives no guidance on sixth-form RE, and the need for a supporting handbook. As a result, it was intended to set up an ASC to review the structure of the AS. The ASC was to have a core membership similar to that of SACRE with additional RE specialists, on which SACRE's advice had been sought.

In addition, in one or two cases in the sample a new AS whose production had been put in hand prior to ERA had been published before the establishment of SACRE. SACRE was now concerned with features of its implementation, such as overseeing the production of a teachers' handbook.

In some places, the ASC was taking priority over SACRE and receiving a greater input and effort, but in other cases the work of ASC and SACRE proceeded in parallel and was complementary (see also pp.124-126). However, in one or two LEAs movement towards revision of the AS was proceeding at a slower pace:

> In one LEA the RE inspector was concerned about: the balance between Christianity and other world faiths in the current AS; and the discordance between the AS and the County policy on multicultural education; the lack of correspondence with thinking about key stages; and an absence of sixth-form RE. Yet he did not wish the SACRE to decide on a revision of the AS until some time had been spent thinking about the nature of RE. Teachers' union nominees on SACRE were working with a task group of RE teachers (alongside other National Curriculum areas and supported by LEATGS money) on curriculum development and INSET for RE and were writing papers for the SACRE. They were thus a catalyst for raising with SACRE the issue of the need for revising the AS and enabling it to make a well-informed decision.

Several LEAs had raised with SACRE the issues of attainment targets (ATs), assessment arrangements (AAs), INSET and staffing.

> In one Metropolitan LEA, where responsibility for RE was divided between a primary advisory teacher and a secondary adviser, they had made presentations to SACRE on RE in primary education and RE's relation to **assessment, recording and achievement.** Revisions of the AS, being undertaken by four age-related working parties, were being linked to PoS, five ATs and advice on assessment.

> In a County LEA one of the early decisions of SACRE had been to **set up a working party on assessment arrangements** which, in turn, had led to questioning of the AS, and an attempt to develop a better infra-structure in terms of continuity and progression and elaborating explicit and implicit RE.

> In one largely rural LEA the adviser thought it important to keep SACRE informed on INSET and on teacher supply — *'that RE teachers are ''few and far between'''*. He felt that with a greater awareness of the issues SACRE could be more supportive and by reporting back to their church groups across the County could help to provide better understanding of the local situation.

On the whole however, at this early stage, **relatively few LEAs in the sample had referred teaching methods, materials or training for SACREs consideration as the DES Circular suggested** (see p.81). In a few LEAs, at their invitation, SACRE had been involved in drafting its own constitution or in considering what its role on RE in the local complaints procedure might be; these more democratic consultations could result in significant changes such as the SACRE wishing to elect is own Chairperson rather than have the Chair appointed by the LEA (see pp.59-60) or to ensure the inclusion of the RE adviser in the LEA representatives on SACRE (see p.111).

The second major function of the SACRE—to advise on collective worship and consider applications for determinations—was anticipated by many LEAs and subsequently proved to be a major preoccupation of SACRE in its first year. It is interesting that there is no prescribed statutory body or procedure (in parallel to the ASC for the AS) for reviewing CW policy as such. This appears to allow for significant inter-LEA variation (in relation to local religious and ethnic considerations) in the extent to which LEAs perceived SACRE to have a contribution to make to local guidelines on CW in general (as distinct from its specific statutory role to decide on applications for a determination). In a few LEAs, especially those covering urban multiethnic areas, there was a felt need for SACRE to be made aware at an early date of its responsibilities with respect to CW and determinations. Indeed, one or two interviewees reported that there had as yet been little scope for raising anything else with the SACRE. Conversely, other LEAs deliberately avoided raising CW with the SACRE, preferring to keep it in the hands of professionals. Other authorities anticipated tensions over raising CW which did indeed result in much heated debate and controversy, often in contradistinction to discussion on RE issues.

Where the complex matter of issuing guidelines for CW locally was brought to the attention of the SACRE this usually involved presentation of a paper or a draft document by the RE adviser/inspector. There was often an educative role here for the adviser. Discussions could be protracted and impassioned. Collective worship, especially its application to determinations, was viewed as a critical issue and function for SACRE on which it expected to have a significant say, if not to hold sway (see also pp.138-139 and pp.152-153). In some LEAs the nature of CW was a sticking point and clearly raised the question of the **status of the advice of the adviser**.

> At the request of the DoE, in response to a need expressed by schools, the adviser wrote a paper on CW which was given to the pre-SACRE meetings and then the main meeting. It was amended by the majority political party in the local authority group which comprised evangelical and traditional Christians. A controversial point was the difference between corporate and collective worship. The revised paper was sent back to the next pre-SACRE and SACRE meetings where it was amended, by the Church of England group, back to its original version and passed by SACRE to be sent to schools. However, the DoE (possibly taking the interests of councillors into account) had asked to review the situation with the adviser. A possible solution might be to send out an advisory document rather than one from the DoE or SACRE.

> In another LEA the inspector had written papers on SACRE's involvement in the complaints procedure, assessment and review of the AS as well as CW guidelines. The inspector, in setting out a range of options, emphasized that

of individual schools applying for whole-school determinations as part of a borough-wide policy. Although CW had been a major focus in SACRE, it had disliked what it perceived as an imposed recommendation. In effect consideration of decisions on this and other papers had been deferred because of SACRE's preoccupation with its role, function and powers.

In a third multiethnic authority CW had been referred by the LEA to the SACRE at its commencement. SACRE had dealt with a considerable number of applications for determination during its first year, although no CW policy was publicly available. It was proposed, as part of an attempt to expand the role of SACRE, to develop a resources pack on CW with an AEO and ATRE working with a nominee from each of the four SACRE groups and considering any material put forward by them.

The following examples, according to interviewees' reports, indicate the **range of issues considered by SACREs,** in differing local contexts for RE.

In one Metropolitan LEA where RE had a low profile the LEA had referred to the SACRE: the AS and a related curriculum input; SACRE's constitution; the HMI report on RE (GB. DES, 1989c); the Religious Studies bulletin; and the lack of time the Humanities Adviser had to give to RE — this was raised by the DoE.

In a County authority, where SACRE and the professionals were said to be mutually supportive but where there was a strong LEA input, SACRE had considered: its own role and duties, staffing, training, RE provision at different levels, attainment targets, publications on CW, the aims and objectives of the AS and RE in relation to core curriculum areas;

In a Metropolitan LEA with a long-standing SACRE with strong Church connections and a proactive approach (*'there is no hang-up over SACRE locally it can do what it likes'*) a recent meeting of the reconstituted SACRE had included consideration of: the number of LEA members; the Saltley SACRE forum; the need for a RE co-ordinator; attainment in RE; the PCFRE conference on Records of Achievement in RE; whole curriculum issues, resulting in the formation of a working party to support the AS; discussion of the review of the AS in the light of INSET and school development plans; use of the Westhill handbook on attainment targets (Regional RE Centre, Midlands, 1989); and discussion of the SACRE Chair writing to schools about finance and concern about lack of staffing for RE.

Overall the very business of referring matters to SACRE and the nature **of these matters epitomised the central issue in relation to SACRE — the balance of power between the SACRE and the LEA. This seemed to revolve around three main, interconnected aspects:**

Information = Knowledge: is knowledge power? Some advisers/inspectors saw it as their function to provide SACRE with information on national and local RE matters (see pp. 102ff) to write papers or make regular reports about school-based RE and INSET — in general to bring to SACRE's attention issues which needed consideration. Others reacted more defensively and indicated some reluctance to share knowledge about some issues or details.

Education = Understanding: how well versed are SACRE members in aspects of religious *education*? How much do LEAs/advisers/ inspectors want them to understand? How much effort are they prepared to put into raising SACRE's awareness and generating its appreciation of the complexity of issues and the relevance of context in RE and CW?

Many advisers/inspectors recognized that individual SACRE members generally had a framework for understanding RE, but one of the challenges of such a body was that by the very nature of its statutorily defined composition both different individuals and different groups within SACRE represented, and were in place to represent, a range of relevant interests — religious, educational and political. Thus some were well informed about their faiths, others about teaching and school management, yet others about LEA policy and financial implications.

In some SACREs there were considerable proactive attempts by professionals through inputs of content and working/meeting procedures to *'educate'* the SACRE (see p.101ff) and raise the level of discussion and range of issues; in some, individuals or groups were aware of the need to educate one another and were beginning to engage in a self-educating dialogue. There was an underlying concern that SACRE should not be *'a political football'* or *'talking shop'*. Yet in others where LEA or professional control was seen as of overriding importance SACRE could be perceived as *'ill-informed'*, *'uncomprehending'* and *'not a professional group'*, despite its membership.

Application = Skills + Motivation: would the LEA/adviser/ inspector use the SACRE to ratify or support LEA policy and implementation or to raise the profile of RE? Or would the SACRE exercise a certain independence and have a distinct influence?

Some LEAs seemed to have made pre-emptive strikes, producing documents of advice and guidelines, in some cases within a local framework for curriculum reflection and development, just before the constitution of SACRE with its statutory powers. Thus materials were presented to SACRE as a *fait accompli* with a view to its adopting and endorsing LEA recommendations. Locally the criterion was the document's utility not its status. SACRE was not yet perceived as the kind of body to produce a practically oriented developmental document related to programmes of study and assessment or assembly.

But elsewhere SACRE's imprimatur was seen as significant *'cementing a triumvirate between the SACRE itself, the LEA and schools and colleges which are in symbiotic relationship'*.

In other LEAs where the RE profile was lower SACRE could be viewed as a potential ally, a pressure group in support of RE vis à vis the LEA, Education Committee or schools. Thus it was difficult for some LEAs/

officers/advisers to come to terms with the fact that SACRE is a separate statutory working group. LEAs and SACREs were learning about each other and how each could be used. Professionals were beginning to realize that it might be advantageous to influence SACRE members (especially elected members) so that they, in turn, could exercise influence for RE.

SACRE's Requests to the LEA

ERA, as elaborated by the DES Circular, obliged the SACRE to offer advice on any matters related to its functions (see p.174ff). **In undertaking their agenda in the first year of operation most SACREs evidently felt the need to request additional information of various kinds in relation to RE and CW** (in addition to observing practice, see pp.91-92 or promoting religious and educational contacts, see p.92ff). However, a few interviewees indicated that their local SACRE had not made any such requests. The matter of SACRE's requests for information, as with observation, were, in some LEAs, regarded with apprehension and real concern, not least because of their implications for resourcing and work loads. They were seen as time-consuming, expensive and potentially embarrassing. These were uncharted waters where the boundaries were unclear. Was SACRE entitled to ask for information? Who was responsible for providing this, especially if it required further research? Could SACRE ask schools directly about RE and CW? Could the SACRE demand that the LEA take up with schools their responsibilities for RE and CW? These questions were certainly discussed within LEAs and sometimes openly in the SACRE meeting itself. LEAs' responses were once again diverse, depending on the perceived power balance — the extent to which there existed mutual respect and trust between LEA and SACRE — and the local context and resourcing for RE. Nevertheless, many SACREs comprised some influential, informed and persistent individuals or groups who were able, where necessary, to press their requests and the importance of their being met. In addition to meetings and their formal minuting the Annual Report (AR) was seen as a medium for formalizing advice and further recommendations and some SACREs took other independent actions (see p.176).

Just over one-third of interviewees (11/28) reported that their SACRE had requested a survey of secondary RE provision and just under one-sixth (5/ 28) reported a request for a survey of primary RE provision. At both age ranges proportionately more SACREs in Metropolitan Boroughs than London Boroughs or Counties had made such requests. In two or three LEAs surveys at both age ranges were being conducted. The greater number of secondary surveys was generally not related to better knowledge about primary RE but out of a sense of greater pressure on secondary provision.

> In one Metropolitan LEA SACRE asked the LEA **for information on resources for RE, exam entries and the status of RE.** LEA officers were happy to draw up a questionnaire and analyse its findings. The LEA would probably not have done the survey but it was influenced by the SACRE, especially the persistence of an RE lecturer in Group C. Broadly, secondary RE in Year 10 and 11 was found to be suffering. In some cases RE did not have the status necessary to deliver the requirements of the law. As a result, schools were being requested to include RE in their development plans and the inspectorate were to keep a watching brief over the next year.

> In an Outer London Borough a **survey of secondary RE provision** had resulted in a dialogue between SACRE members and headteachers (see p.92). Subsequently the ATRE was undertaking a **survey of RE provision** in a sample of two-thirds of the **primary schools**, inquiring about delivery methods, allowances, implementation of the AS, INSET and school documents on RE.

> In two or three LEAs SACRE had specifically requested a **survey about staffing**. One had asked for a list of RE Heads of Departments (HoDs) and assistants. Staffing was a local constraint and a management issue, partly because of good local teacher training (ITT and INSET) provision. There was a constant flow of teachers on INSET and a person power drain, as those who were well qualified and up to date through INSET tended to move on.

A further three advisers/inspectors reported that SACRE had asked for information on these kinds of issues: they might request a full survey, which required acquiring data from schools, but some were content to rely on professional perceptions.

Interestingly, seven interviewees (proportionately more in Counties) claimed that they were undertaking a survey of RE, usually of secondary provision, independently and often in anticipation of a request from SACRE.

> One County ATRE had independently surveyed secondary heads of RE about exam courses and wanted to follow up on the qualifications of secondary RE teachers, possibly tying this in with a curriculum audit. He was indifferent as to whether it was a task for him as an adviser or taken on board for SACRE. The approach was pragmatic as SACRE was supportive and in line with his view on RE. He was providing a report to the SACRE Chair. He wondered if this was his role, but was happy to cooperate as it was not a '*them/us*' relationship.

> In another County the inspector had anticipated SACRE by initiating a survey of secondary RE in the annual curriculum return of schools. He was

aware, however, that they would not be very accurate because *'schools will fudge the time'*. SACRE had talked about secondary and primary surveys but recognized there were insufficient resources to undertake two detailed surveys and accepted his views and perceptions of local provision.

In an Outer London Borough although SACRE had not made a request, the ATRE had drafted a questionnaire and was visiting all secondary schools. The findings were *'gloomy'* with less than one quarter of schools having an RE specialist. There was uncertainty as to whether the information would be brought to the attention of SACRE as it had implications for local complaints, and SACRE was not part of the complaints procedure.

In another case the adviser had initiated, and received SACRE support for, a survey of secondary provision, practice, resource and support needs in relation to exam entries, curriculum analysis, staffing and qualifications — with a 75 per cent response rate.

Thus in about two-thirds of the LEAs sampled a survey of RE provision was currently underway or had been undertaken during the last year and in a further few there had been informal but explicit taking stock with reckonings reported to SACRE. The very existence of the SACRE, as well as its requests, seems to have brought about initial local reviews of provision and practice as well as of policy for RE and CW.

Reports to SACRE about local RE provision could provoke considerable discussion and further questions or recommendations. In so doing the adviser could be treading a tight rope.

In one case an adviser presented a report on local resources for RE (teachers, others, RE Centre, materials) with a focus on INSET. Questions were raised about teacher qualifications in relation to current and previous staffing levels and ITT. One member of Group B persisted with a minuted request to the LEA for a full-time RE adviser/inspector (otherwise indicating that an official complaint would take more LEA time) after it became clear that the adviser's role was general and the ATRE post was a secondment. This was despite an interjection by the Deputy Director about the relatively good advisory provision on RE, moves towards inspection and the shift towards LMS.

Elsewhere, although SACRE did not appear to have requested a survey of RE provision, it had debated a number of issues with some controversy. Among these was the question of what constitutes a reasonable amount of time for RE. This embarrassed the LEA as some schools were breaking the law. This was acknowledged and the LEA insisted that it was taken off the agenda. There was uncertainty as to what extent SACRE could question whether schools were complying with the law. Subsequently SACRE put down a motion to Education Committee on provision for RE and the percentage of time given to it in schools.

There were, in addition, a wide range of other issues connected with RE which SACREs were said to have raised for discussion including:

- the possibility of studying Islam in GCSE;
- the withdrawal by Exclusive Brethren of their children from Information Technology;
- requests for school visits;
- requests to be included in the LEA complaints procedure; and
- requests for legal advice on the nature and extent of SACRE's role.

The second major preoccupation of SACRE and about which it made requests was CW and determinations. This took many forms.

Faith Survey: in one LEA in 1989/90 a pre-existing SACRE had supported a borough-wide survey of the faith backgrounds of pupils with a form going to every parent/guardian. This was used partly as a basis for consideration of applications for determinations (elsewhere surveys were undertaken on a school basis).

Patterns of CW in Schools: a few SACREs asked for surveys or reports on current practice in CW. Sometimes requests for information were included in RE surveys, but as CW was both more complex to report and raised similar issues of resourcing it could sometimes be deferred.

Guidelines on CW, Definitions of CW: procedures including SACRE varied; in some cases advisers/inspectors wrote draft guidelines, submitted them to SACRE for amendment and then circulation with SACRE's imprimatur; a few SACREs were centrally involved in producing guidelines, through discussion in small groups, and in drafting proformas for applications for determinations. This often raised other questions and a few SACREs pressed for definitions of CW and for INSET. Some LEAs perceived the influence of SACRE on CW, especially whether it could communicate about this directly with schools, as a key issue.

INSET: in a few LEAs, as part of its role with respect to CW, SACRE became concerned about the preparation of staff to conduct CW: a few SACREs requested advisers to undertake INSET on CW as there was an awareness of need. In one LEA the absence of any senior management training for CW became an issue which SACRE took to Education Committee; INSET money was subsequently found and training was being implemented by secondary and primary advisers.

Reports on Determination Decisions: occasionally SACRE asked advisers for feedback about how determination decisions had been received: where a determination had only been granted for a year it had become necessary to institute a review; one or two SACREs involved their members in counselling about seeking determinations (see p.149).

Monitoring and Inspection of CW: many LEAs were moving towards a more inspectorial role vis à vis schools; a few SACREs thus requested monitoring of CW to be included in school reviews and inspections and some LEAs were developing such plans, including checklists which could be implemented by non-RE specialist colleagues in the inspection/advisory service.

The major issue with respect to SACREs' requests (apart from their perceived legitimacy) was how they were to be met and serviced. This was sometimes particularly controversial in relation to conducting surveys because of the implications for advisers'/inspectors' time. Responses varied:

- some were happy to cooperate as the SACRE and LEA were largely in agreement and mutually supportive;

- a few took a pragmatic view — that information needed to be acquired and that it was the LEA's role to communicate with schools and to provide this; occasionally an adviser or ATRE was able to enlist the help of an AEO to organize the survey, chase non-respondents and analyse the findings;

- some LEAs and officers were cautious about and reluctant to allow SACRE to appear to have any monitoring role in relation to schools: *'The LEA drew the line at SACRE's policing of schools'*, *'the LEA took a firm view that no one was to speak to schools about CW except the LEA — definitely not the SACRE'*;

- in some instances the response was clothed in a plea of lack of resources. There were indeed genuine issues about the priorities for the limited time of advisers/inspectors who often did not have RE as their sole responsibility: some advisers reported that SACRE accepted and appreciated that the time they could reasonably spend on servicing SACRE was limited and its requests were tailored accordingly;

- relatively few LEAs and SACREs had worked together to discover information about local provision, practice and resource and support needs which could help them in their mutual task:

    - in one LEA the inspector was planning to survey schools together with a head teacher in Group C and another head teacher member of the erstwhile ASC;

    - in another a planned survey of primary and secondary RE by means of a questionnaire was to be sent to schools with a covering letter from the SACRE Chair. The adviser would have liked the SACRE itself to draft the questionnaire and to initiate and undertake other work before making recommendations about RE.

It was interesting to note that, despite initial reservations about data collection, a few interviewees recognized, on reflection, that their researches had been informative, needed follow-up, perhaps annually, and could provide a baseline for any subsequent evaluation of the AS and its delivery. Clearly, however, there was scope for harnessing the influence and interest of SACRE — especially the offices of the teachers'association representatives — in a more collaborative effort with the LEA and schools to discover the priority and significance of issues in resourcing and supporting RE, not only from a management perspective, but also from the view point of RE teachers in contact with students and their spiritual needs and interests.

Communication with Schools and Colleges

In order to gauge the extent of communication with schools and colleges about SACRE and its work, interviewees were asked whether schools had been given information on the SACRE's role and function and the extent of direct contact between SACRE and schools. The circular had also requested a copy of any *local* statement about the role and function of SACRE. Although over two-thirds of circular respondents (and three-quarters of LEAs sampled) had sent such documentation, on inspection many of these documents appeared to be a reiteration of relevant sections of ERA or DES Circular 3/89. Some appeared to be (part of) the SACRE's constitution, standing orders or terms of reference intended for SACRE's own use and to inform its members (see p.63). Only about half of the statements of SACRE's role and function were apparently intended as information for schools or governors.

Indeed, about one-quarter of interviewees reported that schools or colleges had not been given specific information about SACRE and claimed it *was not needed — 'schools know its there'*. By the summer term 1990, in addition to awareness of SACRE in general from ERA and DES Circular 3/89, schools may well have been aware of the *existence* of their local SACRE. As advisers/inspectors indicated, this could have been brought about in a number of ways:

- by the existence of a previous local SACRE and especially through its public fora;
- because of requests from teachers' associations for nominees to be representatives on SACRE; and any subsequent reporting back from them;
- most likely , and after their first intimation of SACRE, because of information about and forms of application for determinations on CW, and documents of guidance on CW or locally publicised controversies related to CW;

-   indirectly due to revisions to the local AS;
-   through INSET of various kinds;
-   because of requests initiated by SACRE, for information on aspects of RE provision and practice as part of local surveys.

Nevertheless, in one LEA where there had been no previous publicity to schools about the role and function of SACRE, when a recently appointed inspector had written to schools reminding them of their responsibilities for RE and about SACRE some heads had evinced surprise about SACRE's remit.

In the majority of LEAs where interviews were undertaken there had been some specific communication with schools about SACRE. These had taken a variety of forms. **Yet there were only two or three examples of the SACRE itself initiating a statement.**

In one LEA the Chair of SACRE (who was also Chair of the County Council) had sent various letters to schools about RE in ERA and informed them regarding the complaints procedure on RE and CW.

In one Metropolitan Borough the opening remarks of the SACRE chair (also Chair of Education Committee) at its inaugural meeting were subsequently circulated in a letter (via the CEO) to all members of the SACRE, elected members, heads and principals, and members of the local teachers' panel. The Chair expressed the hope that SACRE members *'would not only communicate effectively with those whom they represented, but that they would see a responsibility... to help and support school-based RE'* and welcomed *'a new and exciting partnership between the Authority, the faith communities and the schools.'*

Otherwise **communication with schools** about the existence of SACRE, its role and function **had been undertaken at the instigation of the LEA,** sometimes in more than one way.

Letter: one of the most useful examples was a letter from the CEO enclosing several papers, recently considered by the SACRE, aimed at clarifying the position of RE in the curriculum. These included: the SACRE's membership, terms of reference, policy and objectives (including presentations to SACRE on methods and resources for RE and CW, review of training needs of teachers and INSET programme; paper on attainment targets; recommendation of methods and resources to support good class practice; consideration of need for a new AS and monitoring of RE); and practically oriented thoughtful guidance notes on CW, an action plan for heads and a RE bibliography.

RE Newsletter: although this was a fairly popular way of informing RE teachers and schools about SACRE, a surprising number of interviewees noted that there was no RE newsletter, usually in abeyance because of lack of staff or shortage of time, but planned with the advent of an ATRE. One inspector had written an article about SACRE for an issue of the newsletter and had invited members of SACRE to write in it.

Other Local Curriculum (especially Humanities) or General Education Newsletters.

The AS, especially if this was new or recently reissued; sometimes this included quite an extensive outline of the SACRE and its members; in one LEA a PEO (Clerk to SACRE) had written to schools informing them of the role and function of SACRE and its work to date, and of the ASC and AS, encouraging comments on the AS, but none had been received.

Local RE Handbooks and Guidelines: one LEA which had recently produced a loose-leaf format 60-page guideline (to which the school's own syllabus and materials could be added) to complement its three handbooks and the AS, included a paragraph on the local SACRE.

INSET on ERA, National Curriculum etc: in one LEA schools involved in an implementation unit on the NC received an input on RE and the SACRE; elsewhere in National Curriculum training the RE adviser was able to address all primary heads alongside English, Maths and Science advisers.

As well as the underlying issue of who (the SACRE, LEA officers/ advisers) should communicate with schools and colleges about SACRE and its work, there was the sensitive consideration of whether the names and addresses of SACRE members should be released. This was a matter which generally needed resolution prior to the publication of the AR which was seen by some advisers/inspectors as the first main communication about SACRE to schools. Advisers expressed different views about publicising SACRE membership:

- in one County a list of names of members of SACRE had, with their permission, been sent to churches and headteachers; members were said to be happy to be approached on issues relating to RE;

- in another nearby the membership had deliberately not been publicised as the inspector wanted them to *'feel part of SACRE before they became public targets for RE'*. Efforts had been put into education and training at the SACRE. The AR would make public SACRE's membership.

There was a widespread sense that the AR might be the first real occasion for SACRE to consider self-presentation, and, as a means of direct contact with schools, to indicate what had been done and what would be addressed. In future it might need to deliver a clear message on policy and practice and not just one which was reactive.

However, some SACRE members had, during the first year of SACRE, also had personal contact by visiting schools, not just as clergy, governors or parents, but in their role as SACRE members. As yet this controversial practice was not widespread, even in one or two LEAs where paired visits had previously been undertaken. Some LEAs and RE advisers/inspectors clearly feared such requests by SACRE and wished to limit direct interaction with schools and hence the possibility of inspection, (mis) judgement and giving advice directly to heads or teachers.

As one inspector, who felt the local SACRE was aware of the constitutional position, put it: *'This has not been a problem as with other LEAs whose SACREs had members who wanted to inspect schools.'*

Another reported a request of SACRE to visit schools to see CW. The LEA agreed to facilitate this, but not individual visits; schools were expected to be quite accommodating, though visits were not necessarily encouraged. The adviser was concerned about *'how to look at what they see: they must consider themselves as visitors and not as having any power to tell schools what to do.'*

Other RE advisers/inspectors, whilst recognizing limits and the need for preparation, seemed to see visits to schools by SACRE members as a legitimate aspect of their role:

-   in one LEA, it had been suggested to SACRE members that after current INSET they might like to visit RE classes;

-   in another the Chair of the SACRE (a councillor) visited the schools which made applications for determinations, and was well received as schools were used to receiving LEA visitors;

-   elsewhere the Chair of SACRE (an ex-teacher and Chair of Education Committee) and its Vice-Chair (a Church of England theologian and school governor) undertook observations of three primary and secondary schools. The matter was not controversial because of their background. However, a Muslim member of SACRE (*'an extreme fundamentalist and trainee Imam'*) *'took it upon himself to inspect RE in his local school'* and was found questioning children about RE and CW in the playground. The inspector had to reassure the head that the SACRE member had no right as such to do this and that the head had a right to expect to be notified of his presence in school. At the same time the SACRE member had to realize that whilst the school could be open to the public various conventions needed to be observed. Such an incident highlights the need for clear agreed objectives and preparation for such visits.

In several LEAs there had also been indirect communication between SACRE and schools when SACRE had requested the LEA to undertake surveys of RE provision and practice, which had been mentioned by advisers/inspectors in their school questionnaires or interviews, thus raising schools' awareness of SACRE's remit. Two contrasting examples, from two politically, socially and ethnically different Outer London Boroughs illustrate the differential effect of such an exercise.

> In one case, at SACRE's request, the inspector organized a user-friendly questionnaire to secondary schools on staffing, qualified staff, time allocation for RE and the nature of assemblies. There was a *'reasonable'* response but the majority did not respond. Heads were not convinced of the importance of the survey, were used to having responsibilities in these matters devolved to them by the LEA and were unsure of the implications and were therefore wary of putting information on paper. However, a prominent local councillor demanded to know the non-responding schools, wanting to follow the matter up personally — a situation which required the diplomatic skills of the RE inspector.

> By comparison, on receiving a report of a survey of secondary provision (delivery, resources, exams, staff development), undertaken at its request by the ATRE who interviewed HoDs of RE, SACRE was concerned as to how it could help. A meeting was held between five representatives of SACRE, who made brief presentations of their concerns, and secondary heads, who welcomed the meeting and expressed current constraints as well as appreciation of SACRE's support. SACRE subsequently made a number of recommendations (see p.175). Outcomes were an advertisement for a RE specialist in one school which lacked such a post and two upgrades of RE staff who agreed to take on responsibilities for CW.

Despite some examples of communication with schools about SACRE's role and function there was relatively little evidence of direct contact between SACRE and schools - even less directly with *RE teachers* in schools. Thus opportunities had not yet generally been made either to enable SACRE members to have a realistic appreciation of the demands on schools or to explore ways in which schools might be effectively supported in their delivery of RE and potentially to create the chances of having their resource needs realised through SACRE's recommendations. **If schools' perceptions of SACRE were to be enhanced and the school's own responsibilities for RE provision to become a higher priority in future, further consideration needed to be given to developing closer links between SACRE and its constituency.**

Consultation with Others

The statutory composition of SACRE suggests that it was intended in part to be a consultative body, its members, being consultants by virtue of representing their organizations, institutions and associations. To what extent have SACREs, in turn, seen fit to consult, liaise, publicise or be publicised nationally, regionally or locally in an attempt to be better informed or to communicate their objectives and concerns? This may be considered by examining their contacts with other SACREs through RE advisers and HMI, with parents, governors and religious organizations locally and through involvement with the media (see also p.101ff and p.160ff).

Since it was RE advisers and inspectors who were interviewed, it is not surprising that some cited the **support of peers,** through the sharing of experiences with SACREs in other LEAs, and especially through the ongoing regional network of AREAI as a significant feature of consultations for them personally. In addition to some national INSET arranged for SACRE members which some RE advisers and inspectors had attended (see p.102), mention was also made of an AREAI National Conference which included consideration of setting up SACRE and its constitution and devising applications for determinations for CW. Further consultations were taking place on assessment (see p.130ff).

Almost all interviewees reported that they were in contact with their district HMI for RE who had requested to be kept informed through SACRE agenda and minutes of meetings if unable to attend meetings themselves. At least one district HMI had undertaken a survey of the 20 SACREs in the division, summarizing data on their size, composition, local AS, determinations and examples of action by SACRE. In some cases advisers also exchanged information with HMI on the ASC and AS development and samples of school survey questionnaires. (Differential access to some of these types of information as between HMI and NFER was an interesting issue in some LEAs.) In addition to HMI involvement in investigating a complaint about sixth-form college RE provision in one LEA, and giving advice to heads on CW in another, there were only one or two reported examples of HMI having direct roles with SACREs, such as a proposed seminar to include an HMI speaker on RE since ERA, alongside speakers from local HE institutions on teacher training for RE.

Reported examples of **local consultation with parents, school governors and religious organizations** were also fairly rare. **Parents** were sometimes said to be generally more aware about RE, partly due to the direct involvement of some in surveys of faith background in schools applying for determinations on CW. This might be seen as foreshadowing the collection of statistics on pupils' faith backgrounds on entry to primary and secondary schooling from September 1990 (GB. DES, 1989b). In some localities publicity about complaints about RE had also given rise to greater parental awareness. But even in the most high profile reconstituted SACREs there did not seem to have been direct contact between SACRE and parents, though where SACRE was a public meeting it was said they would be welcome to attend. A few advisers interviewed indicated that some SACREs had, in addition to communicating with schools (see pp.89-90), attempted to reach **governors** through newsletters or, as was evident from other documents sent by respondents to the circular, through letters or pamphlets of advice. In some LEAs there had been governors' training sessions on the role of governors in relation to RE and ERA and discussion of the role of SACRE. These sessions had sometimes included SACRE members, as in the case of an HMI lecture on 'RE in the Curriculum' supported by SACRE and open to Chair of governors, heads, RE teachers and members of Church communities. **Wider public relations initiatives** by new SACREs were as yet few and far between.

> A SACRE, whose elected members comprised the Mayor, decided to use the occasion of his opening a local Jewish exhibition to publicise the SACRE and liaison between the Christian and Jewish faiths; the event was supported by the elected members and teachers, but showed that it was not easy for SACRE as a whole to give support.

> Elsewhere a SACRE had planned a 'Meet the Faiths' event (see pp.104-105).

Just over half of the interviewees reported some **local or national media interest** in the SACRE or related aspects of its work, usually CW. Normally this was minor, but in two or three of the LEAs in the sample there happened to be a controversial complaint or determination which was picked up by the media — a situation most advisers were fervently trying to avoid. Even though the local press were usually invited to Education Committee meetings, where SACRE might be an item, SACRE in itself seems to have provoked little interest.

Only a few SACREs or local councils had issued press releases about the formation of the SACRE which had received brief notes in the local press.

> In one LEA there had been some adverse press comment *'muddying the waters about representation'* on SACRE due to a perceived attempt by the new County council (with a majority of only one, after losing a seat to a Muslim Conservative) *'to be friends with the ethnic minority communities'*.

> But at the other end of the country in Britain's most multiracial Borough a local free newspaper devoted a whole page to a glowing review of the SACRE and its work.

Two or three LEAs were expecting more press contact with the issue of a press release on the SACRE's first AR.

Similarly, in a few LEAs a press release on the **publication of a new AS** had been given *'a nice write up'*.

In one case the local press had reported the debate about the AS in the Education Committee.

Elsewhere there were comments like *'The press is only interested in RE when there's a local axe to grind, but usually its along the lines of "Pupils don't know enough about Christianity so why should they learn about other faiths?"'*. In one LEA the local press carried headlines such as *'Schools throw out Jesus'* and *'RE without God'*.

CW and associated determinations were more likely to prove of national or local media interest.

One LEA's statement on CW had been mentioned in a national daily paper.

In a few LEAs statements made by local councillors giving their personal opinions on CW, which were different from those of LEA professionals, could make for local difficulties if publicised.

A classic example of press misreporting occurred when a local reporter who attended SACRE's second meeting which considered an application for a determination subsequently misquoted the head's letter of application by the strategic insertion of *'not'* in *'Collective worship does [not] play a unifying role in the life of the school community and that view is shared by parents and religious leaders.'* (The report in the local paper happened to be situated alongside headlines about a documentary on Salman Rushdie and his photograph.) The RE inspector wrote to the paper's editor, who did not insert an apology or correction, but ran another story asserting that the inspector denied claims that as a result of the determination (for some separate assemblies at festival times only) many other schools would be likely to opt out of *'collective Christian worship'*. In fact local consultations with Muslim community leaders and heads had indicated general agreement about RE and the unifying role of CW, as the inspector's letter noted.

In two LEAs where CW is the subject of local complaint, supported by Parents' Alliance for Choice in Education (PACE), there had been interest from national TV.

In one instance a school, known since its inception for a strong equal opportunities and antiracist policy, which had been granted a controversial determination, was invaded by a TV crew wanting to make a programme.

Elsewhere what began as an admissions issue became a parental complaint about lack of Christian input in CW in the allocated school. A decision on appeal on that count to admit the child to an oversubscribed in-catchment school (thus requiring erection of temporary accommodation) became the subject of a TV programme. SACRE had been kept informed of events, even though it was not part of the LEA complaints procedure. Moreover as advisory guidelines on CW had been issued prior to SACRE's formation it was seen as inappropriate for SACRE to openly support the school in question.

Such examples indicated that media interest in the SACRE and the complex issues with which it deals could be a very mixed blessing given the oversimplification and increased local controversy likely to be engendered.

LEA Support to SACRE

As several RE advisers/inspectors interviewed made plain, the inquiry came at an early stage in the life of the SACRE when LEAs, having passed the first hurdle of establishing its membership, were now coming to terms with the issues raised and the implications of its existence and operation. The majority of LEAs had no previous experience of the formation and functioning of a SACRE, and even those which had were likely to have found that the statutory requirements of ERA extended both its composition and remit. What provision did LEAs make to prepare for, support and service the SACRE in its first year and beyond? How is LEA support influenced by the local profile of RE and perceptions of the status and influence of the SACRE in the light of other current changes in curriculum delivery and local educational management? The interview explored the nature of and issues arising from three possible types of LEA support to SACRE: financial support through a SACRE budget; educational support to members through INSET; and servicing, advisory and inspectorial support from the RE adviser/inspector and other clerical and officer assistance.

A Budget for SACRE?

One of the clearest indications of the extent to which planning to support the work and functioning of SACRE occurred is revealed by the financial provision made for its first year. A body, such as SACRE, with many members, required to meet regularly and report on its proceedings is likely to need financial assistance in relation to such matters as costs of salaries, meeting rooms, refreshments, travel and materials, as well as meeting the statutory requirement of publishing an annual report. DES Circular 3/89 (Para 18) placed responsibility for financial support of SACRE firmly in the hands of the LEA, but offered no guidance as to how this should be met:

> '...The Secretary of State expects each LEA to provide.... sufficient funds for it to perform its functions.... the LEA should satisfy itself that the arrangements are sufficient for the performance of the Council's functions.'

To what extent had LEAs directly and specifically addressed the likely financial needs of SACRE in order that it might operate efficiently and in keeping with the status which might be presumed to attach to a statutory body?

Advisers/inspectors often set their responses about specific funding to support SACRE in the local context of the profile of RE compared with other curriculum areas in the LEA (see p.182ff) and the budget for RE as a whole. Clearly these varied widely from LEA to LEA, but several advisers reported that RE had benefited from recently being a national priority area in terms of Education Support Grants (ESGs), Grant-Related In-Service Training (GRIST) or the Local Education Authority Training Grants Scheme (LEATGS), under which training for RE was allocated £1 million in 1988-9 and £1.1 million in 1989-90 (GB. DES, 1989a, Para 56). However, there was also said to be *'increasingly less flexibility'* and one graphically described it as *'hitting the buffers because of the reduction of central resources and the introduction of LMS'*. As part of the basic but not core curriculum RE may be in an anomalous financial position, particularly where LEAs are operating through divisions and channeling money directly into schools which may leave a gap at the LEA level for RE resourcing. A further factor to be taken into account was the way in which LEA budgets are organized and administered, given that resourcing for a SACRE might be seen as coming under all or any of the following budget headings: curriculum, INSET, ERA or Committee.

Overall **only three SACREs in the 28 LEAs (one County, one Outer and one Inner London Borough) where interviews took place were said by advisers to have specific discrete budgets.**

> In a County with a SACRE since 1974 the budget covered: working parties, including supply cover for work done out of SACRE but related to it; part of the salary of the SACRE clerk; and members' travel.

> The budget of over £7,000 for 1988-9 in one Outer London Borough with a SACRE since 1986 covered: publications arising from the work of SACRE (i.e. faith community survey, AS, handbooks etc); photocopying of the many papers submitted to meetings; members' travelling expenses; their INSET and conference attendance; and publication and postage of SACRE's AR.

> The SACRE budget of £1,800 in one Inner London Borough (calculated on a per capita figure plus ten per cent) covered: INSET, publication of the AR and refreshments, but not travel.

Two of these SACREs pre-dated the statutory requirement. However, the pre-existence of a SACRE at the LEA's option by no means necessarily implied a separate budget. As regards both the previous and current SACREs **several advisers indicated that some financial support was available to SACRE from general, RE, ERA, LEATGS, INSET and other budgets. However, a few were quite unclear about funding sources and nearly all were vague about how much was available.** Resources were obtained from *'here, there, and everywhere'* and it was often a matter of *'wheeling and dealing'*.

Despite the general lack of a specific SACRE budget, almost half of the RE advisers/inspectors interviewed claimed that available financial support to SACRE (which in these cases usually covered: members' travel; teacher supply cover; materials; and publication of an AR) was adequate, given what they saw as the economic reality in their LEA. However, some expressed mixed feelings and felt it was *'a fudge'* or *'messy area'*. A few considered the lack of available funding as completely inadequate. But one or two saw it as an administrative issue for which they did not want responsibility.

Several issues were implicit in consideration of the adequacy of funding for SACRE.

> There were **hidden costs**, most particularly in respect of the **time of the RE adviser/inspector and that of any ATRE or educational officer** involved as observers, advisers or servicers of SACRE (see pp.109-111). In almost all cases the **services of the SACRE clerk** from the LEA committee or administrative section was an additional hidden cost.

> Another, more explicit, issue was that of **supply cover for teachers** in Group C where SACRE meetings were held during the school day. Whether such funding were available could be the determining factor in the timing of meetings, although there was a reported preference for daytime meetings by elected members who were entitled to claim expenses. A few advisers expressed awareness that daytime meetings could involve other SACRE members in time off work and there was a concern that minority ethnic members in Group A could be adversely affected. Only one or two anticipated possible claims for **loss of earnings** which did not yet appear to have been made. Lack of resources for supply cover could affect teacher attendance at daytime meetings. On the other hand, evening meetings could cause resentment by teachers' union members. There was a need to decide if SACRE was to be counted as a full formal committee of the LEA/Council, and, if so, whether payments were available.

> **Travel** expenses were more likely to be an issue in the larger areas covered by the Counties. Although some LEAs met any such claims, it appeared that the availability of such funds had not often been made clear or that claims had not been made. There was frequently an underlying assumption that travel costs depended on the goodwill of members or that they might be covered by nominating bodies. One or two advisers expressed concern that this might discriminate against certain members, especially from minority ethnic backgrounds. Controversial cases also occurred when Church of England members attempted to claim from the LEA when resources had to come out of an RE centre budget and when the LEA met teacher supply cover and the Church of England member was also a teacher.

Money for national **INSET** for SACRE members could also be problematic and linked with the assumptions or lack of clarity besetting travel or other aspects of SACRE funding; sometimes it required specific application to the CEO or DoE. Support for local SACRE INSET, where it occurred, tended to be found from other budgets, if not directly available from SACRE funds.

The costs of **meeting places and refreshments** could also be an issue. In some cases the SACRE was perceived as a full formal LEA committee and met in Council chambers and adjacent rooms - thus the costs were hidden. Provision of refreshments, affording more informal interaction among members with a variety of backgrounds, depended on Council policy. Where SACREs met in local schools the possibility of being charged rent could arise.

Provision of **materials** (e.g. AS, handbooks, guidelines on CW, SACRE constitution, working party reports, draft ARs etc) for consideration during the proceedings of SACRE required resourcing. This could be not inconsiderable where SACRE had a large membership and met frequently. The writing, printing and distribution of SACRE's own **annual report** was an exercise which had implications for time and production costs, even if it were not envisaged in glossy format for local and national LEA-wide dissemination.

Advisers were divided as to whether a *specific* SACRE budget would be allocated in the foreseeable future. Several thought it was needed and probable; one or two did not see the need for a specific budget and some were doubtful it would be provided. A few indicated that separate financial provision for SACRE and the amount were under consideration, and in one or two cases it had been included in the estimates for the following year. In some LEAs where the AS had come under review the activity generated by the ASC and its working parties (including those on CW), the need to publish an AS, and to provide INSET related to implementation, necessitated financial support. This, in turn, raised the question of resources for SACRE, even though this had not been contemplated initially. The requirement to produce an AR was also a direct major factor in raising the question of budgetary support. In some cases a separate budget for SACRE appeared to be a controversial issue. There were a few proactive examples of SACREs making direct requests to the DoE or Education Committee for funding. As a result, in one Metropolitan authority with a ten-year-old SACRE £2,300 was to be allocated for the first time for SACRE work to include printing, members' INSET and governors' training.

Overall the survey revealed that very few of the quarter of LEAs contacted had thoroughly considered the financial underpinning likely to be required by SACRE in its first year or made specific budgetary provision to support

its operation. Resourcing was most likely in the form of hidden costs and met from other LEA or RE budgets. Various anomalies associated with other LEA practices and curricular revisions were beginning to bring the question of a SACRE budget into the open. But **there was no evidence of long-term financial planning for an on-going statutory body.** Any SACRE which pre-dated ERA was optional and maintained (in whatever way) at LEA expense. Yet the obligation now placed upon LEAs to constitute a SACRE to advise on local provision and practice in CW and RE as part of the basic curriculum for all pupils up to 18 — a function being undertaken *nationally* for other curriculum areas by the NCC — might give rise to the question of the availability of national funding to support the work of local SACREs. It would appear that the issue of financial support to these new mandatory bodies — with their curriculum remit and potential to enhance positive cultural and community relations has been a preoccupation of neither the legislators nor the implementers.

INSET for SACRE

Another aspect of LEA support to SACRE was the extent to which provision was made for SACRE members to be involved in local or national INSET in relation to undertaking their tasks. LEAs and advisers varied in their approach: a few saw it as up to SACRE to identify their own needs for education and training; but **the majority saw it as part of their role to offer SACRE members opportunities to develop their knowledge and understanding of current practices and issues in RE and CW, as well as informing them of their duties and responsibilities and, in some cases, of facilitating the working procedures and social interaction of these disparate groups of people.** Even if no specific local or national INSET were expressly aimed at SACRE, it was rare for an RE adviser to claim that INSET was not needed or that there had been no opportunity to involve its members in some kind of local INSET activities. There was wide recognition of the different starting points of members in their awareness, interests and experience, and of the need to ground the SACRE's agenda and concerns in local everyday educational reality. Thus, in addition to *ad hoc* incidental learning *'on the job'*, the majority of LEAs contacted had, during the SACRE's first year, offered members at least one form of INSET which included: buying into types of national INSET; inviting participation in local RE INSET; providing specific local INSET for SACRE; and, in a few cases, making task-related INSET part of the business proceedings of SACRE itself.

As an introduction to the role and function of SACRE many LEAs had circulated SACRE members with copies of the relevant sections of ERA or DES Circular 3/89 or included this, in modified form, in a local constitution, standing orders or terms of reference (see p.88). As well as a variety of local documentation on RE and CW some LEAs provided SACRE members with reports of research such as that by HMI on *Agreed Syllabuses and Religious Education* (GB. DES, 1989c) or advice and guidance, for example, the REC's *Handbook for Agreed Syllabus Conferences, SACREs and Schools* (1989a). Significantly, as part of the recruitment and induction process, a few LEAs had involved potential member institutions or their nominated representatives in consultation meetings about their duties and responsibilities prior to the inauguration of the SACRE itself. **Where the AS is under review and the SACRE is also (with some additions) operating as an ASC, greater attention has often been given to members' INSET in relation to overseeing the production and eventual implementation of the revised or new AS.**

About half the LEAs contacted had at least notified SACRE members of available **national** INSET specifically geared to the role and function of SACREs. The Saltley Trust in Birmingham held at least two national fora, in December 1989 and July 1990, and a day conference was organized in London by CEM/CLEA in March 1990. Although LEA funding for members' conference attendance and travel was an issue in a few LEAs, others invited and facilitated or encouraged SACRE members' participation and involvement. Whilst a few advisers indicated that take up had been slow or that other members could have benefited, in some cases up to four SACRE members attended. As the CEM/CLEA list of delegates confirms, the 43 participating English LEAs and SACREs (19 Counties, 15 London Boroughs, nine Metropolitan Boroughs) were most likely to be represented by the RE adviser/inspector or the SACRE chairperson (although other members of Education Committee, SACRE and education officers also attended). A few advisers were sceptical of national SACRE-related INSET, even labelling it as '*an industry*' and querying its value for money. Others indicated that these events had provided formal and informal opportunities for the transfer of information about operating procedures, forms of support and discussion of ideas on and handling of concerns.

> One adviser reported that a **regional** Church of England initiative involving five Bishops and their suffragens, 15 CEOs/DoEs plus SACRE Chairpersons and RE advisers had proved valuable in raising awareness of the interests of the Church and LEAs and varying aspects of SACRE operation.

Apparently the Muslim Educational Trust have sought information on Muslim representation on SACRE with a view to establishing education and training.

Some LEAs, especially those which did not provide specific local INSET for SACRE members or which had long-standing SACREs, invited members of SACRE to participate in **local** RE and CW INSET, most often with teachers or governors. There were also a few examples of SACRE members engaging in education and training with local clergy, local colleges of education, representatives of racial equality and equal opportunities units and visiting places of worship with teachers.

> In one LEA SACRE members were regularly invited to participate in the activities of the Inter-faith Education Centre and were involved in a two-day INSET programme in upper schools. This incorporated a local theatre group which was addressing spiritual issues.

Whilst there was a recognition of different starting points among such mixes of INSET participants — especially likely between the level of knowledge of RE teachers and non-teaching SACRE members — these engagements often afforded valuable learning experiences.

Several LEAs involved SACRE members in, or responded to requests for INSET specifically directed at their needs and interests. One adviser reported offering INSET which was not taken up. Specific INSET for SACRE took a variety of forms and covered a range of issues in RE and CW.

The most common approach was that of a **presentation** to SACRE, either as part of a business meeting or a separate event.

> RE advisers, and occasionally outside speakers, talked about the history of RE or current developments in the light of ERA; teachers from different school types spoke about their work in RE and CW and showed slides, videos and artefacts. These events could generate interest and discussion. As a result of one such presentation a Muslim member of SACRE asked if it could be repeated for Muslim parents in one of the county's towns.

Those SACRE members who were also ASC members were likely to have ongoing INSET on various aspects of the RE curriculum and its delivery.

> In one LEA with an AS from 1987 and a reconstituted SACRE the RE inspector was attempting to introduce SACRE to various local and national documents on the nature and implementation of RE. This occurred both **as an integral part of half-day business meetings and an all-day event which also included a training experience, multicultural lunch and an opportunity to mix socially.** Documents were included with agenda papers in advance. During the training SACRE members were encouraged to look at: the nature of the documents; the implications for schools and colleges,

and for the work of SACRE itself. Through an experiential process members were made aware of the issues, sensitized to other religious perspectives, and began to appreciate the implementation implications in schools and colleges, and particularly in respect of INSET, materials and teaching methods on which SACRE has a duty to comment. This was described as *'enriching'*.

SACRE INSET almost exclusively focussed on aspects of RE and CW, **rarely in relation to the National Curriculum as a whole**, although in one LEA the SACRE had discussed RE in relation to History, English and Geography (see also pp.127-128).

There were also a number of **specific inputs on CW** including:

- **papers from advisers** raising questions and issues in the local context;

- **a day's conference** before consideration of applications for determinations **at which headteachers talked to SACRE members about their plans;**

- **a workshop** as part of the SACRE meeting in which members of different groups worked in pairs **to establish criteria to use as a basis of advice to schools on determinations and for judging complaints.** Members got to know each other better and, interestingly, produced only process criteria rather than focussing on religious beliefs or figures. The next meeting aimed to produce a document, embodying the criteria, as approved policy to be circulated to schools;

- **a seminar to consider teacher training** and contribute to the development of a **resources pack for CW.**

A few SACRE members had been on **visits:**

- Buddhist and Baha'i members had visited the **RE Centre** to check the adequacy and accuracy of available materials on their religions;

- **to schools**; a few advisers claimed this was unnecessary as SACRE members were also sometimes governors or parents; but it was more likely that school visits were perceived as controversial, especially in the absence of a current AS which could form a common basis for observation and judgement. Elected and other members without an RE background in one SACRE requested school visits which took an ATRE five days to set up. However, these proved useful in raising members' awareness of educational reality and enhanced their appreciation of and support for RE.

At this early stage in the life of most SACREs there were relatively few other illustrations of SACRE taking the initiative in respect of its own development.

In one notable example SACRE positively recognized and embraced a possible wider role in promoting community dialogue. Led by the Chair of

Group A, the FCFC representative, it was planning an exhibition, *Meet the Faiths,* followed by six evening workshops. These would include SACRE members, parents, teachers, governors and members of six major world faiths to talk about the beliefs, practices and concerns of the different faith groups.

Despite these specific examples of good practice, in many of the LEAs contacted initial and continuing INSET for SACRE members had only just begun to emerge as an issue. LEA attitudes and approaches usually reflected the SACRE model in operation, spanning a continuum: some SACREs were an open forum and partnership, where the LEA took responsibility for consciousness raising in order that SACRE could be well informed for its decision making and advice giving, so that in its turn it might offer support to the professionals at all levels; other SACREs were largely orchestrated by LEAs, which wished to limit SACRE's influence and restrain all aspects of its legitimate functioning under a tight professional rein.

Nevertheless there was wide recognition of diverse starting points both within and between groups, and **a need to educate many members of SACRE, not least about the local realities of education and RE in schools and colleges.** Representatives of teachers' associations who were not RE teachers could benefit from opportunities to extend their appreciation of RE provision and practice, as could some elected or faith members who had little recent direct experience of the education service even though they might show interest and support. **Another pervasive and underlying issue was the need for a reminder to some faith representatives to focus primarily on the *educational* and not solely the *religious* aspects and implications of their considerations.** Illustrations from several SACREs indicated that keeping such a focus in mind could be problematic for Anglicans and representatives of all other religious denominations who wished to be forceful in their articulation of a religious viewpoint. To some extent this might indicate a need for education in committee procedures, but it could also be seen as **part of the wider process of social, cultural, religious and racial interaction and the learning of mutual appreciation** engendered by the bringing together of individuals representing a variety of interests, backgrounds and life experiences in the formation of the SACRE.

In promoting INSET for SACRE members so that SACRE can develop its own identity and rationale these substantive matters of approach and perspective had to be addressed alongside more practical considerations of funding, timing of INSET (for example, if members worked full-time) and duration of membership, thus necessitating a rolling programme (see p.62). However, INSET has considerable significance if the SACRE is itself to be professionalized — to be enabled to perform its statutory role and functions wisely and efficiently; if it is, in turn, to be able to appreciate the INSET needs of RE teachers in local schools and colleges; and if it is to develop a wider role in promoting dialogue on RE amongst parents and communities.

Role of RE Advisers/Inspectors in Relation to SACRE

Given the prime position of RE advisers/inspectors in respect of their subject area in their LEA and the mandatory introduction of a SACRE as a local institution for overseeing RE, it is important that any evaluation of the SACRE's initial operation should review their roles in relation to this new body. Thus interviewees were asked to describe their function in servicing the SACRE, whether there was a separate clerk, the time given to SACRE and related work, and whether they experienced any difficulties in responding to a possible diversity of interests and demands in relation to RE.

A significant issue was whether there was a separate clerk or not. In all but four of the 28 LEAs where interviews were undertaken there was a separate clerk to SACRE who did not have any advisory or inspectorial responsibilities for RE (in addition one interviewee was a PEO (Development) who acted as clerk to SACRE). The four cases of advisers also acting as clerk varied:

- one long-standing senior advisory officer in a County authority was technically the SACRE clerk but also the DoE's representative and '*voice*' and saw his role to facilitate the meeting; he shared minute writing with the RE adviser;

- one general adviser for Humanities/RE in a large County authority regarded it as quite acceptable to act as SACRE clerk;

- one northern Metropolitan LEA appointed a half-time ATRE from September 1989, primarily to act as clerk to SACRE/ASC and partly to support teachers in schools and liaise with heads on potential applications for determinations;

- in another northern Metropolitan area an erstwhile standing consultative committee had been clerked by an LEA officer, but when reconstituted as a SACRE this function was included in the post of Coordinator of the local Interfaith Centre. As clerk to SACRE he took minutes, and as co-ordinator he informed SACRE of the INSET programme. Currently this ambiguous role was not felt as a clash of interests, since, to date, the

Centre Committee and the SACRE had (with some overlapping membership) been supportive; but there were implications in terms of clerical assistance to service the SACRE with paperwork without additional financial support to the Centre.

However, it appeared that **most LEAs and/or RE advisers had given prior consideration to the possible ambiguity of role if the RE adviser as an officer in attendance were also to be clerk to SACRE.** Indeed, a few advisers spontaneously mentioned the potential difficulties of such a position, such as the hampering of involvement in or observation of meetings. Most preferred not to be absorbed in actual minute writing at the time, but to be free to offer advice if required.

These SACREs with separate clerks were resourced from a range of LEA support systems and at variable levels of post. In the main clerks came from the LEA's committee or administrative section, including schools' or governing bodies' branches, but also from advisory services support or the RE Centre. Clerks ranged in status from secretarial or clerical officers to senior administrative officers, AEOs and EOs or even the County Legal Adviser. Normally, in addition to taking minutes of meetings, the clerk was involved in production of the agenda with the RE adviser/inspector, the Chair of SACRE and possibly another LEA officer. SACRE clerks also made arrangements for meeting rooms and sometimes supervised travel and budgeting matters.

Several advisers expressed a number of **reservations about the adequacy of clerking support** in terms of procedural difficulties and lack of sensitivity to and understanding of issues.

> Most advisers were involved in **overseeing minutes**. Some felt that there was a need for such supervision and checking as minutes could be *'a bit hit and miss'* or that the minutes were *'stunted'* as the clerk *'did not catch all the issues'*. Indeed, the minutes of the first year of SACRE meetings received from 40 LEAs revealed a considerable variation in style, from perfunctory recording of discussion items or decisions to fuller accounts of debates and variation in opinions expressed. Overall there was a tendency to keep to fairly brief reports.

> In a few cases advisers were **directly involved in collecting together and circulating papers** for SACRE members in advance of meetings. These could amount to several substantial documents. One adviser in an Inner London Borough had spent *'a wild proportion of time'* collating papers and getting them to members on time as it was felt this would not have been achieved by the administrative department.

Advisers were also involved in **supervising clerks and other professionals who *'did not know the ropes'*.** Difficulties included: mistaken circulation of a preliminary discussion paper on CW; mis-timing of the issuing of a public statement by the SACRE Chair; and the mis-attribution to the CEO rather than inspectorate of a document of curriculum advice to heads on CW and RE. These clerical confusions could arise because the SACRE introduced another administrative layer into the LEA, thus sometimes indicating a need for clearer established channels of communication. Advisers were, as a result, usually involved in clarifying misperceptions. Moreover some reported that few other LEA officers had an understanding of the legal position relating to SACRE, or displayed a negative attitude to it.

Interviewees were asked whether they regarded their **role in relation to SACRE** as one of servicer, implementer, adviser or inspector. The overwhelming majority, as some lists of SACRE members also made clear, were LEA officers *in attendance* rather than *members* of SACRE. However, there were a few ambiguous and interesting cases, for example:

- in one northern Metropolitan LEA, where Group D deliberately consisted of a mix of elected members and LEA officers, the senior inspector (primary) with responsibility for RE was a member of SACRE; however he had suggested that in future when required to make reports to SACRE he might occupy a *'town clerk'* role;

- in one Outer London Borough the RE project co-ordinator and first full-time advisory teacher on a one-year secondment was also a representative on SACRE for one of the teachers' associations; this resulted in various anomalies and a tension which might have been reduced by a job description;

- in one County the newly appointed inspector for RE had previously been a teachers' association representative on SACRE and viewed the possibility of changing perceptions and of establishing his new role with interest, especially in relation to steering through a new AS.

Generally the chosen self-description of RE advisers/inspectors in relation to SACRE also bore some relation to their respective status or length of service in the LEA. Almost one-quarter were at pains to point out that they did not regard themselves as servants of SACRE although one or two saw themselves as *'dogs body'*. Of the categories suggested, adviser (five), adviser and servicer (four), and adviser, servicer and implementer (four) were most often chosen. One or two saw themselves as adviser and implementer or inspector and adviser, but others were keen to keep inspection at a distance from SACRE.

One County inspector rejected the image of servant of SACRE, preferring to engineer members and feed them with papers and information. He saw his function as to hear and advise SACRE, but not necessarily to do its bidding. He would evaluate any reasonable requests from SACRE in relation to schools, but would *'reserve the right to say no'*. At the same time he adopted a reflective approach and aimed to anticipate SACRE's needs and interests.

Another saw himself as *'conductor'* of SACRE, standing between the LEA and SACRE as an adviser and friend.

One characterized the role as *'manager'*, reporting to SACRE in the broad sense and promoting discussion and openness.

Another described himself as *'consultant'* offering advice, presenting documents and having an instrumental role in training and preliminary discussions to enable members to be better informed to make judgements and decisions — the professionalization of SACRE.

Typically RE advisers/inspectors were involved in a range of tasks on account of SACRE:

- compiling an agenda and overseeing minutes of meetings with the clerk and sometimes other officers and members;

- writing papers and collecting documents to inform SACRE and for discussion;

- liaising with SACRE members to respond to queries or *'behind the scenes'* activity, especially briefing meetings with Chair of SACRE and possibly another LEA officer or the clerk about the issues likely to arise; to give guidance on what is realistic and manageable and hence desired outcomes;

- reporting on local provision and practice in RE and CW;

- offering guidance to Heads about the appropriateness of seeking a determination and, if so, advising about the procedures involved and evidence required.

Advisers/inspectors found it **problematic to specify the amount of time they spent on SACRE work**, most seeing it as difficult to distinguish from other RE tasks. Initially the setting up or reconstitution of the SACRE was generally felt to have been a time-consuming endeavour, depending on the processes of consultation (see p.15ff). Some advisers had also been involved in devising a constitution or terms of reference for SACRE; in one case this had involved a SACRE working party in three meetings. Generally advisers were agreed that the amount of clerical support was not onerous. However, there was again a range of perceptions about the amount of time involved in supporting SACRE, from relatively *'little'* to *'an inordinate and disproportionate amount of time.'* All expected and acknowledged some increase in workload. This was especially noticeable where the adviser was not in a full-time post or had RE as only one of a range of other subject responsibilities. In some cases it proved to be much more than anticipated. Input directly related to SACRE was said to be *'patchy and mixed'* and *'in fits and starts'*. It depended on a range of factors, notably: the number of meetings per term; the number and nature of papers to be written or documents of advice to be drafted; the number and extent of consultations (with Chair, Diocesan staff, other SACRE members); and the extent to which other work — on the AS, CW, surveys of RE provision, and working parties on attainment targets (ATs)— was considered to be associated with SACRE work; and the degree of importance the adviser attached to the SACRE, in terms of its professionalization or in acquiring its support for RE provision. Initiating action from SACRE itself could also result in extra work for the adviser.

Preparation time for meetings and actual meetings varied from half to three days per meeting, most commonly one day. Associated work could be added.

One adviser spent half a day each term preparing for the meeting but considered prior interaction valuable and had consulted the SACRE Chair three times since the previous meeting. Thus it became three or four days per meeting, increased by two weeks developing an associated programme of INSET for SACRE members.

Consulting about CW and applications for determinations could become a major incursion on time ;if there were more than one advisory post for RE in the LEA the more senior was generally likely to be closely involved with schools in counselling about determinations as this was regarded as political and sensitive. For example:

- one County adviser spent three days preparation for every SACRE meeting and a total of 25 days on the AS and CW, mainly because of consultations with governing bodies to ensure correct preparation for seeking determinations and *'to head off questions'*. There remained many applications still to be processed;

- one advisory teacher in an Outer London Borough considered she spent one day a week for a year on SACRE work, including meetings and consultations, especially re CW.

Others found it difficult to distinguish the SACRE-specific aspects of their work (irrespective of its initiation) — whether, for example, they were collecting information on RE exam entries and passes as general adviser or for SACRE:

- one had recently spent 25 per cent of time with a working party on ATs — work related to SACRE but which would have been undertaken anyway. However, SACRE had given encouragement to undertake this work and provided the focus and structure for doing it;

- some advisers/inspectors predicted an increasing involvement of time with SACRE-related tasks in the coming year, especially in relation to monitoring, continuing involvement on CW and determinations. Moreover, if SACRE recommended the calling of an ASC this could involve a '*mammoth*' amount of time both in itself and in subsequent implementation.

Although some advisers interviewed claimed not to feel conflicting demands in responding to the diversity of interests in relation to RE and CW, **virtually all during the course of interviews indicated locally controversial issues which suggested that there was some degree of tension between advisers'/inspectors' own professional views and the requirements of the LEA or the requests of SACRE.** RE advisers/inspectors occupied a pivotal role between the LEA and SACRE and could have varying allegiances, according to their own interests or what they perceived to be those of RE locally. It was clear that they had a critical role in setting up the SACRE initially — often being the only officer in the LEA who appreciated the implications of the legislation. Even so, there could be anomalies regarding the presence of the RE adviser/inspector at SACRE meetings — one group of teachers' association representatives noticed that the constitution did not specify the attendance of the adviser and insisted that this be added. There was, additionally, the issue of whether the RE adviser was an officer in attendance or a member of SACRE (see p.52ff). This related to the important questions of the function of the adviser at SACRE (see p.106ff) and ultimately, vis à vis SACRE, who is the adviser responsible to? Even when advisers had a clear job description how the SACRE work fits in remained to be seen. It appeared that some had requested clarification, or had been put in the position of making clear to SACRE that, as an LEA employee, they were responsible to the Chief Adviser, Inspector, CEO or DoE. Several advisers felt that their role with respect to SACRE was evolving and suggested various degrees of control over this. For example:

one adviser wished to see herself as an adviser to SACRE but, unlike her relationship with schools, was asked for answers more than advice. Her role in SACRE was not defined and her position was mixed and unclear. The LEA saw her as a servant of SACRE but also to direct it, and '*not to raise questions or to give information about what they do not need to know about.*'

Overall interviewees indicated a range of views about responding to varying demands on RE: some found SACRE very supportive; others were

testing the boundaries of responsibility and influence; some experienced considerable role tension or conflicts of interest; and others foresaw their possibility.

One or two RE advisers/inspectors felt **supported** by other advisory colleagues who happened to be members of SACRE as representatives of religious bodies. Several felt supported by SACRE as a whole.

> In one northern Metropolitan LEA where an adviser with secondary and an advisory teacher with primary responsibilites, both relating to SACRE and RE, were interviewed, both felt that SACRE wanted to be helpful and that it gave *'personal support and commitment'*. A briefing meeting was held with the Chair and clerk. In the SACRE meeting the advisers gave definite guidance on what is manageable (e.g. they advised against monitoring of CW in the summer term), having freedom to argue back about the extent of their responsibilities and the purpose of the work. *'A real dialogue'*: the advisers *'listen'* and *'don't feel the only experts'* , although they tended to pull the ideas together. SACRE and advisers work as *'mutual support'*.

A few other advisers reported that SACRE understands what is reasonable and is motivated by what is helpful to schools; for example, one saw SACRE's request to undertake a survey of primary provision as providing information for INSET needs for a future programme. A few reported a change over time:

> *'not as difficult now as in the early days when we were all watching what we said'*. The LEA expected issues to debate and there had been open debates of high quality. Even though some members wanted to take a fairly religious rather than *RE* line, the teachers were *'no shrinking violets'*.

In one or two cases SACRE had been directly supportive of the RE adviser; for example, in two Counties SACRE had recommended and pressurized the LEA to make a full-time appointment for RE which influenced and expedited the process. But in other instances there seemed some uncertainty on the part of SACRE of the extent of its powers or even a lack of willingness to *'flex its muscles'*.

> One interviewee reported a discussion with the Chair of SACRE about the extent to which SACRE should be proactive, particularly with respect to finding out what was happening in schools; the Chair (a councillor) did not want the SACRE to have too high a profile. After discussion with the DoE it was decided to give priority to reviewing the AS.

Elsewhere advisers were wanting to **test the boundaries of SACRE's influence in relation to the LEA**, especially where RE had a relatively low profile or where the LEA wanted to take firm control over SACRE. This could be especially difficult if the adviser were relatively new or felt that some SACRE members lacked sufficient background knowledge or experience. Occasionally, it was felt that the membership of the SACRE itself was inactive and lacked initiative. A few advisers would have liked SACRE to put pressure on the LEA to appoint an ATRE or on secondary schools with regard to teaching qualifications for RE. Others were able to gain the ear of the Chair and SACRE's support or imprimatur (see p.121).

Nevertheless the majority of advisers gave illustrations of **overt tensions or conflict with the LEA and SACRE.** In one or two cases these were more directly associated with local restructuring, where a county subject brief for RE sat uneasily with a divisional role as inspector, or other responsibilities, such as for the Humanities in general, so that, although in the short-term priority was needed for RE, other subjects were also clamouring for attention.

> In one situation where it was made clear that SACRE was not to use the adviser *'on errands'* and that the LEA was to decide how SACRE's requests were to be dealt with, the adviser nevertheless felt that some of the tensions between the groups on SACRE could have been avoided, as he considered that he had closer knowledge of the groups over many years and would not have raised some of the issues.

> An inspector for the Humanities, including RE, who claimed to have spent one-third of his time in 1989-90 on RE because of the political context of SACRE ,RE and CW, openly asserted *'considerable tension in the role'* which he saw as *'neither fish nor fowl'*. He saw it as partly executive and to provide information for EOs and elected members' decision-making, but complicated by his inspectorial role. He did not regard himself *'at the beck and call of SACRE but to take account of their requests and provide for them'*. It was a new area with closer working relationships with elected members. He considered he was appointed because he felt comfortable dealing with politicians.

> One SACRE appeared to have become inert because of preoccupation about its role, function, chairperson and extent of influence. The RE inspector had prepared a number of papers — on CW, review of the AS, assessment and SACRE's role in the complaints procedure — but consideration of them had been consistently deferred, with attendant implications for RE and CW in the LEA.

A critical issue in several LEAs was any request by SACRE to review local RE provision. This was often resisted or deferred by the LEAs for a range of reasons: the lack of a viable AS; resourcing implications for the adviser's time; or an apparent desire to shield schools perceived to be under pressure on other curriculum counts. Some respondents also clearly distinguished the role of SACRE as to advise and that of the LEA to inspect.

> Some advisers reported that they or their superiors had had to point out to SACRE that there were inadequate resources for undertaking surveys of secondary or primary provision.

> In one authority the inspector thought SACRE's request for information about teacher shortage and exam results should be met by the meeting secretary (from the LEA secretariat) with his advice on data collection and analysis. In future it would be part of LEA surveys every four years.

> In another LEA where the adviser, at SACRE's request, had carried out a survey of primary and secondary provision which provided a baseline for subsequent evaluation and implementation of the AS, some schools reported using their own rather than the LEA's ten-year old syllabus. A councillor requested to see these with a view to inspecting school provision. The adviser advised against this, trying to be careful of both the school's and councillor's interests. He wanted to play down any inspectorial role so that schools would not see SACRE as a watchdog and so that SACRE would operate more in line with the joint review model operated by the LEA with schools.

Another major area of contention was reported to be difference of view within SACRE and between SACRE and education professionals about the nature of RE and CW.

> In one SACRE, for example, there were some contentious discussions about the place of world faiths in RE and the extent of multifaith approaches. In this largely white area the prevailing view of elected members was for minority ethnic groups to be assimilated and for little recognition to be given to their views and interests in religions other than Christianity. Discussions could result in direct confrontation between elected and co-opted members with the advisers holding the middle ground. Yet this was not reflected in *'clever minute writing'*.

Other advisers reported tensions over guidance on CW: whether this were to be issued by the LEA or SACRE; the degree of consultation with SACRE; policy and procedures on determinations; and monitoring practice in schools (see pp.91-92). Some advisers claimed no tensions currently, as SACRE was said to operate by consensus, but they could foresee that CW could become problematic, especially if the CEO/DoE were to be particularly influenced by elected members' views, or, if the composition of SACRE were to become more evangelical or fundamentalist and take a narrow line.

It was clear that some advisers/inspectors adopted or wanted to adopt a firm line on their role vis à vis SACRE and that they would not be responsible to SACRE in terms of the tasks they thought it appropriate to carry out. This was not by any means incompatible with the view that part of their role was *'to educate and raise the quality of the activity of the SACRE'* to encourage a healthy dialogue between the groups, especially between Group A—C and Group D. Advisers were thus sometimes seeking an independent role.

> One felt able to offer advice, was not constrained and would not hesitate to say if perception or judgements were incorrect — *'no toady'*.

> But for others it was more difficult: another was keen *'not to be locked into the LEA group'* and to be free to say what she wanted as appropriate and not be constrained to a particular line.

> Others were more pragmatic or even ruminative: one inspector found SACRE an additional factor to consider; it did add a certain tension. He asked himself *'Shall I carry on as before and write directly to schools regarding RE and attainment targets, or, should I share with SACRE the fact that I'm holding a day INSET course with primary teachers?'* The tension was worth living with if SACRE could be used for support when wanted if its backing was sympathetic. But if SACRE's advice did not agree with his professional views then he could dissociate himself from its recommendation. For example, if SACRE were to recommend separate acts of CW then he would say SACRE's role is only to advise and that as a representative of the LEA he did not have to accept SACRE's advice. Then the CEO would write to schools. But *'its fine as long as there is consensus and they share the same message and viewpoints.'*

The advent of SACRE placed RE advisers/inspectors in a more political role than usual. Some were prepared to seek to use opportunities creatively. Much seemed to depend on whether the adviser/inspector regarded the SACRE as friend or foe, but also on the degree of openness in the LEA and the reasonableness and informed understanding of *RE* by SACRE members.

Perceptions of Status and Influence of SACRE

Other important aspects of the level of interaction and degree of support between the LEA and SACRE are indicated by the number of senior LEA officers and Education Committee members attending SACRE meetings and perceptions of the status and influence of the SACRE locally by LEAs and schools.

Involvement of Other LEA Officers

In an attempt to gauge the level of interest in the SACRE, RE advisers/ inspectors interviewed were asked about the possible involvement of other LEA professionals, especially those in the most senior posts, and other members of Education Committee in addition to those in Group D. It was fairly common for a senior officer in the LEA to have been involved with the RE adviser/inspector in determining SACRE composition and formation (see p.16) and in setting up the constitution and operation of the SACRE in its initial stages (see p.66). Several RE advisers/ inspectors reported an *'interest'* in SACRE by their CEO or DoE; others that an active *'watching brief'* was kept, either through their reporting directly — occasionally *'being in close touch'* — or via the Chief Adviser/ Inspector or a Senior Education Officer. One or two suggested the CEO or DoE would like to attend SACRE meetings but did not have time; but it was more frequently claimed that the CEO/DoE would attend if issues being discussed were particularly controversial, or if their active support was requested. Participation was related to LEA *'committee style'*, perceptions of influence of the SACRE and the personal (religious) interest of the CEO/DoE.

In addition to the participation of RE advisers/inspectors and any ATREs as advisers or observers (or members - see p.108) of the SACRE and of an LEA officer as clerk (see p.106), **just over half of the LEAs where interviews were conducted had SACREs whose meetings other senior LEA personnel had attended at least once.** In almost half the LEAs senior officers such as Chief Inspectors/Advisers, Head of Schools Branch, SEOs or AEOs had been present at SACRE. In addition, in one-third of these LEAs either a CEO/DCEO or DoE had attended SACRE at least once.

In a few cases it appeared that a senior LEA presence at an initial SACRE meeting had been fairly **nominal** as if to check all were in order and operating as desired/envisaged.

In other instances attendance had been related to **particular purposes**:

- specific occasions such as when the CEO attended the inaugural meeting of the reconstituted SACRE, or the Head of Schools Branch (rather than the RE adviser) presented a report to SACRE on the LEA's interpretation of a *'reasonable amount of time'* for RE in its schools;

- or on-going support/involvement related to the priority given to the production and publication of an AS.

In two or three LEAs the DoE was reported to attend SACRE meetings regularly out of *'personal interest'* and as a *'committed Christian'*. RE advisers/inspectors regarded this degree of involvement as very supportive:

- in one LEA with a controversial SACRE the DoE attended and was consulted about the agenda and meeting strategy;

- in another the DoE attended as an observer but also answered questions about financial and policy matters;

- in a third the DoE showed considerable interest in the SACRE's first year, had himself made secretary of SACRE, and attended meetings regularly until latterly handing over to his Deputy who had a critical interventionist role in meetings. This SACRE was well supported by other LEA officers (RE adviser, two AEOs (one the SACRE clerk) and one curriculum adviser) and seven elected members — some of the most senior politicians including the Vice-Chair of Council and several members of the Education Committee.

A high level of LEA officer support built into the institutional structure of the SACRE was often, but not invariably, associated with a strong team of elected members, especially from Education Committee (see p.118). In some cases the implications of the SACRE's role for wider community and race relations were also acknowledged in the LEA attendance (see p.53). Although it could indicate a degree of wariness and appreciation about demands SACRE might make, a range of high-level officer support integrated into the SACRE meetings was more likely to reflect a recognition of local interest in the SACRE and that the LEA saw it as important and wanted to treat it seriously by giving it strong professional input.

Involvement of Other Elected Members

In none of the LEAs where interviews were conducted did members of Education Committee additional to those in Group D attend SACRE meetings. Many interviewees evinced some surprise at this question, indicating that the number and status of elected members represented on SACRE was adequate (see pp.51-52). It was sometimes claimed that elected members wished to take on these roles for local political and community reasons. Nevertheless elected members represented on SACRE could have considerable status on the local Borough or County council and many were on Education Committee, often in senior positions. For example:

- in one Labour-led County authority the five elected members included: Chair of Education Committee (Chair of SACRE), Chair of Equal Opportunities Committee and Chair of Schools Sub-Committee;

- in one Conservative Outer London Borough the five elected members on SACRE included: the Mayor, Chair of Education Committee (Chair of SACRE), Chair of Primary and Chair of Secondary Sub-Committee;

- in one Conservative northern Metropolitan Borough Group D comprised (Conservative four, Labour two, Liberal Democrat one) all on Education

Committee, its Chair also being Chair of SACRE and the Vice-Chair of SACRE also being drawn from this group.

The number and seniority of elected members on the SACRE varied according to LEA *'committee style'* and also perceptions of the significance of the SACRE. Even where elected members in Group D were not senior members of Education Committee other members of Education Committee did not attend SACRE meetings. Recruitment could be an issue:

- in one newly formed SACRE in an Inner London Borough it was suggested that elected members had to be *'press-ganged'* to belong to SACRE;

- in a County with a ten-year-old SACRE there was reported to be almost a queue by elected members for vacancies on the SACRE; it was said to be regarded positively as a lively committee with good debates, and to have high standing in the Education Committee.

The representation of Education Committee members on SACRE and their senior status could prove influential in gaining Education Committee's support for SACRE's recommendations.

In one Outer London LEA with an influential pre-existing SACRE, SACRE was always an item on Education Committee meetings where it and RE were perceived as making a positive contribution to local race relations. Education Committee was pleased with SACRE's AR and found extra money to have it published and given a high profile and wide distribution.

However, many RE advisers/inspectors were ignorant or unclear about whether SACRE and its advice was a matter for discussion in Education Committee. This reflected their absence of involvement at this level, due generally to their lack of seniority. Conversely, although elected members of Education Committee were usually fairly well represented on SACRE, the absence of wider involvement of Education Committee members (like the general public) as observers at SACRE meetings indicated that SACRE had not yet been perceived as a more open forum for education dialogue.

Perceptions of SACRE by LEAs and Schools

As much of this overview has revealed, LEA attitudes towards their SACRE, its role, status and influence, varied greatly according to local educational, religious, political and socio-economic circumstances. Perceptions were also related to different interest groups, with, for example, possible variation between senior LEA officers, RE advisers/ inspectors and elected members. These attitudes and responses could be highly situational, context-bound and time-dependent.

118

For the majority of LEAs where the experience of a SACRE was new, local perceptions were still being formed. Naturally enough, in the first year priority had been given to the formation of the SACRE, with concentration on its actual working within the meetings of SACRE itself, rather than giving attention to its public image. For many LEAs it continued to be a process of *'feeling the way'* and testing boundaries in relation to decision-making and implementation, responsibility and support affecting matters of educational principle and practice. In many cases LEAs, including RE advisers/inspectors, approached the business of the formation and operation of the SACRE with a certain, if not considerable, apprehension. Some reported that LEA professionals were wary of SACRE, conscious of the demands it would make, and were expecting it to cause tensions. In other cases it was more directly a matter of establishing LEA control where there was a strong concern that RE issues should be the province of professionals — officers, inspectors and advisers — rather than religious or political representatives. Thus some LEAs were proactively trying to restrict power to the professionals and *'keeping SACRE sweet'*. Others were said *'not to want SACRE to flex its muscles'*, restricted available information given to SACRE and did not provide INSET in an attempt to curtail its access to issues and practice and limit its authority. Some LEAs appeared not to realize the remit of the SACRE and its potential influence. Such approaches could be sources of tension for advisers/inspectors (see p.111ff); others appeared in support, whilst some regarded it as a challenge to use SACRE creatively to enlist its influence and assistance to raise the local profile of RE. Undoubtedly in a few LEAs the establishment of SACRE was seen as a necessary chore to comply with legislation. In some cases attitudes to SACRE were less than enthusiastic because of local restructuring of schools and finance and more generally because of demands of implementing the National Curriculum in other subject areas, against which RE appeared to lack parity of esteem. Nevertheless, as shown by examples of innovative approaches or interesting practices already highlighted, many of the LEAs where interviews were conducted had either approached the formation of the SACRE and its operation in a more open, flexible and supportive manner or were gradually moving towards a more collaborative partnership with it and the various interests represented. Indeed advisers in several LEAs with long-standing SACREs reported that they were locally perceived to be influential and respected.

SACREs also have a direct role in relation to schools in conveying advice and deciding on applications for determinations on CW. It was thus important to gauge schools' perceptions of the SACRE locally as mediated by their RE advisers/inspectors. Whilst a few advisers disliked generalizing about schools' views, the range of reported perceptions to some extent reflected those of LEAs. Most advisers claimed that schools were aware of the existence of the SACRE (or had no excuse for not being aware) through DES Circular 3/89, if not directly from local documentation on the role and fuction of the SACRE (see p.88), guidelines on CW (see p.138) or in connection with applications for a determination (see p.143ff). In addition, some heads and teachers were aware of SACRE because of requests for nominations from their professional associations and possibly by reports back through these channels. However, some advisers queried schools' awareness of the role and function of SACRE: such consciousness-raising was a task for the adviser in local RE and CW INSET and with individual schools, especially in relation to applications for determinations. Since ERA and DES Circular 3/89 some advisers reported changing concerns and perceptions on the part of schools: whereas some had initially viewed ERA in respect of RE and CW with worry and disquiet, to be overshadowed by the need to address the implementation of the National Curriculum in core subjects, others were said to have gradually become more aware of the obligation to review their RE provision or CW practice — perhaps as a result of a local SACRE-initiated survey or by seeking a determination on CW from SACRE.

Reported schools' perceptions varied widely and usually in relation to the local profile of RE and the LEA/SACRE approach to CW and determinations.

Some were said to be 'terrified' of SACRE and of any possible inspection or evaluation of RE and CW. Heads were 'terrified lest their school be named' or 'feared a court case about "broadly Christian" worship' and were 'wised up to the complaints machinery'.

Others, despite under-provision and under-resourcing, largely ignored SACRE.

Others, it was claimed, were suspicious of SACRE and felt it was unnecessary. They looked to the adviser and advisory teachers for guidance and support.

Elsewhere schools were reported to have little direct contact with SACRE except through staff members, yet it commanded authority and respect because of its position and values; SACRE was not feared but seen as the support to an influential inspectorate.

In several other LEAs schools tended to see SACRE as influential, though some advisers queried the extent of its actual influence.

Whilst some schools showed interest in SACRE and asked advisers 'What is SACRE doing now?', others, at least initially, apparently saw SACRE as 'a watchdog' and could seem in awe of it—one secondary school where RE had not previously been timetabled was now referring to it as 'SACRE time'; other schools looked to SACRE for support inquiring 'Is SACRE to give us *advice on this or that?' or 'When is SACRE going to tell us about attainment targets?'*.

These reported school concerns reflected worries about legal interpretations of ERA in domains where parental rights of withdrawal are safeguarded. They also to some extent mirrored LEA ambivalence about the status and influence of the SACRE and lack of clarity about the extent to which it should have direct relationships with schools. This was particularly so in respect of giving advice on RE rather than its obviously legitimate function to grant determinations.

RE advisers/inspectors usually had a critical, if sometimes circumspectly interventionist role, in relation to the SACRE, LEA and schools and in respect of the profile of RE and the direction of CW. Thus there could be differences in perceptions of the SACRE by the adviser and those reported for schools. Some advisers saw SACRE as personally supportive of them and their task as well as concerned to maintain or enhance local RE provision (see p.112). Clearly at this initial stage many perceived the extent of the SACRE's potential influence on RE and CW and its possible independence of the LEA to be yet realized (see pp.171-172). The SACRE itself was often still *'finding its feet'*, Due to the emphasis on establishing working procedures and decision making *inside* the SACRE and the general lack of attempts at building of relationships with schools, usually only those schools with direct contact with SACRE through seeking determinations had actual experience of its operation and influence. Some advisers shrewdly saw their task to use SACRE creatively to support and enhance their professional views about the direction of RE and CW as well as enabling SACRE to feel it had a public profile. They saw the imprimatur of SACRE as significant but also to be used sparingly. For example:

- some included SACRE's name or dropped the name of the Chair of SACRE, if a well-known local councillor, in any letters or documents sent to schools; these were perceived to have weight and influence also because of the implied agreement of teachers' unions represented on SACRE;

- one was aiming to produce a series of baseline documents on RE reflecting inspectorate views but with SACRE imprimatur, indicating the attention of SACRE. SACRE's endorsement of guidelines on CW was seen as supportive to schools - it was a strength to have SACRE's backing for implementation of a realistic policy on CW for which guidelines are a starting point;

- in another LEA RE professionals perceived the local SACRE's role with respect to RE and CW on a par with that of NCC for core subjects; thus some argued that advice from SACRE should have statutory force, but such views were not shared by other LEA officers who wanted to limit SACRE's status and influence.

Many SACREs had made significant starts in their first year of operation. Yet as many advisers' comments on promising lines of development for SACRE emphasized, the SACRE had some way to go in developing its coherence as a policy-making body and in image building. There remains considerable scope for enhancing its sphere of influence and winning the confidence of schools and LEAs in supporting the implementation of sound policies and realistic meaningful practices. In this task of liaison and feedback, the teachers' association members of SACRE, especially RE teachers, have a special, but seemingly so far largely undeveloped, part to play. Perceptions of the status and influence of SACRE thus formed one of the key issues in its first year of operation (see p.171ff).

SACRE Concerns and Policy

SACREs are given a wide-ranging statutory remit open to local interpretation and with variations in practice according to local circumstance, LEA referrals and SACRE requests. In becoming involved in LEA policy and practice SACREs had three main spheres of concern: RE, CW and the local complaints procedure, specifically in relation to the AS, teaching methods, materials and training. Its statutory duties obliged the SACRE to give advice on these matters and some SACREs also initiated action (see p.174ff).

Religious Education

The extent and depth of SACRE's concern with RE at this initial stage related to several factors, such as: whether the balance of its time was taken up with CW and especially determinations (see p.143ff); to what degree the LEA raised RE issues with the SACRE and/or it was itself proactive in making requests for information or visits to school and was successful in having these interests met; and whether there was a local SACRE tradition on which the approach and work of the new body could build. The main RE issues which preoccupied SACREs were: the AS and its revisions; related curricular matters (cross- curricular links and with CW), assessment, organization and delivery.

The Agreed Syllabus

In over one-third of the LEAs sampled one of the first tasks of the LEA had been to bring to the attention of SACRE the need to recommend a revision of the AS and therefore that an ASC should be constituted (see pp.187-188 and p.78). There seems little doubt that in some LEAs ERA had prompted them to consider the status, age, relevance and currency of their AS — *'it would not have been done otherwise'*. Indeed, in some cases, it was a question of trying to find copies (the AS could date back as far as 45 years). Some LEAs quickly perceived the need for urgent action; in others ERA seemed to have brought to a head a quiescent situation, *'a sleepy consensus'*, where RE had previously not enjoyed such a high priority or the local context had been perceived to be potentially too contentious to initiate a review. As time passed, some LEAs, occasionally in conjunction with SACRE, had taken a harder look at the content and approach of their AS and considered to what extent it would be seen as in line with ERA's (S.8) requirements that any new AS '*shall reflect the fact that the religious traditions in Great Britain are in the main Christian whilst taking account of the teaching and practices of other principal religions represented in Great Britain*'. A third factor which had sharpened the focus on the AS was the attention given to programmes of study (PoS) and especially attainment targets (ATs) and assessment arrangements (AAs) for other subjects in the National Curriculum (see pp.130-133).

In addition to the fact that Group A—C of SACRE could '*require its LEA to review its current AS*', there were other direct connections between the SACRE and the AS through the ASC, in respect of overlap of membership, meetings, working parties and INSET. Continuity of membership between the SACRE and ASC was perceived as important by the LEA and RE advisers/inspectors. Available information indicates that where ASs are currently under review the membership of SACRE and ASC overlaps by at least 75 per cent, may be identical, or sometimes the ASC had additional members from other religious backgrounds, Humanists, or teachers with particular experience. Partly for this reason, meetings of the SACRE and ASC are often held on the same day, consecutively, with a change halfway through proceedings. In some cases, SACRE/ASC members are involved in working parties undertaking the main business of AS revision and occasionally advisers/inspectors had mounted INSET in this connection. The following examples illustrate these aspects of SACRE interaction on AS revision.

> In one or two LEAs SACRE members were invited to become members of ASC and to nominate others, even though the LEA made the appointments. An adviser convinced the LEA that it could no longer ignore the lack of an up-to-date AS, especially in the light of an objection by a small group of white parents to an Eid party held in a school with one-third pupils from Muslim backgrounds, as it was difficult to justify the school's RE programme in the light of the current AS. It was expected that the SACRE would recommend the establishment of an ASC, so the LEA decided to call the tune and at SACRE's first meeting informed it of the LEA's intentions to review the AS, that SACRE had no legal involvement in developing the AS, but that it hoped SACRE would want to be involved and consulted (including on membership) and attend seminars.

> In a County with a 20-year-old AS and changing community structure the Education Committee suggested that SACRE should recommend an AS review and that it might become the ASC. Members (many in full-time employment) expressed some diffidence about attending more meetings. A professional working party was established of primary, secondary and post-16 teachers. Advisers put on a one-day conference on RE for the ASC, suggested what sort of AS should be produced and '*got them on our side*'.

In a Metropolitan authority the recommendation to review the AS, dating from 1944, went to a full council meeting for a decision. Although it was debated whether the SACRE should be transformed to an ASC, it was felt that the teachers' association representatives needed strengthening with a secondary HoD and primary co-ordinators. The onus was put on SACRE members to opt out of the ASC. An informed consultative group of inspectorate, teachers and communities had started to bring together good practice and identify background materials.

Elsewhere in another Metropolitan authority, the SACRE and LEA saw the AS as having priority. A working party of teachers had actually started work on a draft AS prior to SACRE. Although it was claimed that the LEA would have formed an ASC irrespective of setting up SACRE, the formality of the establishment of an ASC via the SACRE '*set the work back a bit*'. In fact, the SACRE members agreed, with slight additions, to continue on the ASC because of the urgency of the need of an AS in schools. The chair of the teachers' group worked with other groups and when wording was agreed this was put to the full conference. It did not always accept the chairpersons' recommendations, though unanimity is required of the ASC for a new AS to be adopted.

In another Metropolitan LEA with parallel ASs (one dating back to 1949) the SACRE converted itself to an ASC and the AS revision more or less absorbed the SACRE meetings. A working party on aims was formed with one member from each of the SACRE/ASC groups; a teachers group drew up objectives; and these, together with an overview of other ASs, were presented to the ASC. The adviser was largely responsible for writing the AS, but found this '*unbelievable and unnerving*'. When the syllabus was agreed the ASC reverted to the SACRE. Work was now focussing on school-based implementation, and the development of a handbook. The adviser was resisting a directive role from SACRE, not '*You will teach this*' and '*This is how you will teach it*', and an introduction to the AS by the SACRE Chair, although the role of SACRE needed to be acknowledged.

Interestingly, in three Counties the AS was undergoing some revision with SACRE's knowledge, but without the setting up of an ASC.

In one an adopted AS, in use for three years, was out of print. It had not been discussed by SACRE but the Chair, CEO and the adviser were in agreement that it would be a waste of time and money and potentially controversial to revise the AS. However, it might need to be considered by SACRE in relation to ATs. The SACRE might then issue guidelines in the form of a letter from the Chair or an appendix to the AS (unlike the position of CW where the LEA took a quick lead).

In another LEA SACRE requested the LEA to '*re-present*' the AS. It was to have a key word system for aims and objectives and a new layout including a flow chart illustrating the development process. SACRE (not an ASC) was to consider, modify and support the document.

Elsewhere, one of the early tasks of SACRE was to set up a working party on AAs which had led to the questioning of the AS. The erstwhile adviser had initiated a review of the AS which had previously been influential, adopted and modified in several other LEAs. It was felt to be philosophically sound, but needed to communicate more clearly with practitioners about continuity and progression, have a clear structure across age-related phases and to untangle explicit and implicit RE. The new adviser and a working party had consulted with teachers and revised the AS linking it to a PoS with key stages (KSs) and five ATs. There seemed to be uncertainty as to the contribution of an ASC and whether SACRE could perform this role. Reports on the AS and AAs to be trialled in schools were made to SACRE. It expressed concern that the lack of teacher advisers for RE would lead to postponement of implementation of the new AS and that this would be seen by schools as giving less importance to RE compared with other National Curriculum subjects, such as history and geography, which needed teacher advisers to fulfil the statutory requirements of implementing their PoSs and ATs. SACRE also recommended that a summary of the AS, accessible to governing bodies and parents, should also be prepared.

Such examples of revisions to ASs indicate certain anomalies. In particular they raise questions about the necessity of a separate ASC, distinct from the SACRE, especially when no such statutory parallel body exists for producing a local policy on CW (often perceived to be more controversial). This applies *a fortiori* when the ASC, so closely mirroring the membership of SACRE, frequently effectively sub-contracts the actual process of producing a new syllabus, partly to increase professional RE involvement and to minimize the demands on members' time.

In a few other LEAs interviewees mentioned that revision to the AS had been discussed in SACRE or was likely for various reasons. Others, especially those with ASs produced in the 80s, were less likely to feel that a revision would be thought necessary or desired unless there was pressure from groups within or outside SACRE. Different approaches were taken.

In one County SACRE had discussed the AS's possible revision and assessment. They had accepted the adviser's view that it would be unwise to launch an ASC to revise the AS during the next two years. He saw current legislation and local arrangements as an opportunity to push RE alongside history and geography and to obtain joint funding. Revision to the AS would, in his view, prejudice chances of promoting a less Bible-based teaching of RE, a broader view of Christianity and more about other world religions.

In one of the new Inner London authorities, previously covered by the 1984 ILEA syllabus, SACRE had discussed whether or not to adopt this at its first meeting. Three groups wished to, but the LEA group wanted a revision and to add a local '*stamp*'. Thus the question of review was to receive further discussion at pre-group meetings and a later SACRE.

Elsewhere the inspector, aware of the deficiencies of the AS, thought the time was ripe for revision. He was trying to prepare SACRE for making an informed decision by presenting to it various papers on all aspects of RE in order to raise their consciousness about the nature of RE (see p.79).

The preoccupation with current AS revision, consideration of it or preparation for it amongst the LEAs sampled meant that many SACREs were deferring serious or detailed consideration of such matters as teaching materials, teaching time and INSET until after revision of the AS. Implementation was not necessarily seen as an integral consideration, but bolt on, even though a recent HMI Report (GB. DES, 1989c) recommended that implementation of an AS required a plan which includes a role for SACRE. In one or two cases SACREs were considering drafts of teacher handbooks in relation to (relatively recent) ASs, but more attention was being given to developing guidelines on CW (pp.138-139) and currently these apparently outnumbered AS guidelines or handbooks (see Table 2). In some cases encouragement was being given to schools to produce their own plans for RE showing how their own syllabus fitted with whole-school development. But school-based curricular appraisal of RE content and teaching approaches was seen as a process for SACRE to develop over time. More immediately interviewees generally expressed concern about the perceived status of RE in the National Curriculum and its need for parity in schools with other (Humanities) subjects in relation to staffing, teaching time and exams. During their first year SACREs were becoming better informed on the curricular and organizational aspects of RE, often through involvement with revision to the AS, so that their sympathy for RE could be converted to active concern.

RE and Cross-Curricular Themes

The overwhelming majority of advisers/inspectors indicated that SACREs had not considered RE in relation to Personal and Social Education (PSE) (despite the frequent overlap in the upper secondary years) or cross-curricular themes, such as citizenship or the environment. Even a long-established SACRE was reported to be more concerned about the survival of RE as a separate subject against a yardstick of other Humanities subjects. Some interviewees evinced surprise at the question, indicating that SACRE '*would be out if its depth*' or '*could not cope*' or that they would not want it to concern itself with what was generally regarded to be a sophisticated curriculum exercise. Indeed, few advisers/inspectors suggested that RE in relation to cross-curricular themes had been considered at LEA level or in INSET: one mentioned that local advisory teachers were beginning to look at this in relation to inputs in KS 1-3; another that it would arise apropos of AAs for RE links with cross-curricular work with PSE. Some indicated they were awaiting a lead from DES or NCC.

One or two questioned whether such considerations should be part of SACRE's role and that it might be seen as *'pontificating'* — it was a school or LEA responsibility.

A similar number thought that it would be a matter for the ASC rather than SACRE — RE in the AS could be discrete or cross-curricular with RE leading or supporting. In one LEA INSET for the ASC had addressed RE's contribution to cross-curricular themes through staffing and topic work. In another cross-curricular themes were raised at a meeting of SACRE with a view to fleshing out the AS (under revision) in relation to PSE and citizenship, but SACRE did not express a view.

Elsewhere the inspector had introduced a discussion in SACRE of RE in relation to PSE through the new LEA PSE policy, which mentions SACRE and the place of RE in the PSE curriculum; also by means of a map for the RE curriculum whereby schools could review which curriculum subjects include RE and thus plan work developmentally. The approach was through common concepts, skills and attitudes, age-related and taken from the AS. Schools had found it useful — English teachers, for example, realized how they were dealing with the spiritual dimension. But it was felt that although SACRE had some understanding of the larger concept the mapping exercise rendered them *'gob-smacked'*.

However, as a result of a local survey, one SACRE had renewed concerns about the management of RE in PSE and Humanities at secondary level, exacerbated by increasing pressure on timetabling from the National Curriculum. It was anxious that RE teachers should be consulted from the beginning and that, even if modular, RE should meet the aims and objectives in the AS and, as indicated in its AR, that RE should be clearly identifiable.

Links between RE and Collective Worship

Advisers and inspectors were asked whether SACRE saw RE and CW as linked or separate. This somewhat loaded question may have lent itself to some opaque responses, but it was also perceived to be a difficult issue on several counts. Statutorily, it was felt that ERA seemed to suggest RE and CW are connected, as they have been on historical, religious and educational grounds. Yet in curriculum terms there was seen to be no clear line management or responsibility for CW beyond the local SACRE itself, unlike the same acknowledged responsibility by the NCC towards RE. Moreover, there was an implicit difficulty in advisers'/inspectors' responses about distinguishing SACRE's view from that of the LEA or their own or even, in some cases, generalizing about '*a*' SACRE view.

This said, some interesting judgements and comments were made: with responses being almost evenly divided between those who claimed SACRE saw RE and CW as linked, separate or both separate and linked/ unclear.

Linked: since many members of a SACRE had been involved in the ASC, it was claimed most in the LEA understood the difference between RE and CW, although they perceived them as closely associated both in educational and religious terms;

where a new AS had just or was about to come into force a few reported that it would include reference to CW and that in INSET, especially at primary level, they would be linked;

a few said CW is supporting RE in class: experiments in forms of school worship may help with the exploration of RE; or what happens in worship is seen as good if it is reflected in the life of the school.

Separate: in a few cases the LEA had '*encouraged*' or even '*told*' SACRE to keep CW and RE separate; but it was claimed that some SACRE members (especially Muslims) had difficulty in seeing them as separate; or that not many understood the *educational* aspects of CW; or that in practice they were linked through the work of the local RE Centre.

Separate & Linked: in one or two instances the approach was pragmatic: SACRE realised that RE and CW are two different aspects of the task to which it has to respond even though it has no overall concept of the relation of CW and RE;

another SACRE had a good debate on RE and CW links: it saw them as separate and complementary, the latter in so far as CW is about RE; the link was recognized but it saw them as distinctive areas;

elsewhere the adviser/inspector found it '*difficult to think*' about SACRE's view or suggested that it was too early for it to have a view as it had not yet realized its full role on CW.

In responding some advisers/inspectors indicated that their own view differed from that they perceived SACRE to take: whilst they tended to share perceptions about RE there were more likely to be differences of viewpoint on CW. Moreover, SACRE's view could differ from that of schools — in practice schools were said to see CW and RE as linked, especially informing each other in curricular practice at the primary level and sometimes through a supporting school ethos and underwritten by LEA policy on whole-school development. There was a concern that heads should understand they do not have a right to think of the RE teacher as responsible for CW.

Another issue which seemed to arise, especially at secondary level, was that some schools were said to count CW as coming within their RE provision and to specify this in their annual curriculum returns. A certain confusion appears to have arisen in interpreting the draft DES Circular (GB. DES, 1989d) on *The Length and Control of School Sessions,* where it was suggested that time for CW should be *additional* to the minimum recommended period of teaching per week. However, in one LEA at least, a letter from the CEO about the SACRE stated that '*collective worship is an important aspect of school life and may be counted in a school's reporting procedures* [in line with *The Education (School Curriculum and Related Information) Regulations,* GB. Statutory Instruments, 1989] *where it can be shown to fulfil particular curricular objectives.*' It is interesting to note that the final reissued DES Circular 7/90 on the *Management of the School Day* (GB. DES, 1990, Para 27) reiterates that the suggested minimum weekly lesson times:

> '*include religious education, but they do not include the statutory act of daily worship. The Secretary of State regards it as important that schools make adequate time available for collective worship in addition to the suggested minimum hours for lesson time. Collective worship has an important general contribution to make to school curriculum objectives and a particular role to play in the promotion of the spiritual and moral development of pupils which Section 1 of the 1988 Act requires.*'

Thus it appears a distinction is drawn between formal teaching and worship, whilst at the same time it is acknowledged that worship can complement school curriculum objectives and make a specific contribution to certain aspects of pupils' development which are not necessarily addressed through the formal curriculum. However, the legislation and guidance here appears to be confused and to admit of anomalies.

Attainment and Assessment

To what extent have SACREs been involved in local consideration of attainment and assessment in RE? How do we know children are religiously educated? What are the criteria for assessment? ERA recognized RE as part of the basic curriculum — a broad and balanced curriculum that should be available to all — and, standing alongside the core and foundation subjects. As such, some have argued that RE should be related to educational goals (ATs), learning experiences (PoS) and the processes involved in enhancing children's learning and development (AAs). However, unlike the core and foundation subjects, in RE these must be established in a local form. Over the last two years this situation has given rise to considerable local, regional and national activity directed towards attainment and assessment in RE. Advisers/inspectors interviewed held strong opinions on these matters and their relevance to local RE which were reflected in the involvement of their SACRE.

Several interviewees suggested that moves towards linking ATs with local ASs was not just '*a sign of the times*' but related to a general unease amongst advisers/inspectors that RE syllabuses should be more specific, especially about progression and continuity, particular curriculum objectives and appropriate educational processes. Contrary to the philosophy of many syllabuses of the late 70s and early 80s, which broadly prescribed aims and objectives leaving content to teachers — many of whom, especially primary teachers, had no training for RE — there appears to be a growing concern, in some quarters, that teachers of RE need clear guidance on learning experiences (PoS), goals (ATs) and evidence of and criteria for learning (AAs). All these have training implications that need to be addressed. Such views are also linked to fears about perceptions of the status of RE — that if RE were not couched in the same language as the core and foundation subjects it would be even harder for it to maintain or develop its status.

For such reasons **many RE advisers/inspectors have been involved in one or more national, regional or local initiative on attainment and assessment in RE.** Each of the following enterprises were connected, either by personal or LEA participation and SACRE awareness with at least one, and mostly several, of the LEA advisers/inspectors interviewed.

> **AREAI**: a group of RE advisers and inspectors worked together in 1988-9 to produce an interim consultative report, exploring ways in which the national curriculum framework might be applicable to RE (AREAI, 1989b).
>
> **REC**: building on this, a working party of RE professionals from constituent bodies of REC is looking at the way in which PoS, ATs and AAs might affect LEAs and the development of ASs.
>
> **Westhill Project**: in association with 30 LEAs (including a quarter of this LEA sample who bought into the project using LEATGS or INSET money) the Midlands Regional RE Centre has published a teachers' handbook which includes a model for developing ATs and PoSs for RE in four KSs (Regional RE Centre, 1989) and is producing a follow-up on assessing, recording and

reporting in RE (1991); LEAs sponsoring this work would need to render it locally relevant.

FARE: based at Exeter University and operating over two years with six south-western LEAs this project is working with teachers to examine forms of assessment, PoS and ATs appropriate for RE (Copley, *et al.*, 1990). In one LEA SACRE approved local involvement in piloting this work which was seen as commensurate with the current AS.

Some reservations were expressed by some interviewees about these various initiatives which were seen as having '*vested interests*'. There was also a sense, as one put it, that '*as the DES has encouraged do it yourself attainment targets in RE everyone is reinventing the wheel*'. Some felt strongly that this work needed a national platform and that NCC should take a lead.

However, **others expressed markedly less interest in attainment and assessment in RE, for a variety of practical, local and educational reasons.**

A few saw **assessment as far too inspectorial**: one inspector had '*kept SACRE away from ATs*' — teachers needed to work in an area where they were allowed free expression and not constrained by assessment; criticizing the National Curriculum model as '*philosophically flawed and empirically untested*' he predicted LEAs which had gone down the line of assessment in RE would subsequently retract, but was keeping in touch with developments.

A few recognized that the **lack of resources for RE locally and its low profile would not support any national or local involvement**; advisers' views varied: between the sceptical, indicating that, in the light of current debate, work on ATs and AAs might be wasted — a view accepted by SACRE; and those who were waiting for outcomes from existing initiatives before the matter was raised with SACRE.

A few others held **particular views about the nature of assessment**; for example, one inspector was against assessment in RE — seeing it more as a matter of untestable values and attitudes — but was in favour of it in relation to Religious Studies which could be linked to work in History and literature, whilst reflecting the AS. In an LEA where assessment had been discussed in relation to the AS and exams another inspector voiced concern that RE would be '*degutted by ATs and that teaching will be linked only to these*'. Involvement in ATs was '*only for the status of RE*'. He preferred local work to focus on children's needs in RE, especially the opportunity to encounter various types of religious experience, and relate what religious people believe in and act upon to the development of children.

Several interviewees indicated that many of these arguments had been raised and aired in discussions in SACRE, particularly in relation to the local AS and its current state of development or implementation. In some cases advisers/inspectors had presented papers and information about various national and regional initiatives. Sometimes it was felt that some SACRE members experienced difficulty in grasping the practical details or implications; in other cases there was disagreement within SACRE about whether to link assessment with the AS, or differences of view between SACRE and the LEA adviser/inspector for RE about LEA involvement in national initiatives. Variations in the amount of time available locally for RE adviser/inspector/ATRE involvement with ATs and AAs were very evident.

> In one LEA which had bought into the Westhill project SACRE had a stimulating discussion about ATs as many SACRE members are teachers. It was decided not to mount a local initiative on ATs — particularly as teachers of younger children were adamantly against this — but that the LEA would offer support to any school wanting to consider using ATs in RE and would make recommendations as to how the Westhill suggestions could be adapted locally.

> In one or two LEAs SACRE was about to establish a working party on ATs: in one case to discuss links with the AS and produce guidelines on objectives and content — probably a year's work related to SACRE's three meetings; elsewhere a SACRE member with long experience in RE was to chair a steering group to decide on the nature of work and key ideas, probably operating through teachers' groups, drawing on other initiatives and tailoring them to the AS, KSs, progression and continuity.

> Elsewhere SACRE's early setting up of a working party on AAs had led to revision of the AS (see p.126).

> By comparison, in another LEA trials of ATs developed by local teachers were already underway in 70 primary and secondary schools. Evidence was to be analysed and presented to SACRE as part of the informing and credentializing process, prior to a decision about adopting the framework.

Local diversity was much in evidence in respect of views expressed on attainment and assessment in RE, the degree of involvement in national, regional or local initiatives, and the extent of SACRE's awareness and appreciation of the details of content, process and implications for practice and training.

Aspects of Organization and Teaching RE

SACREs are specifically empowered to consider teaching methods, materials, INSET and ITT but, in addition, may give advice on other aspects of organization and teaching RE, such as teaching time, staffing and teacher qualifications as they may see fit. To what extent were these subjects of attention for SACRE in its first year?

Teaching time for RE was only beginning to be a concern of SACREs, largely as a result of evidence obtained from local surveys of RE provision initiated by SACRE or the LEA (see pp.83-85).

> One SACRE had an extensive and controversial discussion about what constituted '*a reasonable amount of time for RE*' (see p.85).

> Another SACRE was interested in such a discussion but it was postponed to come up in relation to the handbook rather than the AS. The adviser wanted it to become a recommendation for teachers as to what was practically viable.

> Elsewhere the inspector had sent a letter to schools (to be subsequently brought to SACRE's notice) drawing their attention to the need for parity of RE with foundation subjects and suggesting that RE should have five per cent provision. This resulted in some complaints from schools of insufficient available time.

Teaching time was often seen by advisers as an issue more at the secondary level, especially in Year 10 and 11 when RE might be integrated with Humanities or PSE, or in the sixth form. There was less available evidence on RE in primary education. Schools were perceived as clever at disguising RE provision in survey and curriculum returns. There was concern that RE, in line with the local AS, should be identifiable as such, and in one or two cases SACREs were making recommendations to this effect (see p.175). **Thus there was tension between SACRE and LEAs, on the one hand, and schools on the other about available teaching time for RE and time for CW (see p.130).** This was likely to become more of an issue in successive years where schools were to be required to indicate RE's particular contribution to whole-school development and with changes in local ASs, ATs and AAs and closer monitoring by governors, LEA and HMI.

Staffing was another matter to which some SACREs were starting to attend. Teaching qualifications or incentive allowances were rarely addressed. Some SACREs had requested information and had received reports from RE advisers/inspectors, some of which were based on survey evidence for schools. Interviewees' reports indicated considerable LEA diversity in the staffing situation for RE. Whilst for some authorities it was a concern if one school lacked an RE specialist, in others it was a question of reducing the number of schools where this obtained.

> In one County 94 per cent of schools were said to be staffed for RE with a 1:300 teacher-pupil ratio and most primary schools had a teacher with curricular responsibility for RE. The adviser considered no school should be prevented from fulfilling SACRE's recommendations, only if its staffing policy was at fault.

Elsewhere in the range of LEA types there were reported staff shortages, especially at secondary or upper school level and for HoDs; in one LEA four out of ten secondary schools were attempting to recruit RE HoDs; in another six schools had probationers who were HoDs. But an adjacent County was less well staffed at lower levels; and in one rural County many small primary schools had only two or three teachers to cover the entire curriculum. Poor fields of candidates were blamed for recruitment difficulties. But elsewhere strong INSET programmes had resulted in out-of-LEA promotions (see p.84).

Where staffing was discussed within SACREs, advisers/inspectors appeared to have taken SACREs into their confidence and requested support (see p.84). Some felt that SACREs could put more pressure on the LEA on teacher supply and advisory posts. But in some LEAs it had been made clear to SACRE that schools were responsible for staffing levels and the LEA role was one of monitoring rather than direction. **However, a few SACREs were making explicit recommendations about staffing levels in schools in their ARs and about LEA advisory support (see p.175).** Whether these were to be successful appeared to be related to perceptions of the status and influence of the SACRE locally and the degree of communication established.

Teacher training (both INSET and ITT), teaching methods and materials were matters explicitly referred to SACREs by ERA, but evidence from the study indicated that as yet they had received only perfunctory consideration despite some considerable and creative local INSET programmes. These had at least usually been brought to SACRE's notice, and were sometimes included in ARs. A few SACREs had also requested or been given more detailed reports. In one or two cases advisers/inspectors were additionally deliberately trying to raise SACRE's consciousness about the INSET needs of teachers of RE by involving SACRE members themselves in experiential learning whilst undertaking their own role (see pp.103-104). **Given the proportion of LEAs where the AS was under revision, it is not surprising that many respondents indicated that INSET would become a matter for SACRE's attention when implementation of the AS was reviewed.** Meanwhile, teaching methods and materials were likely to be left to consideration of working parties, mainly of teachers. SACRE was, however, viewed as a potential ally on INSET in relation to the Education Committee, LEA and schools:

in one Metropolitan LEA INSET would be a concern of SACRE in overseeing implementation of the AS because no money was forthcoming after a request by the DoE to Education Committee: *'RE is regarded as small beer locally'*;

in a County authority being reorganized into divisions, RE funding was county-wide and INSET centrally organized whilst responding to divisional returns and school requests; there could be difficulties in reconciling advisory responsibilities if they were to be divisionally oriented; but SACRE might give added weight to supporting inspectorate requests and recommendations;

another SACRE was moving towards recommending that school reports should mention INSET for RE.

Not surprisingly, ITT had not yet become a matter of interest of SACREs. Indeed, **several interviewees, even those with ITT connections, gave the impression that this had not been fully recognized as a SACRE responsibility.** On the other hand, a few saw this remit as very important.

One noted that the survey of secondary RE provision would provide insights relevant to ITT for the AR and had been in contact with local institutions of HE on ITT.

Another bemoaned the lack of class expertise in local teacher training, especially in the primary area, going as far as to claim that two local colleges had little to contribute to INSET and there was a need to '*retrain*' probationers.

National and local changes — the fact that RE is no longer a national priority area for LEATGS funding; LEA reorganization and moves from advisory to inspection services; and patterns of INSET provision which may be more LEA or school-focussed, with buying in of support from local colleges — will have considerable implications for institutions undertaking training in RE. It was not part of this study to inquire to what extent training institutions had realized SACRE's remit to address itself to INSET and ITT or whether any SACRE recommendations might influence such bodies. However, it was clear that SACREs had not yet developed particular links with training institutions to enhance mutual understanding of needs and interests.

Collective Worship

Guidelines on Practice

The other main aspect of the SACRE's function is to advise on '*religious worship*' and to consider school applications for determinations. ERA (S. 7 (1)) defined collective worship for county schools as '*wholly or mainly of a broadly Christian character*'. DES Circular 3/89 (Para 34) subsequently elaborated:

'*For those acts which are broadly Christian, the main emphasis should be on the broad traditions of Christian belief.*

....an act of worship which is "broadly Christian" need not contain only Christian material provided that, taken as a whole, it reflects the traditions of Christian belief. Any such worship should not be distinctive of any particular Christian denomination. It is not necessary for every act of worship to be of this character, but within each school term, the majority of acts must be so.'

Interpretation of these prescriptions and their implications for the organization of CW in schools as appropriate to the faith backgrounds and ages of pupils, has been a critical issue for schools and LEAs and has formed a major consideration for many SACREs. Indeed, a few SACREs have been preoccupied with issues concerning CW and particularly their role on determinations to the virtual exclusion of other matters in their first year of operation. The requirement for CW came into force on 1.8.89, except for Inner London Boroughs where it was 1.8.90.

In many LEAs there was seen to be an urgent need for guidelines on CW for schools, especially in view of the initial perceptions and concerns of heads, parents and communities. Some SACREs had themselves requested guidelines or information on local CW practice (see p.86), but occasionally in more monocultural areas CW had not even arisen as an issue for SACRE. Some advisers/inspectors reported considerable anxiety and disquiet on the part of heads about the practical implications of interpreting ERA: some were reported to be *'losing sleep'* over the meaning of *'broadly Christian'*, the requirements for *'daily'* provision, and whether these would necessitate a change in approach. Others were aware or appreciative of the sensitivity of some faith communities (especially some local Muslim communities, and partly in response to pamphlets circulated by the Muslim Educational Trust (1989a and b)) to the wording of the Act and a feeling that their faiths had been overtly marginalized. In some cases consciousness had thus been raised, leading to specific requests. There were also reports of concerns expressed by parents from Christian and other faith backgrounds that ERA would alter their local school's practice on CW with which they had previously been content. To an extent heads, parents and others had been influenced by misleading and inaccurate press reports instead of referring to ERA itself. But many schools, especially those with pupils from a range of faith backgrounds, were genuinely exercised as to how they could best meet the needs and interests of their pupils: to provide them with educationally valid experiences which minimized any discordance with their or their parents' beliefs and values whilst at the same time conforming to the Act. It was often a question of *'unpacking the meaning of the Act with practitioners'* so that they could begin to see it as *'less of a bogey that they thought'* and gradually bringing about a change in the climate of opinion.

These tensions and the complex issues surrounding the requirement for *'religious worship'* in schools were often reflected in the discussions within SACREs. **For herein lay an issue: the urgent need for guidance to be produced for schools and, more specifically, for applications for determinations to be considered — complex conceptual and policy decisions with practical implications — by a body intentionally composed of different interest groups, with a range of knowledge, experience and understanding, which had not yet learnt to work with one another.** Collective worship was thus a concrete test: as one adviser put it *'to find a way through in relation to age, aptitude and faith background, collective not corporate, educational not theological, and worship in relation to God'* in order to produce guidelines for school practice.

By the summer term 1990 almost two-thirds of the 28 LEAs in which interviews were conducted had issued policy guidelines on CW. A total of 32 respondents to the national circular sent copies of recently produced guidelines on CW and a further 11 indicated that guidelines were in preparation. In the LEAs sampled there was no difference in the proportion with or without CW guidelines relative to those with or without determination requests. One or two LEAs without local guidelines wanted schools to develop their own up-to-date policies as part of a process of self-evaluation.

> One LEA in which SACRE members had pressed for a definition of CW when considering requests for determinations had a policy not to give a definition but to offer guidelines to schools to produce their own. SACRE put its name to this document. The County adviser believed this put the onus on schools to think more about making their practice appropriate to the community. He suggested a principle had been misunderstood if it was thought that heads' and governors' duties regarding CW could be determined by another body such as SACRE and the LEA had sent out a circular to this effect. Few schools in fact had their own policies.

In terms of the **status of issue of the CW guidelines:**

> almost two-thirds were issued by the local SACRE — its imprimatur generally being seen as a strength. Included were such variations as a letter to schools, an LEA policy adopted subsequently by SACRE, and a consultative document which set out available options with an implicit recommendation for one option — a cross-borough policy for whole-school determinations — although there were difficulties of implementation as the LEA was committed to decentralization;
>
> in only two cases were the guidelines issued by the LEA alone;
>
> one had only advisory status;
>
> and one or two instances were controversial and, as yet, unclear.

SACREs were involved in varying degrees with the working out and drafting of guidelines:

in several cases **the adviser/inspector wrote guidelines**; some found an AREAI workshop on CW helpful preparation; drafts were tabled at SACRE meetings, discussed, often at length, and amended; occasionally if there were serious disagreement within the SACRE this process could continue over several meetings (see p.80 and p.113);

a few SACREs had set up **sub-committees or working parties** to consider CW guidelines on strategies and delivery; at its first meeting one SACRE had established a group to draft a letter to schools with suggestions about definitions, aims and means to multifaith CW, to establish criteria for determinations and to produce an application form for schools; sometimes, however, these working parties were composed of teachers, possibly from a cross-section of schools, and with diocesan representatives rather than SACRE members;

occasionally the **whole SACRE** could be directly involved in experiential learning processes to develop guidelines (see p.104); in one SACRE a special meeting was held to discusss CW at which each faith community was invited to make a presentation of its views on ERA requirements and the role and nature of CW, headteachers outlined organizational issues and the inspector described existing LEA policy in relation to ERA.

However, there were sometimes **anomalies:**

even when there was advisory input with a paper and much discussion there was sometimes continuing disagreement so no policy or guidelines resulted;

in one or two instances SACRE had not realized its remit on CW which had not '*cropped up*', had not been introduced to SACRE by the LEA, and was not planned to be so until after the AS were developed; an adviser in this context claimed that even if it did arise it would be necessary to point out to SACRE that it had no statutory power to change practice and no money to implement recommendations: it would be a matter of '*sabre rattling*';

even after agreement about guidelines there could be delays about their production and circulation;

quite often, as meeting minutes reveal, there remained differences of viewpoint between advisers/inspectors and members or Chairs of SACRE about the degree of emphasis on '*broadly Christian*'.

Examples of guidelines revealed considerable **variation in the extent and presentation of documents:**

some user-friendly documents had a question and answer format and provided further reference sources;

a few were age-related, and focussed on the secondary or primary whole-school context of community as a starting point;

in one case guidance was the basis for a fuller document which would include exemplar material of good practice;

in two or three instances initial CW guidelines predated ERA and, as was evident from different sources or drafts, had subsequently evolved, sometimes being influenced by work from other LEAs with relevantly similar catchments or policy; in one LEA with a proactive determination policy a new working party was following up issues, definitions and guidance for three particular groups of schools: those which had not applied for a determination and on which information on CW practice was therefore inaccurate; schools with a determination which were seeking to operate worship in separate faith groupings for one period per week; or those with a whole-school approach; in another LEA a working party was considering examples of practice, which related to acquiring knowledge, gaining understanding and respect for the beliefs of others, which were to be co-ordinated into a handbook on CW to parallel that for the AS.

Naturally advisers' views on CW in the light of ERA and how it might be interpreted were influential in SACRE discussions and the production of local guidelines. Most advisers/inspectors considered that ERA had generally raised the profile of thinking in schools about CW, although for some there was an underlying concern about an element of complacency, especially where schools had not shown evidence of their practice. Advisers themselves often thought ingeniously about **ERA's interpretation in principle and practice, as have trainers of teachers of RE** (e.g. Cox and Cairns, 1989; Hull, 1989). Interviewees' views of CW in ERA ranged across a spectrum.

Some viewed it as a **'minefield'** and those who **focussed on organizational features** such as the space, time, planning, preparation and monitoring needed for *daily* worship, thought it **'unworkable'**; several interviewees were aware of schools in the LEA which were breaking the law and were reluctant to make this a major issue of contention with schools in the current climate of National Curriculum implementation.

Some reported that heads, teachers and communities had taken the Act **literally,** particularly as they had not known how to interpret the '*broadly Christian*' basis; perceptions of a heavy emphasis on Christianity had been a problem, especially in some areas with large numbers of pupils from Islamic backgrounds; in one Metropolitan LEA it was claimed that a determination had given the school more freedom, whilst continuing to place on it the obligations of meeting *daily* worship and, where parallel separate acts of worship were arranged, to provide worship according to all the faith backgrounds represented in school. Thus, providing acts of worship for pupils from Islamic backgrounds meant also providing confessional acts

140

of worship for pupils from Christian and other faith backgrounds.

Some advisers had advocated a **broad definition** and encouraged schools to follow the **spirit rather than the letter of the Act,** sometimes through a letter or guidelines which described and supported a range of current practices; such an approach was also seen as helpful to schools in multiethnic localities and had sometimes obviated applications for determinations; in one case the LEA was said to see community relations with schools as very important and that *'being comfortable'* with communities should take priority, although compliance with the law was also important.

Some advisers, albeit after initial disquiet, saw ERA as **flexible and enabling** and an opportunity to enhance previous good practice; interpretations of this varied, for example: some viewed ERA as giving support to multifaith collective worship and local effort was focussed on how to use resources from several religious traditions to good effect — accepting and recognizing differences without being syncretistic; elsewhere schools were encouraged to move from *'the lowest common denominator of assembly'* (not worship but with moral and value overtones and focussing on festivals), to an approach based on broadly conceived principles attached to worship (like adoration, valuing, contrition, thanksgiving, supplication in prayer) common to religions and which are valuable for faith and non-faith groups alike;

Some felt that **the concept of 'broadly Christian worship' was 'nonsense'.** Efforts were expended on exploring worship as a theological and **educational** concept and what was appropriate for a school context. There was much mention of the notion of *'worthship'* — to see CW as an opportunity to reflect, celebrate and value through a range of activities (e.g. story telling, listening to music, appreciating nature, silent reflection (e.g. on bullying)) not defined by an object (e.g. God) but by their characteristics, in a variety of contexts (year, tutor group, PSE lessons, whole school). The school as a human community with its own values (such as caring, understanding, loyalty, achievement) could also be celebrated.

Thus in some contexts there appeared to be a move towards *school* worship — focussing on concepts and methods — differing from worship in religious settings, traditional assembly, collective worship of a *'broadly Christian'* character or separate acts of faith worship — or none — all of which were to be found across, and, in some cases within, LEAs. The two major questions to be addressed were: 'Who or what are you worshipping?' and '"Collective" for whom?'

Although it was not a focus of this study to consider school-based worship, SACREs did need to concern themselves with **implementation** of policy and guidance on CW, **training** to enable schools to meet the requirements of ERA, and **monitoring** of their ability and effectiveness in making provision. These matters raised issues which were often distinctively local to the context of the LEA or school.

Implementation. It was generally seen as up to schools as to how they chose to adopt and implement local guidelines — thus there were some on whom ERA had little effect, whereas others were involved in radical reappraisal of their provision and practices. Some LEAs took a more proactive line than others, both in respect of schools developing their own policies and in terms of cross-LEA policies, such as encouraging schools to seek determinations. A particular issue was the extent to which schools, whether or not they sought a determination, had consulted staff, parents and faith communities and attempted to involve them in their worship practices; again diverse practices were reported, some with little success with parents, others where good community relations enabled local Imams, for example, to attend worship. Certain bodies, for example the BHA and FCFC, have produced a guide for staff, governors and others (including Church leaders) on principles and practice for CW in county schools (BHA, 1990; FCFC, 1990). The teachers' associations have also been actively giving advice (e.g. NAHT, 1989; NUT, 1989; SHA, 1989).

Training and the implications for delivery of CW were issues for schools and staff in county schools whose contracts of employment since the 1944 Act continues to give them freedom not to attend CW without penalty, though they may be required by the headteacher to attend school assembly where worship is not taking place (DES Circular 3/89, Para 46-8). The Circular assumes there should be staff willing to lead CW, but where not, it suggests heads might seek advice from the LEA or SACRE in finding *'persons not employed at the school who would be willing and able to conduct such acts'*. There were no reports of such consultations with SACRE, though in a few cases SACREs were concerned that training opportunities should be available for managers and deliverers of CW (see p.175) and some LEAs had mounted day conferences or short courses, sometimes in advance of or using local CW guidelines, and produced seminar reports for wider circulation. Some interviewees expressed concern that RE staff should not be automatically expected to take on CW responsibilities, or not without incentive allowances — but this level of detail had rarely been raised with SACRE.

Monitoring of CW and indeed RE was a critical issue, though again one which was at this stage likely to be an awareness of advisers/inspectors rather than SACRE. Although there was evidence that monitoring and inspection was generally under active review in many LEAs, and some consideration was given to the place of RE, there were considerable time implications for already hard-pressed advisers/inspectors. Only two or three gave any concrete indications of plans for inspecting CW: one had devised a set of ten criteria for inspectorial colleagues to check on concepts observed and developed during proceedings. More generally, however, there was an awareness of a lack of national and local inspector-power — a fact upon which some schools traded.

Applications for Determinations

One of the particular functions of a SACRE is

> '...on application made by the headteacher of any county school after consultation with the governing body, to consider whether it is appropriate for the requirement for Christian collective worship to apply in the case of that school, or in the case of any class or description of pupils at that school.

> ...the council shall have regard to any circumstances relating to the family backgrounds of the pupils at the school or of the pupils of the particular class or description in question which are relevant for determining the character of the collective worship appropriate in their case.' (GB. Statutes, S. 12 (1) and (2)).

DES Circular 3/89 makes it clear that

> '...each SACRE, once constituted [is expected] to inform the county schools in its area as soon as possible of the date by which requests for a determination should be received in order that it may operate from Autumn 1989.

> It is for each SACRE to decide how applications should be made, and to promulgate any necessary guidance to schools.' (Para 39 and 40).

The power of SACREs to make a determination allowing alternative worship came into force on 1.3.89, except for Inner London when it was 1.4.90. Determinations may be given for up to five years. DES Circular 3/89 suggests that the extent of withdrawals from Christian CW may be a factor which influences an application to SACRE. It also makes clear that '*it is for the headteacher to decide what form the alternative worship will take, although the SACRE should be informed of the proposed arrangements*'. The Circular also suggests that, just as consultation with the governing body and parents is necessary prior to making an application, so they will need to be notified of new arrangements. Furthermore it clarifies that

> 'Where a determination has been granted in respect of a class or description of pupils of a particular faith or religion, the alternative collective worship may be provided for these pupils as a whole. It may not be distinctive of any particular **denomination** of any faith or religion, but **may be distinctive of a particular faith or religion.**' (Para 37).

Here, and elsewhere, parental right of withdrawal from CW is noted. Indeed, the Circular goes on to say

> 'Nothing in the Act prevents any maintained school from allowing, at the request of parents, religious education to be provided or religious worship to take place according to a particular faith or denomination where parents

have withdrawn pupils from the RE or collective worship provided in accordance with the law.' (Para 42).

Schools are encouraged to respond positively to such requests, unless the effect would be denominational worship, provided arrangements can be made at no extra cost, and that alternative provision is consistent with the overall purposes of the school curriculum — all points open to interpretation. As an addendum, it is perhaps interesting to note that DES Circular 16/89 (GB. DES, 1989b) on the collection of statistics on school pupils on school entry, which includes data on religious background, suggests that *'the classification to be used in grouping children by religion is: Christian, Hindu, Jewish, Muslim, Sikh, Other (specified) and no religion'* (Annex A. 3). Whilst in due course this will provide interesting statistics on the religious background of young people, it may have earlier implications for withdrawal from RE and CW and for provision, especially perhaps vis à vis the meaning of collective *worship* for those who are officially recognized as having no religious background.

The legal requirements raised many issues in respect of determinations for schools, LEAs and SACREs, including: LEA policies or attitudes towards determinations; the local school, community and religious context; actual applications in LEAs; timing of applications; SACREs' application procedures; school consultation and preparation; submission and consideration of application by the SACRE; criteria for granting a determination; and types of alternative provision.

LEAs and SACREs took a variety of attitudes to schools seeking determinations which were communicated to schools in their policies or guidelines on CW, by letter to heads and governors, in INSET or in informal dialogue with schools. Although interviewees usually claimed it was up to schools to make up their minds, schools would be aware of LEA/SACRE views alongside those of parents and communities.

Occasionally there were **differences of views between groups in SACRE** which prevented it from coming to a decision about whether schools should be encouraged to seek a determination or not; in one SACRE the LEA group wanted to **discourage** applications and was making it as difficult as possible. However **attitudes could change**: one inspector reported that they had *'leant over backwards to stop determinations'* as there had been anxiety about segregation and splitting the communities, but felt that they had now *'grown in confidence'* — determinations must be sensitive to particular localities, school values and policies and pupils' needs.

Many LEAs in the sample made it clear that they were not expecting any applications from schools for determinations, this could be for at least two reasons: because determinations were seen as awkward and controversial, or because of the view that the experience of CW could bind the school community, and schools were therefore encouraged to continue and develop a variety of good practices; one SACRE Chair was said to see applications for determinations '*as a failure by the LEA to transmit what the Act is really saying and that its intention is not to threaten particular groups*'. **Generally considerable consultation between advisers/inspectors and heads was not to dissuade but to make sure an application was the only option.**

A few LEAs/SACREs had taken a proactive stance to encourage schools to seek determinations; in one or two cases confidence already built up with the faith communities facilitated this; elsewhere it was a question of schools wishing to do something *positive* for children from a variety of faith backgrounds which made them both *special* and *equal;* even so, despite LEA/SACRE communications, decisions about applications were very much left to the initiative of heads, the character of particular schools and parental choice.

Thus, although determinations on CW were more likely to be an issue for urgent consideration in LEAs with relatively high proportions of the population from faith backgrounds other than Christianity, procedures and outcomes were very much dependent on particular localities and often the specific school, religious and community mix. Objective factors which appeared relevantly similar, such as proportions of pupils from faith backgrounds other than Christianity, LEA policy and school consultations, could result in opposite decisions on applications for determinations. More subjective factors such as perceptions of ERA, sensitivities and divisions between and within religious communities, how these were dealt with by schools and the basis of past practice, school values and heads' attitudes were, it seemed, more germane. At the heart of this was genuine and sensitive consultation at a variety of levels especially by LEA RE advisers/ inspectors with schools and, in turn, heads and governing bodies with communities and parents. In the latter case particularly as the REC Handbook (1989a, p.34) pointed out, it was important to be '*very sensitive to the wide range of attitudes and deep conviction*' and '*to avoid defining the realities of "minority" faith communities for them*'. An example illustrates how potentially negative perceptions could occasion challenging opportunities for improving school—faith community relations and also respond to the diversity of interests within local faith communities.

One SACRE had developed a CW policy circulated with a covering letter from the CEO indicating a particular stance about CW — that it binds the school community together and that it should be broadly Christian in its approach. The Muslim community in one town were disquieted by the Christian emphasis in ERA. As a result, the County inspector set up a termly meeting between Muslims and heads of local primary and secondary schools to talk about matters of interest to the community. During discussion the Imam made forceful pleas for separate faith worship, though the local Muslim representative on SACRE held a broader view which encompassed the need for Muslim children to have opportunities to be aware of Christian worship to promote mutual understanding. Subsequently there was only one request for a determination though more had been expected.

Advisers/inspectors indicated a range of **locally specific perceptions as to why determinations had not become an issue locally.** These included: LEA advice that a determination was unnecessary because of a deliberate liberal interpretation of ERA; because of LEA investment in INSET on CW for heads; because LEA policy stressed schools should work in partnership with their communities and practice should be based on what is appropriate and in the interests of families and children; and because some schools were actually said to have '*superb relationships*' with their parents and communities, to the extent that determinations were often not an issue in some schools with over 60 per cent of children from faith backgrounds other than Christianity. One interviewee mentioned this even applied in one Church of England primary school with all its pupils from Muslim backgrounds. On the other hand, in a few LEAs determinations had actually been encouraged *because of* the goodwill which existed between schools and communities and the perception that schools could support community interests by positive recognition of pupils' values and beliefs stemming from their faith backgrounds in granting determinations to provide CW of other than a broadly Christian character in various ways and for different groups of pupils.

Differences of local philosophy and approach are well illustrated in relation to a particular episode: the national circulation of a pamphlet in the summer term 1989 by the Muslim Educational Trust (MET, 1989a) which set out a range of options for Muslim parents in respect of CW and RE, but appeared to advocate that parents should exercise their right of withdrawal. This differentially affected schools in, for example, northern Metropolitan authorities.

In one LEA the existence of a pilot scheme of separate faith worship in up to 20 schools, facilitated by staff of the Interfaith Centre, pre-empted expressions of dissatisfaction by Muslim parents. The local Council of Mosques circulated the pamphlet and a specimen letter of request for withdrawal to be used by parents but also listed schools with parallel CW or determinations. The existence of a process of community dialogue meant that any pressure on schools came through Muslim members of governing bodies but there was also a process of parental consultation on withdrawal.

In two other LEAs, as a result of circulation of the MET pamphlet, schools received applications '*in vast numbers*' from parents to withdraw their

146

children from CW and RE. Heads were advised to speak to parents individually to discover their real interests and they also talked to mosque leaders. In one LEA *'some activists had a one-sided view'*, but it was made known that interested parents could observe CW in schools and if still unhappy could withdraw their children on an individual basis. In both LEAs goodwill prevailed and there had subsequently been no school applications for determinations, despite initial disquiet and expectations.

Another LEA was deeply affected by the MET pamphlet's circulation; a legacy of this was that one primary school, for example, had 122 pupils withdrawn by Muslim parents. The LEA's policy with respect to deter-minations was *'pragmatic'* but to ensure it was the only option. In this case it was viewed as *'no earthly way to continue'* and a determination was given on the basis of pupils' faith background.

Usually in LEAs where no applications for determination had been expected none had been made to SACRE. There were also LEAs with fewer actual applications than expected, even to the extent of none where 20 per cent of schools had been expected to opt for a determination. In some cases applications were under consideration or had not been taken to completion at some stage in the consultation or preparation phase (see p.149 and p.151). **In the sample of one-quarter of LEAs where interviews were conducted 12 out of 28 SACREs (43 per cent; six Counties, four Metropolitan and two London Boroughs) had actually received and considered applications for determinations during their first year. Interestingly three-quarters of these SACREs (and a higher proportion of Metropolitan LEAs), had also been responsible for recommending and often were also centrally involved in revision of the local AS (see p.123ff). Thus a high degree of activity and debate was likely to have been associated with these SACREs in their first year.**

Although DES Circular 3/89 had suggested that SACREs would need to decide on procedure and timing for applications and communicate this to schools, once again practice varied. **The timescale of applications seemed to have been a particularly unclear issue,** notwithstanding differences for Inner London Boroughs (see p.143). Moreover, it appears to have been more likely for LEAs rather than SACREs to have notified schools of their right to apply for a determination. No doubt this was related to the often lengthy process of SACRE formation — a timescale not necessarily envisaged by ERA — and the possibility that schools could apply for a determination before the SACRE was in place — although there was no evidence of this occurring. Interviews indicated that **in almost all the LEAs where applications for determination had been received by SACRE this was still an on-going process.** Indeed, although one or two advisers/ inspectors opined that some schools with a high proportion of pupils from faith backgrounds other than Christianity were slow in making applications, many more showed that they considered it very important to give schools time to consider all the options, consult widely and to find the most compatible way in which the needs of all pupils might be met. However, in at least one County LEA where determinations were not encouraged the timescale appeared somewhat rushed: heads were sent letters informing them of the process for making applications and a 'closing date' only two months ahead. Since this included the Easter holiday and applications required the collection of evidence and consultation with parents, governors and the RE adviser the timescale must have been a debarring constraint for many schools.

Many of the sample LEAs had a **form for school applications for determination**, variously issued by the LEA or SACRE. However, a few SACREs which had considered applications and granted determinations lacked a form and clear procedures. Application forms, which advisers were prepared to show, often followed a fairly standard format, which may have been influenced by an AREAI workshop. Forms usually required information on:

- name, type of school and number on roll;
- religions represented in school and number of pupils;
- present arrangements for CW;
- reasons in light of ERA for seeking a determination;
- consultations with governing body, parents and staff and views expressed;
- type of determination (whole or part school);
- reasons for each group;
- proposed arrangements for CW (groups, time, location, personnel);
- length of determination sought.

Deciding to make an application for determination thus required much thought, preparation and consultation by a school. It was not to be entered into lightly, especially as it involved specifying current CW practice and, usually, though strangely not invariably, intended CW arrangements. In these cases monitoring by SACRE or LEA advisers/ inspectors was expected to check on school's responsibility for the quality and legality of CW. Guidance on CW and determinations usually emphasized the **importance of the process of consultation** prior to making an application. This was often controversial, time-consuming and uncertain and usually involved governors, advisers and parents.

Governors should legally have been involved, however, some schools seemed to have kept governors at a distance; some governors were said to be uneasy about the process of consulting with parents and making an application to SACRE: '*governors are fearful of applying for a determination because they think it admits they are profoundly wrong in what they have been doing in the past and tend to back off and give credibility to a mish mash*'. Governors did, however, also support heads and therefore required further advice and support.

RE advisers/inspectors were critically involved with schools in offering guidance and help to prepare their application to SACRE and, in some cases, in counselling or following through with schools after SACRE's decision. In one or two cases RE advisers had only just begun to be involved in such consultations whereas elsewhere this had already involved many person hours.

Consultation with advisers could result in **clarification**, as in one LEA where four schools expressed the likelihood of applying for a determination '*without understanding what this meant*'; according to the inspector it was evident that '*three didn't need a determination*' although one put in a formal application, but the process helped schools to define CW for themselves.

Elsewhere advisers could help to **reconcile perceptions and interests**: in one middle school where Muslim parents were sensitive to the wording of ERA and there was a concern that this might change practice, advisers were able to explain how this could continue and, as a result, a shared statement was issued. **There were relatively few examples of consultation between advisers/ inspectors, SACRE members and schools**, but in one case a Muslim member of SACRE accompanied the inspector to a school which had a predominantly Muslim intake to consider ways in which CW could be conducted, including acceptable hymns. As a result of this exercise in coming to a mutual understanding the school did not seek a determination. Some advisers felt they trod a fine line not to recommend to schools or dissuade them from making an application for a determination, but to fully explore the issues in their particular context.

Parents needed to be consulted individually about their views on school CW provision and their faith backgrounds in order for schools to seek a determination, and withdrawal of their child if they wished separate faith worship to be provided. It appears that LEAs or SACREs may have given guidance on questionnaires to be used or occasionally to have undertaken surveys directly. Careful attention was required to the format and wording of parental questionnaires and the presentation of alternatives if they were not subsequently to be challenged. In one LEA where groups of heads had met regularly and devised a letter inquiring about parents' wishes for CW, local Sikhs had subsequently contended that parents should have been asked about mounting separate faith worship for each faith group, not just whether they wished to opt out of broadly Christian worship.

Applications for determinations seem usually to have been considered by SACRE as a whole. Occasionally a 'Determinations Working Party' was established, as in one LEA where the Chair and one representative from each of the four groups undertook initial consideration of applications. A few SACREs considered 'mock' applications for practice. Most SACREs invited heads to attend the meeting to speak to their school application, though they did not always attend. There had rarely been direct contact between SACRE members and heads prior to application. In one or two SACREs any application seems initially to have been more or less granted automatically, although changes in attitudes were reported by some groups, with part determinations becoming more significant. **Indeed, treatment of heads in SACRE meetings could become quite adversarial.** Some advisers/inspectors saw it as part of their role to deflect difficult issues from heads. If known, a head's personal religious views, especially if atheist or agnostic, or the head's antiracist convictions could underly some difficult questioning. But in other cases, heads' justification of applications in terms of a spiral curriculum could be bemusing for some SACRE members. Nevertheless, there was a perception by SACRE members and advisers that heads were often '*on trial*' or '*put on the spot*' in defending their applications. This had led at least one SACRE to table reconsideration of its procedures at a future meeting. Consideration of applications could involve quite close questioning from various SACRE members about a range of inter-related factors such as: perceptions of the local communities, statements about CW in the school prospectus, current CW practice, the spiritual content and delivery of proposed practice, and the presentation of the application as well as the age, aptitude and faith backgrounds of the children.

In a few SACREs some applications had been referred for further information. This could lead to withdrawal, especially if the political context were contentious or the grounds for application were based on equal opportunities rather than numbers of pupils from other faith backgrounds. **Across the sample the number of determinations granted in the 12 LEAs concerned ranged from one to 66.** In only four LEAs did the number of determinations exceed three.

> In one County five applications had been granted and 30 were reported to be in the pipeline; some schools were said to be reluctant and to show a certain degree of insensitivity when the pupil population was predominantly non-Christian.

> An Outer London SACRE had approved 26 applications although its initial circular had indicated that ERA was sufficiently broad to encompass school practice in CW:

'within a multifaith context it is possible for schools not only to use materials from all faiths but also to reflect the religious composition of the school. For example, in a school with a large number of Sikh pupils, the choice of materials for use in collective worship would more often be from Sikh sources than any other faith. In practical terms multifaith worship is likely to be thematic reflecting the values and experiences common to all faiths.'

In one Metropolitan LEA 66 out of 300 schools had been granted determinations; half for parallel acts of separate faith worship for one period per week and half for a whole-school approach. LEA policy had suggested that a determination might be an appropriate course for schools with large numbers of pupils from faith backgrounds other than Christianity both to avoid community conflict and to demonstrate an equal opportunity philosophy.

In another Outer London authority with a proactive determination policy, 61 determinations had been granted; only three schools had not applied and one of these, which undertook a survey of faith backgrounds, discovered that most parents were Christian.

Only a few SACREs, ironically those which had not yet actually been presented with an application for determination, appeared to have explicitly considered criteria for determinations in full SACRE meetings, subcommittees, workshops or working parties, and then had not necessarily come to agreement. Some interviewees claimed that the SACRE would have a policy on and criteria for determinations if the necessity arose; others that CW guidelines were effectively that.

The inspector in one LEA whose SACRE had granted one determination claimed that it would be discriminatory for SACRE to have written criteria. If provision and practice in schools requesting a determination were to be investigated it would also be necessary to investigate that in other schools in order to say provision and practice in the school requesting a determination was different.

Another inspector where SACRE was looking for evidence from schools of large numbers of pupils from different faith backgrounds as a criterion for determination felt that, on the contrary, schools should be required to demonstrate that they had pupils from faith backgrounds which are broadly Christian.

In practice those SACREs which had received applications predominantly used the number of pupils from faith backgrounds other than Christianity as the main criterion for granting a school determination. However, each application seems to have been considered on its own terms and specific context, *which included the differing CW policies and guidelines of LEAs.* Perhaps for this reason **there seems to have been a lack of**

151

consistency in the grounds for granting determinations both between and within some LEAs. In effect some determinations appear to have been granted on grounds relevantly similar to those which in other LEAs were used as justification for continuing current practice and obviating the need for a determination. There were examples of confusion and anomalies.

In one LEA, where two schools had been granted determinations on numerical/faith background grounds, Group B had challenged another application on **the nature of current and proposed CW practice.** This became an issue to the extent that the LEA sought DES guidance, although Circular 3/89 (Para 37) makes it clear that it is '*for the headteacher to decide what form alternative worship will take*'. Schools should indicate their plans and SACRE may comment but its advice is not mandatory. Neither ERA nor the Circular appear to indicate whether or not a determination needs only a majority or a unanimous decision by each of the constituent groups of SACRE.

In another LEA which had considered 11 applications only two were granted '*where the overwhelming majority of pupils were of a faith other than Christian*' and all, but one, were refused on grounds of compliance with the Act. One for a **part determination for two groups** was also refused but the grounds were unclear. In other LEAs part determinations were allowed, as specified in ERA.

Elsewhere, **faith community sensitivities to the wording of the Act** had been grounds for making applications for a determination. This seems to have been admitted where it was associated with parental withdrawals and provision of separate acts of faith worship for a large proportion of children from a faith background other than Christianity in the school. But where the number of pupils from the faith community was small practice was not seen to require change — instead they were put under pressure for withdrawal. This may be due to interpretation of '*broadly Christian*' or resource and cost implications.

The critical issue here seems to be that of parental withdrawal or, alternatively, opting in (see p.149). This also needs to be viewed in relation to parallel acts of CW for different faith groups which predated ERA and which have not necessarily gone through the formal process of determination. Moreover, where in one case Jews applied because they wanted their own form of worship three days a week the application was seen to be unnecessary because it was previous practice for parents who had withdrawn their children.

Determination applications have also been considered on equal opportunities or **antiracist grounds** but these were again confusing and controversial.

In one case an acting head who was active in the local CRC strongly believed that '*Muslims should not be lumbered with Christianity*' — a reading of the

Act. The school had over 80 per cent children with faith backgrounds other than Christianity. Alternative plans for worship were not specified or apparently well thought through, but it was suggested that at some times separate faith worship might be necessary. Although a school representative was not called to the meeting a determination was granted for one year and was being followed up.

In a multiracial authority, where the advocated approach was multifaith and thematic assembly, 26 applications for determinations had been granted, two referred and one withdrawn. All but one of those approved had been on numerical grounds. But a controversial determination had also been given to one school where the majority of pupils were Christian but the head saw multifaith worship as *'part and parcel of the school's equal opportunities policy'*. The school had, since its opening during the 80s, heavily emphasized its equal opportunities and antiracist principles and a strong presentation was made to the SACRE. There had been a split vote on the determination and a representative of one of the religions other than Christianity had subsequently complained that schools in different parts of the borough had been treated according to different principles. There was a possibility that the determination would be reconsidered and rescinded.

Elsewhere an authority had facilitated separate faith worship in some schools on equal opportunities grounds (see p.151).

These examples demonstrate the lack of clarity and wide interpretation of ERA in local authority and school contexts. There appears to be a lack of consistent application of principle, irrespective of actual practice. Moreover, there was relatively little evidence of follow through on determinations — another task which required resourcing — despite the requirement on LEAs to provide annual returns *'of the number and effect of any determinations made by their SACRE'* (GB. Statutory Instruments, 1989. No. 954, Para 12).

As has been indicated, current patterns of worship, which include at least the following, raise many questions.

Separate Act of Faith Worship. This emphasizes worship in a particular faith tradition. There are many issues here. Have the parents/pupils (even in discussion) opted out or in? Even if Christian parents have also opted for parallel acts of Christian worship rather than withdrawal is this allowable under the Act? Does positive parental choice rather than negative choice make a difference? Does worship then become confessional, or is that part of the meaning of the concept of worship, if it is made to depend on faith? How appropriate is this in a school context? Is it *education* or indoctrination? What are parents' expectations, teachers' perceptions, pupils' responses? How does worship fit with their other experiences of schooling and their lives beyond school?

Organizationally there are major logistical, personnel, timetabling and resource implications, either if ATREs are timetabled to conduct worship (rather than advise on RE), or if schools themselves are able to draw upon staff or members of the communities able to undertake these roles. What provision is made for those pupils from non-religious backgrounds who are withdrawn from worship? In one such case, where green issues were to be discussed, is this adding to religious or spiritual development? How does it differ from other aspects of the curriculum where such issues might arise?

'Broadly Christian' Collective Worship. Should the focus here be on *'broadly Christian'* or *'worship'*? If the latter, then do similar concerns about confessional acts arise? What about non- believers, seekers, those of other faiths? What could *broadly* Christian mean? Does it mean Christian or not? How would it differ from say, broadly Islamic? Or is the *'broadly'* meant to suggest what is common to religious beliefs and values? Does this suggest Christianity is a filter through which other forms of worship should be approached or that Christianity is a religion *primus inter pares?*

Or again consider *'wholly or mainly broadly Christian'* — does this necessarily imply a 51/49 per cent distinction over a school term? Schools and LEAs have been addressing such issues in reconsidering their provision in relation to their school composition and faith community interests. Responses vary, partly according to resourcing, including preparation time, to plan, review, check — for example, progression and continuity, explicit and implicit features, incorporate aspects of a range of traditions and involve faith members. There is concern that constraints of time, staffing, status may lead to a *'lowest common denominator'* approach which does not adequately or acceptably reflect *any* of the religious traditions or worship.

Collective School Worship. Some guidelines on CW emphasize a collective approach through shared values to individual development. Thus, as one SACRE recommended approach puts it: CW can contribute to spiritual, moral and cultural development through the knowledge, awareness and understanding of each individual pupil, but also to *'a sense of cohesion, stability and shared values in the school as a whole and in this way provides a secure framework in which pupils may develop their own spiritual and moral values and commitment'*. These guidelines reiterate the AS view that *'a child's own personal faith and lifestyle is the product of the home and the faith community'* and that the school role is to support these — to the extent of providing facilities for individual faith communities to organize and worship on the school site in addition to CW required by the Act. This is conceptually difficult and requires practical skill in relating approaches relevant to the age, aptitude and faith background of pupils. But it represents a creative and challenging opportunity to bring to bear all the educational strategies available to teachers to enhance their pupils' spiritual development as persons, which may be broader than or encompass their particular religious beliefs. The question arises: Is this allowable under the Act? Would it sufficiently reflect *'broadly Christian'*? By what means (e.g.

silence for prayer, in pupils' own faith traditions, reflection or meditation) would it constitute worship? How would it differ from good assemblies which emphasize common values, celebrate achievements and skills and pose questions for reflective awareness?

In their first year many SACREs have been brought to consider such issues in greater or lesser detail as part of developing guidelines for local CW and reviewing applications for determinations. The future role of some SACREs would be to review implementation of the local recommended approach or the school's own proposals and to monitor the quality of delivery. But it would also need to consider whether what was provided was both legal *and* educational. Such evaluations would be made all the more difficult across schools because of the varying baselines of practice and interpretation of ERA. The complexity of issues raised require further conceptual unpacking and empirical evidence. But, in principle, the question remains: is *worship*, collective or confessional, an appropriate activity for an educational form of life which is part of the school day and curriculum?

SACRE's Involvement in Local Complaints

ERA required LEAs to establish a complaints procedure to consider matters relating to the curriculum and CW and DES Circular 3/89 suggested that LEAs might wish to give SACREs a role in this *'where the complaints relate to SACRE's area of expertise'* (Para 12):

> *'Every LEA is required by Section 23 of the Act to set up arrangements for consideration and disposal of any complaints related to the curriculum or religious worship made on or after 1 September 1989. These include complaints that an LEA or governing body of a county, voluntary or maintained special school has acted or is proposing to act unreasonably, or is in default of its duties, as respects the provisions of the Education Acts relating to RE or religious worship. The new procedures will cover among others things the establishment of the LEA's SACRE and the LEA's actions in relation to the establishment of a Conference and implementation of a new agreed syllabus ..... complaints must be considered in accordance with the local arrangements before the Secretary of State considers them .... LEAs may wish their SACRE to have a role in the machinery in particular circumstances.'* (GB. DES, 1989a, Para 52).

The RE Handbook suggested that:

> *'If the Council is given responsibility by the Local Authority to deal with complaints regarding religious education and worship by parents and others, then it must decide on its procedures for handling such complaints.'* (REC, 1989a, 9. 2. 3 (3)).

These new arrangements envisaged parents and others — such as local religious organizations — having better opportunities to make local representations. It is thus of interest to review to what extent and how SACREs have been included in the local complaints procedures — particularly as this may be seen as a key indicator of the degree of trust and confidence in the SACRE — and the number and nature of local complaints reported in the LEA sample over the past year.

In the quarter of LEAs where interviews were conducted:

one-third (9/28) of SACREs were clearly included in the local complaints machinery in various ways;

almost one-third (7/28) it was claimed would be included if a complaint arose, though there might be no specified procedure for inclusion or handling complaints;

in two cases inclusion of SACRE was still under consideration: in one LEA with a paper on complaints procedure the adviser had written to the Head of Schools Division suggesting SACRE's involvement; in another SACRE's role was being debated and was unspecified — the LEA had dealt independently with a previous complaint about uniform which had religious connotations;

in two other cases the involvement of SACRE was not automatic or specified but it *might* have matters referred to it by the LEA;

in six cases whether SACRE was included or not was very unclear both from respondents' replies and from supporting documentation including ARs; this could be the case even where the SACRE had a constitution or a publicly available document on its role and function; in one case the SACRE had made it clear that it wished to be included;

in two cases SACRE was not included in the complaints procedure. *Interestingly, in these two LEAs (out of four in the whole sample) RE/CW were currently a matter of formal complaint which was under consideration by the Secretary of State.* In one of these LEAs SACRE had no formal role in the complaints procedure and in the other it was '*a grey area*' — SACRE's constitution said that '*at the discretion of the authority*' it might be involved.

Relatively few SACREs among the almost two-thirds in the sample (and others about which documentation was sent in response to the circular) which were included in the complaints procedure appeared to have written procedures for handling complaints or which indicated whether the whole SACRE or nominees and, if so, from which groups, would be involved. It seemed that SACRE might both be more likely to be included in consideration of complaints if it included strong Education Committee representation and that elected members might form a

SACRE complaints sub-committee or working group.

> In one SACRE members were informed that the proposed complaints procedure for RE and CW would be heard by a panel of SACRE — its Chair or Vice-Chair and two other members, at least one of whom should be a member of the County Council.

> Elsewhere, however, faith representatives were critically involved (see below).

Some SACREs had been included in discussion about their role in the complaints machinery, though it was occasionally questioned whether this had been fully realised. In only one LEA in the sample had SACRE actually been called upon for its advice on a local complaint through the local complaints committee and had suggested to the investigating officer that there was compliance within the law.

The following examples indicate thoughtful ways of effectively involving SACRE in the complaints process and of building on the strengths of its diverse and locally informed membership.

> In one Metropolitan LEA, as the result of '*a spirited debate*' about dealing with complaints it was felt that it would be useful if SACRE were to be the first to be consulted and were to give its advice direct to governing bodies to save potential mistakes because of lack of understanding.

> In an Outer London Borough SACRE was consulted about its role in the complaints procedure and made a number of recommendations to the LEA which were largely subsequently incorporated into the LEA's proposals, approved by the Secretary of State. These were, as indicated in the SACRE's AR:

> '(i)   *The faith community representatives on SACRE would be prepared to assist the informal resolution of complaints relating to RE or collective worship, and may be contacted through the Chief Inspector.*

> (ii)   *A termly report will be provided to SACRE. This will summarize the extent and nature of formal complaints about RE or collective worship that have been brought to the attention of the Chief Inspector.*

> (iii)   *SACRE will be involved in any investigations conducted by the Chief Inspector as a result of complaints that have not been resolved at governing body level.*

> (iv)   *This involvement will typically consist of a small ad hoc group of faith community representatives who will express their views on a particular complaint. If the complainant is a member of a particular faith community, then a person representing that community on SACRE will be a member of such a group.'*

In one County it was envisaged that SACRE would become involved with complaints on RE and CW only in a very small minority of cases which could not be satisfactorily resolved by heads or governors. **A clearly outlined document on the local complaints procedure and SACRE's role in handling complaints is available on request and in languages other than English.** The SACRE complaints hearing also allows for *'the complainant to have the right to be accompanied by a friend/interpreter if necessary'*. Information on RE for parents and governors is also available from schools in Bengali, Gujerati, Italian, Punjabi and Urdu.

Generally, however, the potentially pivotal role (and the benefits and issues) of faith members from minority ethnic backgrounds liaising with their communities to explain SACRE and LEA policy on RE and CW, to diffuse misunderstanding and to represent parents' and young people's views, does not yet seem to have been seriously considered by all but a few SACREs or LEAs.

Interviewees were asked about issues or complaints on RE or CW that had been raised locally or with SACRE by schools, religious or community organizations and parents. Clearly the issues of greatest concern and complexity usually related to CW and determinations and were raised with or via schools prior to SACRE — for example, where a group of Muslim parents requested schools to seek a determination. There were also issues surrounding requests for representation on SACRE by various faith organizations and Humanists. Interviewees' reports of community and parental interest in RE were, once again, very diverse. Some reported little interest locally in RE, but, if any, then, they claimed, in relation to the National Curriculum as such, and a general perception that it placed certain and differential values on core and basic curriculum subjects. Others noted that heads had indicated that, for the first time in their careers, parents had asked about RE and CW.

> **The majority of respondents indicated that no issues** had been raised with SACRE by parents or local organizations; in one strongly multiethnic borough this was attributed to the confidence which had been built up locally by establishing a network of faith groups; in a county with a diverse urban and rural mix the inspector was surprised that no formal complaints had yet been received despite the *'severe interest'* of several evangelical groups, but considered that within the LEA there was a clear understanding of what constitutes RE according to the AS.

> **Some reported 'near misses'** in terms of issues being officially brought to SACRE; rather they were **dealt with informally at school level or by advisers/inspectors**; these included: complaints by parents in a Church school that RE should not include material about Diwali or Eid; issues concerning Jehovah's Witnesses; a complaint by an RE parent about poor

provision in one area of the county. It was noted that parental complaints tended to be associated with particular schools or were seen as *'individual grouses'*.

In four LEAs complaints/issues had become more formal, though in only one case had they been raised directly with SACRE:

- in one LEA, as a result of a complaint to government by an ex-college lecturer about lack of sixth-form RE and CW provision, there had been a local HMI investigation. SACRE was informed that colleges had been included in CW courses and some were endeavouring to take provision seriously and *'organize CW in a variety of interesting ways in order to make attendance more attractive to 16-18 year olds'*. SACRE accepted that *'this approach met the spirit of the Act and was preferable to the difficulties which would be created by colleges trying to ensure students' attendance.'*

- formal complaints in three other LEAs, initially made by individual parents, were receiving the support of PACE: these concerned an an admissions issue which was related to the proportion of Muslim children in school and a subsequent complaint about CW (see pp.95-96); complaints about the AS, CW and a determination in one school with a strong equal opportunities/antiracist tradition; and two complaints on CW and lack of timetabling of RE. There was local uncertainty and concern about the outcome of these complaints, how decisions might be received and of the implications of decisions for interpretation of statutory requirements locally and nationally.

There did not appear to be any local arrangements (apart from the Annual Report) for formally reviewing, evaluating or monitoring the SACRE's work. Although DES Circular 3/89 suggested complaints procedures would cover *'the establishment'* of SACRE there seemed no provision for evaluating or monitoring SACRE's operation. Interviewees unanimously reported that this had not been considered and there were no plans in hand. One or two commented that this would be difficult as SACRE was perceived as having no clear objectives — despite its statutory duties and responsibilities; others that it was still trying to find its role; and some that there were already too many local commitments to monitoring or, alternatively, that the LEA did not have a *'heavy'* monitoring policy. In a few LEAs SACRE was, however, perceived as starting to *'flex its muscles'*, issue advice, take action and show the beginnings of a self-consciousness or self-evaluation about its operation and concerns. **The inquiry thus revealed that SACRE's role in local complaints was an issue as was its own operation.**

SACRE'S Annual Report

ERA (S. 11 (9)) obliges each SACRE to publish an annual report on its functions, especially if its representative groups (other than of the authority) *'require'* a review of the Agreed Syllabus.

'The council's report should in particular:

a) *specify any matters in respect of which the council have given advice to the authority;*

b) *broadly describe the nature of the advice given; and*

c) *where any such matter was not referred to the council by the authority, give the council's reasons for offering advice on that matter.'*

The subsequent DES Circular 3/89 (Para 14) added:

'The Secretary of State believes that LEAs should arrange for copies of annual reports to be sent to schools, and to the National Curriculum Council and local teacher training institutions, particularly when the report makes reference to ITT or INSET.'

In addition to teacher training, ERA advocated that SACRE should address itself to particular methods of teaching and choice of teaching materials. Thus, as the REC Handbook (REC, 1989a) observed, it was envisaged that the annual report (AR) should be widely disseminated and play an integral role in the promotion of RE locally:

'The council will need to consider the nature and structure of, and the interested audiences for its first and subsequent reports. In this way it may provide not only for the maintaining of the work of each school but also for the evaluation of the effectiveness of the Agreed Syllabus and of the LEA's policy in carrying it out.' (Para 9.2.3 (2))

The publication of an AR thus appears to formalize the work of the SACRE, in a way which had not necessarily previously occurred if an LEA had established a SACRE prior to ERA.

Review of Audience for the Report

During interviews RE advisers/inspectors in 28 LEAs were asked whether their SACRE had reviewed the audience for its AR. At that time (May-

July, 1990) some SACREs had been operating for a relatively short time (see p.22). One-third of these SACREs (more Metropolitan Boroughs) had reviewed the audience for their AR in meetings: one- third had not (though advisers indicated they were aware of the legal requirements); and in the remaining third the position was either unclear or the matter was on the agenda for discussion at the next meeting during the summer term.

Many advisers seemed to feel that the audience had already been defined, but there also appeared to be considerable local flexibility allowing for wide or restricted circulation. LEAs also differed in their audience orientation: the extent to which they saw Churches or teacher training colleges as being relevant — up to ten of the latter in some cases. **A controversial issue in some LEAs was whether schools would receive a copy of the AR;** some advisers assumed this, others were unsure of it, or indicated it was a matter as yet unresolved. Audiences mentioned by RE advisers/inspectors overall included:

- all members of Education Committee;
- SACRE members and their nominating bodies (e.g. Diocesan Board of Education);
- officers of the LEA;
- schools;
- local university, school of education and teacher training colleges;
- NCC;
- other RE advisers/inspectors in the regional AREAI group;
- HMI;
- national RE bodies (e.g. REC, PCFRE, CEM);
- local MPs.

It was not generally envisaged that SACRE reports would be disseminated nationally to other SACREs or LEAs. Hardly any consideration had been given as to whether it would be appropriate, helpful or financially realistic to make it known that the SACRE report was publicly available locally — for example, for parents or RE teachers.

Amongst some advisers there was a sense that **the diversity of the audience made for difficulties as to what should be conveyed and how it should be communicated** (see pp.163-165). **Another issue of concern, given the lack of clear budetary support for SACRE's work** (see pp.97-101) **was the cost implication of producing an AR for a large audience;** the need for up to

1,000 copies was sometimes estimated. Presentation was influenced by financial considerations. However, since the AR is a legal requirement, there was recognition that the AR would be produced and published and money found to meet the expenses. Indeed, in one or two cases (see p.118) Education Committees acknowledged the potential benefits to local community relations and were raising the profile of RE locally and nationally by supporting wider dissemination.

Report Writing

Who writes the AR proved to be quite an interesting issue - not necessarily one which was debated by SACRE itself, but apparently more often decided internally with the LEA. In the 28 LEAs where interviews were conducted the responsibility for writing the AR devolved as follows: on advisers/inspectors (11; six in Metropolitan LEAs), on SACRE clerks (four) and on other combinations of personnel (13). The 'other' category included one or two cases where the report writer (possibly a PEO or EO) was not yet decided, but mostly involved either the RE adviser/inspector or ATRE plus an AO, EO, SEO or DCEO, or the SACRE clerk, plus EO, AEO, and sometimes in consultation with the adviser/inspector/ATRE and/or the SACRE Chairperson. The extent of LEA officer input suggested that this task tended to be seen as administrative. **Only two or three respondents indicated that report writing was viewed as the responsibility of the SACRE itself.**

> In one case a small sub-group was convened for the purpose consisting of the Chair and his nominees, with editorial input by the adviser.

> In another LEA the DoE and adviser recommended that SACRE should set up a small working party for report writing to comprise heads and teachers, convened by the Director and with the adviser as observer. The group would consider items outlined in the adviser's briefing paper, draft a report and present it to SACRE for comment. The adviser felt strongly that it should be a report written by SACRE, not the LEA.

Procedurally most interviewees indicated that a draft report was tabled at SACRE meetings for discussion and amendment, although a few where the SACRE was LEA-led commented that it *was not that kind of SACRE*. In some cases the draft report was circulated to individuals such as the Chair of SACRE, DoE, or Diocesan Bishop, which could make for delays, and occasionally controversial proceedings within the SACRE itself could postpone consideration of the AR. Thus production of the AR could vary from a convoluted process to almost a formality.

Nature and Structure of the Annual Report

In addition to the matters to be covered in the AR, as specified in ERA and DES Circular 3/89, report writers had two major influences — REC guidelines (REC, 1989b) and other SACRE reports in wide circulation.

Only one or two interviewees were unfamiliar with the two-sided paper, *Guidelines Towards the Format and Contents of the Annual Report From a SACRE,* issued by REC in 1989. This suggested that ARs should report on: SACRE composition; administrative matters regarding meetings etc; policy framework on RE and CW; publications supported by SACRE; consultations; matters referred by the LEA; matters of advice to the LEA initiated by SACRE; and future plans. One or two advisers/ inspectors questioned the helpfulness of the REC guidelines. But the overwhelming majority had found it a handy reference, a useful starting point for thinking and as a guide to headings, and a few indicated that it had been followed faithfully. It had sometimes been circulated within the SACRE, or at least to its Chair.

Advisers/inspectors also showed some interest in other SACRE reports available regionally, which had been gathered for consideration as models, or in two or three cases, which had intentionally had national circulation. Although some liked a glossy presentation and were conscious of its possible public spin off, their enthusiasm was tempered by an awareness of economic constraints in their LEA. But the majority were spontaneously cynical about 'up market' presentations and somewhat unfairly disparaging about content. There were a few indications that sight of other SACRE reports had given some advisers/inspectors pause for thought as to whether their local report were sufficiently comprehensive or could be better presented.

Most interviewees claimed that their SACRE's report would be short and '*not glossy*' in its presentation — '*two A4 pages*' or '*A4 folded three times*'. Only three or four interviewees suggested that their first SACRE AR would be a glossy production — in two cases the same format as the AS — thus connecting the medium and the message. A similar number reported that the SACRE report would run to several pages — ranging from seven to over 20 pages with appendices.

Generally there was little evidence that serious consideration had been given to communicating the first year's work of SACRE and linking appropriate content and style of presentation with the intended audience so as to maximize the effectiveness of the report. Only one or two advisers commented that '*the style will be bland as its not for use by schools*' or, alternatively, that it should be '*user friendly*' (see p.90). Indeed in some cases it was clear that not only in the matter of content but also in its presentation the adviser's/ inspector's view was only one of several; presentation could be a '*political*' decision by the LEA or the Chair of SACRE, especially when an influential member of Education Committee. It was another issue of perception — of striking a balance between communicating with the legislated and desired audiences in a way which was informative and accessible without incurring local opinion that the money could be better spent.

Interviewees indicated that ARs were most likely to be based on minutes of meetings, possibly with additional information from surveys of provision undertaken as a result of SACRE's request. Reports in their first year were expected to be mainly, if not exclusively, descriptive of the aims of the SACRE, getting established, what had been done, decisions taken and in some cases, what was intended or needed in the future. In one or two SACREs, where political and religious tensions were apparent, there was a sense that there was as yet little to report or that could be counted as policy, and the appropriateness of an *annual* report was questioned. The majority of SACRE ARs were expected to follow the format and content suggested by the REC Guidelines and to include information on administrative matters (membership, meetings, attendance, constitution), statements about RE, guidance on CW, and (where appropriate) decisions on applications for determinations. Some indicated that reference would be made to INSET and occasional mention was also made of ARs including issues from meetings, complaints and advice on RE/CW to governors.

In respect of RE the nature of what was to be said in the AR, and especially any likely recommendations, could be an issue which provoked discussion because of the possible implications or interpretations. **Although matters raised with SACRE by the LEA were to be reported, there was a sense of reluctance in a few quarters about mentioning SACRE's recommendations to the LEA, as specified by ERA** (see p.160). An obvious recommendation, which occurred fairly frequently, was for an ASC to be constituted to reconsider the AS. Some interviewees also indicated that statements would be made about current RE provision, links between the AS and ATs and future monitoring of RE.

An inspector in an LEA with a new AS reported SACRE's increasing interest in the delivery of RE and its own role.

Another adviser in an LEA with a long-established SACRE expected its recommendations on RE, based on a survey of secondary provision, to be concrete, specific and supporting change, e.g. *'that RE as part of Humanities does not work well'* and that *'a Head of RE should have particular allowances for taking on CW'*.

Elsewhere an inspector thought it useful for SACRE to make particular statements about RE so that schools could see how they compare.

Another adviser wanted SACRE to ask schools for feedback about its report and suggestions about what SACRE should consider.

But one inspector who felt that most schools had already been informed about SACRE's work to date thought a more valuable approach would have been a document giving timely constructive advice.

Training (INSET and ITT) also proved to be a variable issue. Although ERA also specifically stated that SACREs had a duty to advise on provision of training (as well as teaching methods and materials) and Circular 3/89 envisaged that the AR would make reference to ITT and INSET, it was clear that, in their first year of operation these matters remained largely unaddressed by many SACREs. Indeed, some SACREs may not have been made fully aware of these responsibilities — traditionally the province of advisers, inspectors and advisory teachers. On the other hand, a few interviewees mentioned that the SACRE's AR would report on or make recommendations about INSET or even include an outline of the future programme. It was sometimes said that the teachers' association representatives on SACRE had made sure that INSET was emphasized. Opinions also differed on the matter of SACRE giving advice on ITT: some, even with local teacher training colleges with religious foundations, had not appeared to realize the connection, but others, who did not find it strange in principle, observed that ITT had not yet arisen in SACRE's deliberations. Clearly, however, a few SACRE's had been proactive and influential in making recommendations to the LEA, repeated in their ARs, about appointments of advisers or advisory teachers for RE. One Humanities adviser, where RE was not a high priority, thought the SACRE's AR would provide an opportunity to make some recommendations about provision, funding and training even though he was pessimistic about this being supported by the local Education Committee.

Use

The requirement of the SACRE to produce an AR could be seen as in tune with an increasing emphasis on public dissemination. Yet, in line with the fairly peremptory consideration given to the report's audience, it seemed that uses for for the report had not been a matter for much debate or interest. Opinions of interviewees again varied from those relatively few

who saw little or no use for such a report to rather more who were unsure, and others who saw it as having some or even much value. Possible uses identified included: nationally for other LEAs; locally within the LEA, for parents and general public, with schools, and to raise the profile of SACRE and RE.

Although very few advisers saw a use for *national* circulation of SACRE reports, most had received and openly referred to two or three which had been widely disseminated. The ATRE in one of the LEAs from which one of these reports emanated reported that it had been decided to circulate the AR nationally as many requests had been received for information about the pre-existing SACRE and for copies of its AR. There was a feeling that other LEAs with a new SACRE would be interested in its work.

In terms of *local* use, it was important for RE advisers'/inspectors' names and addresses, as well as those of SACRE members, to be given in the AR in order to facilitate contact and communication on local RE/CW issues. But there were those advisers who saw little or no use for the AR:

- one adviser viewed it as a waste of time and a paper exercise only contributing to the amount of educational paper work in current circulation and not to improving the quality of RE;

- another did not see a particular use, but felt it would have been more useful if she could have written it as she would have liked with recommendations.

Others were unsure of its use:

- one inspector considered it as a matter of going through the motions to meet the legal requirements. Yet he was aware that RE at secondary level had '*had a raw deal*' and was absent in the 16-18 age range; in future SACRE might wish to note such gaps and make recommendations for change.

Elsewhere other interviewees regarded the SACRE AR as potentially valuable and of high profile, possibly with a press release, for example:

- one County adviser reported that it would be '*quite significant locally*' —'*a kind of PR exercise*' for the county, the inspectorate, churches and press to let schools know what SACRE is doing;

- one Metropolitan adviser considered the role of the SACRE's AR would be to educate parents and make schools aware of SACRE. She identified a particular relevance to secondary schools, already overstaffed but without RE teachers, and where RE is subsumed in PSE or Humanities in Year 10 and 11. The revised AS would also have implications for resourcing;

- a County inspector saw SACRE's AR as being influential through established structures — there was a need to inform elected members so they, in turn, could exercise influence.

Interviewees were most likely to consider or mention a specific use for the SACRE AR in relation to schools, although again opinion was divided:

- one suggested that if it were circulated to schools it might be added to their curriculum box with other RE materials, such as the AS, and would have an annual up-date;

- elsewhere the AR was being being sent to schools with a covering letter suggesting discussion by heads and governors.

But in other cases the weight of opinion seemed uncertain or cynical about the usefulness of disseminating the SACRE report to schools:

- in one LEA the AR was circulated to churches and schools, but the inspector doubted if schools would take much notice;

- another was uncertain, if it were circulated, what impression it would give and felt it better to have a briefing meeting;

- elsewhere an adviser was reluctant to send more paper to schools, especially as he wanted to communicate the ideas of the SACRE. The AR would be used in meetings and for public relations via the press, but not INSET;

- another did not regard the purpose of the AR to stimulate schools—there were other means — even though it was recognized as a potential tool in other LEAs.

Most interviewees viewed the SACRE AR as raising and sharpening the profile of the SACRE itself, although some were cautious about its image:

- one thought ERA and SACRE had certainly raised the profile of RE and CW in the LEA but that the local awareness of SACRE was as a political as much as a religious body [*educational not mentioned*].

At the same time many saw the SACRE and its AR as a fillip for RE:

- to be taken up by the local research and development unit which included teacher advisers on secondment;

- to add to weight of opinion about RE as a shortage subject in terms of staffing and timetabling;

- by dealing with INSET and ITT and through circulation to local teacher training colleges to have a practical link with staff development and potential spin off in terms of local teacher shortage.

167

In sum, one interviewee in a Metropolitan LEA, who regarded the SACRE's fairly extensive AR as valuable, saw its use as:

'informative for those outside [the area]. *Locally, it will help schools know that SACRE exists, what it is doing and what is happening generally in RE and CW. Hopefully it will raise the status of SACRE and of the kinds of issues it will be seen to be dealing with.'*

Availability

Although ERA specified that SACREs should produce an AR, no guidance appears to have been given about the due date for the first or subsequent reports. A few advisers queried this in interview. In practice most SACREs appear to have related production of their first report to the first full year of the operation of the SACRE — which was variable and in some cases well after the dates of establishment required by ERA (see p.22). Some SACREs' first reports might relate to a time scale in excess of one year. Indeed, it is possible that the very existence of the inquiry served as a reminder of the need for a report and its circulation.

An issue associated with availability of the first AR was uncertainty about its status vis à vis the local Education Committee and whether it needed approval by this body prior to publication and circulation. Once again practice seemed likely to vary: whilst some interviewees were unsure of the procedure or its significance, a few indicated Education Committee approval would be necessary; many thought it would be at least politic for the Committee to receive the report prior to wider dissemination; but others queried this given the high representation of elected members of Education Committee on SACRE and, for some, the Chair of Education and of SACRE in one person. The latter was sometimes seen as significantly supportive for RE. Some respondents, however, perceived the potential political value of the SACRE's report and its business appearing as an agenda item for Education Committee, even though matters arising for discussion were more likely to be dealt with by elected members than the LEA's officers, let alone the RE adviser/inspector.

Of the 28 LEAs where interviews were conducted: five SACREs had already published their ARs, the earliest dating from April 1990; seven were expected to publish by the end of the summer term; in 14 cases availability was anticipated during the autumn, or at the latest by December 1990; in two cases likely publication date was unknown. By the end of September 1990 a total of 20 SACRE ARs, covering their first year of operation, were in hand and by December 1990, 37. Subsequently an analysis of 79 ARs, available by the end of January 1991, was undertaken by NCC (1991).

SACREs: Present and Future

In concluding the interview RE advisers and inspectors were invited to reflect and comment on constraints on and promising lines of development of the role and function of SACRE in its initial year of operation. As a context for their remarks many respondents were concerned to point out that it was *'early days yet'* in the life of the SACRE and wanted to link their perceptions with general concerns about RE and its status. Many RE advisers/inspectors were anxious about the standing of RE in relation to other humanities subjects and perceived that RE, although part of the basic curriculum, was being treated differently from other curriculum areas, and was not receiving the same attention in schools as subject areas covered by National Curriculum documentation. Additionally, some pointed to financial constraints on RE and hence of development through advisory support and INSET, which, in some cases were low level. INSET for CW was a particular current concern. Despite the evident commitment of these advisers/inspectors to RE (even when it was only one of their responsibilities), in practice it was clear that they did not regard RE as having parity with other areas of the curriculum.

Analysis of advisers'/inspectors' descriptions of constraints on and promising lines of development of their local SACRE revealed **a central pervasive theme —that of the nature of authority and influence of the SACRE which was, as yet, emerging.** It was, moreover, highly variable in different LEAs and the response of advisers/inspectors was, correspondingly, differentiated. The authority and influence of SACRE locally formed the backdrop for respondents' perceptions of constraints on SACRE and its promising lines of development and may be treated here as an area of overlap between a review of issues primarily seen as constraints and reported achievements to date, future needs or strengths upon which to build.

It was interesting, but not surprising, to find that no SACRE, LEA or RE adviser/inspector had thought seriously about evaluating the operation of the SACRE (see p.159). However, it might not seem unreasonable to consider the effectiveness of the SACRE in relation to the effectiveness of RE in school. Being asked about constraints and promising lines of development at least gave RE advisers/inspectors a chance to reflect about SACRE's first year as a whole.

Constraints

Interestingly, four interviewees in the sample claimed that there were **no constraints** on the SACRE in their LEA: *'no hang-ups over SACRE locally — it can set its own agenda'*. Although SACREs varied immensely in the range and depth of their activities and concerns, these were among the most active; two of these SACREs had existed prior to 1989. All remaining interviewees mentioned at least one and usually several current constraints or tensions or foresaw particular difficulties.

The broad political context within which SACRE —itself a political body —was trying to operate was overtly mentioned by some. This could relate to:

> **central and local educational anomalies such as the position of RE** as part of the basic but not National Curriculum and implications for implementing local guidelines, resourcing advice and inspection on an LEA basis in the light of LMS;

> **the view of the status of SACRE taken locally** (see pp.177-178) which was often related to the priority given to RE and local financing of RE — for example, the CEO could be said to recognize the importance of SACRE but that constraints were in middle management and in implementing a budget for SACRE;

> or practical constraints could come from **the elected members on SACRE (Group D)** particularly with respect to views on the curriculum.

The internal characteristics and nature of SACRE itself

One or two interviewees felt **the internal structure of SACRE** with its four constituent groups was problematic in so far as this gives priority to religion when the majority of pupils, it was claimed, do not come from religious backgrounds; SACRE's structure also made it difficult to deal with cross-curricular or equal opportunities issues.

This was related to the **lack of educational backgrounds** or knowledge of education of some members: some found that religious representatives as committed faith members were not necessarily sympathetic to other views and that it was a tension having to deal with extreme viewpoints within SACRE; others experienced some elected members as ill-informed on educational matters and especially on the place of world religions in the RE curriculum and RE's contribution to multicultural education.

After some had experienced difficulties **getting SACRE together, getting**

to know each other and working together as a group was still evolving; some felt SACRE needed to act as a body, to be aware that as a group of people who consider RE important that there are issues to be addressed and that SACRE can have an effect; others thought that with only three meetings a year the amount of co-operation and work of SACRE was limited and that development had to take place over time.

In developing an identity a few thought SACRE's annual report or the production of RE or CW guidelines or documents with a thematic focus would help.

The role of SACRE vis à vis the LEA and schools

Role confusion of SACRE with the LEA was felt by some: there could be an overlap between the 'CEO imprint' and the 'SACRE imprint' and some felt that given insufficient time for RE at LEA level tasks should not be duplicated; several respondents saw SACRE as potentially divisive, as setting up a 'them' (SACRE) and 'us' (RE adviser/inspector) situation especially if, for example, the SACRE were to request a survey of RE provision or monitoring of CW; some relied on the checks and balances in the SACRE itself, others were more manipulative — allowing for example, SACRE to issue guidelines on RE but not on CW; others spoke of a partnership between SACRE and the LEA. But even where SACRE was viewed positively there could be underlying tensions and a hidden agenda, for example, on voluntary-aided schools, representation of Humanism and delays in production of guidelines on CW after encouragement had been given to schools to seek determinations.

Image of SACRE with schools: there was a perception that SACRE needed to develop its role and image in relation to schools, in particular the standing of SACRE and significance of its work and statements in relation to those of other national curriculum and assessment bodies. Some were apprehensive if, for example, SACRE were to issue strong advice on staffing and curriculum time for RE; others were hoping it *would* play such a role.

Limited scope, influence and authority to date

Perspectives varied immensely; one or two lamented that SACRE had not been moving as quickly as it should, but basically wanted it to '*rubber stamp*' the LEA's policy; more felt the SACRE was at present too much '*under the thumb of the LEA*'; others that the SACRE '*has no teeth*' and cannot be proactive. A few felt that it would be premature to expand the role of the SACRE given the local context of RE, e.g. that a limited agenda with regard to oversight of AS was enough; some noted that the SACRE *'has potential but only as an advisory body'*; others would have liked the SACRE to be more aware of its powers, to have a larger influence, for example on the status of RE and to push the LEA more, as in some cases it had begun to do (see p.175) for support and resourcing for RE.

Promising Lines of Development

Several RE advisers/inspectors, rather than seeing the influence and authority of SACRE as a constraint, chose to perceive these as promising lines of development, among its achievements to date. They also reflected on the SACRE's own needs for development and ways in which its strengths could be enhanced. Again many interviewees pointed to more than one way in which it was felt SACRE showed promise.

Developing SACRE's scope, influence and authority

Although most interviewees believed SACREs were **not yet aware of their full power** many saw them as a potential force for good for RE. The local context was integrally related to future developments. One or two advisers saw *'no scope for change - its a question of keeping it amused'*; some counselled a *'softly, softly'* approach for although it was currently *'caring within a lawful framework'* it was also *'a dormant volcano'* which could become more active; others already saw SACRE *'flexing its political muscles'*.

RE advisers/inspectors were very divided about how proactive and influential they wished SACRE to be — views often related to their own status and influence within the LEA. One whose own appointment had resulted from pressure applied by SACRE to the LEA — partly because the SACRE had perceived an adviser as necessary to its own functioning — saw the benefits of having members of Education Committee on SACRE; others were considering their own tactics as to how SACRE could best be used to serve what they judged to be in the interests of RE, and what priority to give to SACRE amongst their other duties and responsibilities.

Essentially RE advisers/inspectors were concerned with the balance of authority and influence over RE locally — *'that the LEA should not put power into the hands of the SACRE yet that the SACRE should not be "under the LEA thumb"'*. One summed it up: *'if the SACRE takes itself*

172

seriously and is treated seriously it could have a great influence'.

Raising the profile and status of RE

SACRE was described as *'good news for RE'* and *'a bonus for RE'*; the majority of interviewees saw it was supportive, helpful to the status of RE and raising its profile; in some LEAs it was regarded as having set up a new framework for RE, the AS and CW; in others it was seen as part of the partnership in education between communities, especially as many bodies were involved in it, and a source of strength to teachers and schools. Naturally advisers wanted the SACRE to be in tune with the professionals and not to *'cause upheavals'*. Some felt it had raised the awareness of advisory/inspectorial colleagues and the Education Committee about RE. Previously RE was *'nowhere'*, the LEA was aware of the deficit but had no obligation to respond. As another described it *'previously RE was a Cinderella subject and now its beginning to come to the ball'*.

Looking to the **future role of SACRE**, RE advisers/inspectors identified several needs.

Communication within SACRE

Several advisers recognized the need to develop INSET for SACRE members in a variety of forms: in some cases it was claimed some Church representatives and minority ethnic representatives of religions other than Christianity needed to be encouraged to have the confidence to speak out in order to make SACRE a real debating forum; others felt the need to provide opportunities to explore SACRE members' knowledge of and views on RE, even though they were wary of uncovering some fundamentalist perspectives; some had plans for encouraging work in small groups alongside teachers on the development of RE policy; others mentioned inter-LEA INSET for SACRE members as useful for raising awareness of working procedures and strategies of influence.

Communication with the LEA and schools

Many advisers perceived the need to develop contacts between SACRE and LEA and schools to enhance mutual appreciation of roles and approaches. Where visits of SACRE members to schools had occurred these were felt to be very beneficial. Interestingly, whereas some advisers wanted more communication between SACRE and schools to raise consciousness in schools of the place of RE and greater concern for delivery and outcomes, others, by contrast, wanted the SACRE invited to schools to see examples of good practice in order to inform its thinking. A few interviewees pointed to a more receptive climate and closer partnership between educational institutions and changing perceptions on the part of some teachers who were initially suspicious of SACRE's role. One or two with a long-standing SACRE knew that schools felt they were receiving advice and support.

Communication between SACRE and the wider communities

Some advisers, because of the composition of SACRE, saw considerable potential for '*building bridges*' between different communities in the locality: one adviser in a '*white highlands*' LEA envisaged the potential for communicating about RE by SACRE members working out a consensus on RE reporting back to their respective constituencies; another in a multiracial urban location saw the potential for community relations with the more active involvement of members of SACRE in schools to raise awareness of the dimensions of several world faiths; another adviser in a County LEA with representatives of religions other than Christianity in two towns had plans for building a partnership with faith communities by seeking sponsorship for a community education project: through a RE resource centre this would link the SACRE, faith communities and schools in the educational process of trying to work toward a common view of the substance of RE and offer opportunities to explore current educational processes in teaching and learning in the school context.

SACRE's Advice, Action, Status and Influence

In confirming promising lines of development interviews with RE advisers/inspectors and ARs of the SACREs in the sample revealed several aspects of local and national policy and practice in RE and CW which were of sufficient concern for some SACREs to issue strong advice or recommendations or to take action. In so doing, issues in respect of channels for communicating advice or recommendations were raised. These, in turn related to local support for RE and the views of the RE adviser/inspector about the SACRE's role.

SACRE's local recommendations focussed on RE, CW, INSET and advisory staffing.

RE. There was evidence that several SACREs had recommended an ASC should be set up to review the AS. A few SACREs had expressed concern or made recommendations to the LEA about aspects of RE relating to staffing, teaching time, exam entries, INSET, resources, subject parity and status. For example:

one SACRE had put down a motion for Education Committee about provision for RE and percentage of school time;

another had been critical of the LEA about the status of RE;

in an LEA where RE had had a low profile for many years SACRE had taken a strong line on the need for INSET in relation to the new AS, teaching time, parity of RE with other subjects, resources and status of RE;

an established SACRE made several explicit recommendations in its AR — for example, that there should be RE specialists in all secondary schools and that all secondary pupils should have one hour of RE per week — and expressed concern about the number of exam entries for RE.

CW. Most SACREs had been much exercised about the nature of and practices in CW; some had taken a proactive approach, for example:

one had set up its own working party to draft a statement of policy for schools and suggestions for practice, establish criteria for determinations and produce an application form;

another had issued a statement condemning the Education Committee's letter encouraging Muslims to withdraw their children from CW and expressing support for schools in collective not corporate worship;

several voiced concern about the need for INSET for CW: for example, in one case a proposal to Education Committee resulted in such INSET for senior management.

INSET was generally perceived as a key area for resourcing to support delivery of RE and CW:

several SACREs were reported to be *'badgering'* their Education Committees for more INSET support for RE; in one or two cases this was linked to funding for RE Centres, especially where resourcing under Section 11 funding was shortly to cease;

Advisers and Advisory Teachers. Recommendations mostly focussed on the need for advisory personnel:

a few SACREs had successfully persuaded Education Committees of the need to appoint a full-time RE adviser or ATRE where there were previous gaps or additional perceived needs; in one LEA SACRE had challenged the new advisory structure and *'prodded'* the LEA for a full-time RE Adviser; elsewhere SACRE's disquiet and dissatisfaction was voiced about discontinuation of part-time ATREs (in favour of history and geography) with consequent delay in the implementation of the new AS, concern about

of RE and any influence was likely to lack the backing of resources. Moreover, the implications of LMS at school level for a basic curriculum subject under local but not national guidelines and monitoring have yet to be fully perceived.

The status of SACRE

For the majority of LEAs SACRE was a new body and was still in the process of being realized. Even those SACREs existing prior to 1988 were being reshaped to function in line with the direction of ERA. Yet there were signals that SACREs were learning to compete with other national curricular changes and to win or maintain status locally. In this the position and views of the RE adviser/inspector were critical as to whether the SACRE was regarded as an integral, influential and supportive body working for the interests of RE, to lead or be in partnership with the LEA, or another quango to be bypassed, mollified or suppressed. At this early stage in the life of SACREs, when there are signs of renewed searching after the religious and spiritual in the life of the nation, struggling to come to terms with its multicultural, multiethnic, multiracial character, there were already promising indications: for the profile of RE; for its contribution to education for all; for dialogue between religious and secular communities about fundamental beliefs and values; and for assisting positive community relations. As a unique statutory body it deserves recognition and support for a status commensurate with the significance of these formal and informal educational endeavours.

References

ASSOCIATION OF RELIGIOUS EDUCATION ADVISERS AND INSPECTORS (1989a). *Directory of LEA Religious Education Advisers and Inspectors 1989-90.*

ASSOCIATION OF RELIGIOUS EDUCATION ADVISERS AND INSPECTORS (1989b). *Religious Education for Ages 5 to 16/18. Attainment and Assessment Interim Consultative Report.* Report of a Working Party. July 1989.

BRITISH HUMANIST ASSOCIATION (1990). *Standing Together.* Advice for Teachers Wishing to Preserve Shared Values Assemblies. BHA Briefing. London: BHA.

COPLEY, T., PRIESTLEY, J., WADMAN, D. and CODDINGTON, V. (1990). *A FARE Deal for RE.* The Interim Report of the FARE Project. Exeter University, School of Education.

COX, E. and CAIRNS, J. M. (1989). *Reforming Religious Education.* The Religious Clauses of the 1988 Education Reform Act. Bedford Way Series. London: Kogan Page in association with the Institute of Education; University of London.

FREE CHURCH FEDERAL COUNCIL (1989). *Annual Report.* London: FCFC.

FREE CHURCH FEDERAL COUNCIL (1990). *Collective Worship in County Schools.* A Guide to Principles and Practice. London: FCFC.

GREAT BRITAIN. DEPARTMENT OF EDUCATION AND SCIENCE (1989a). *The Education Reform Act 1988: Religious Education and Collective Worship.* Circular No 3/89. 20th January, 1989. London: DES.

GREAT BRITAIN. DEPARTMENT OF EDUCATION AND SCIENCE (1989b). *Ethnically-based Statistics on School Pupils.* Circular No. 16/89. London: DES.

GREAT BRITAIN. DEPARTMENT OF EDUCATION AND SCIENCE (1989c). *Agreed Syllabuses and Religious Education: The Influence of the Agreed Syllabus on Teaching and Learning in Religious Education in Three Local Education Authorities.* Report by HMI. London: DES.

GREAT BRITAIN. DEPARTMENT OF EDUCATION AND SCIENCE (1989d). *Length and Control of School Sessions.* Draft Circular, 8.5.89. London: DES.

GREAT BRITAIN. DEPARTMENT OF EDUCATION AND SCIENCE (1990). *Management of the School Day.* Circular No. 7/90. 4.7.90. London: DES.

GREAT BRITAIN. STATUTES (1988). *Education Reform Act 1988.* Chapter 40. London: HMSO.

GREAT BRITAIN. STATUTORY INSTRUMENTS (1989). *Education, England and Wales. The Education (School Curriculum and Related Information) Regulations.* 1989. No.954. London: HMSO.

HULL, J.M. (1989). *The Act Unpacked.* The Meaning of the 1988 Education Reform Act for Religious Education. Birmingham Papers in Religious Education No 1. University of Birmingham and Christian Education Movement.

LODGE, B. (1990). 'Controversies within the meaning of the Act', *Times Educational Supplement,* 2.11.90, p.13.

MARRATT, H. (1990). Analysis of SACREs in England, February 1990. Unpublished paper for Free Church Federal Council Education Committee.

MUSLIM EDUCATIONAL TRUST (1989a). *What Can Muslims Do? Education Reform Act, 1988. Compulsory Christian Worship and Christian Religious Education (RE) in Schools.* April 1989. London: MET.

MUSLIM EDUCATIONAL TRUST (1989b). *Religious Education, Collective Worship and the Education Reform Act 1988. Practicality and Reality. A Memorandum to Muslim Parents.* December 1989. London: MET.

NATIONAL ASSOCIATION OF HEADTEACHERS (1989). *Education Reform Act 1988. Guidance Notes. Religious Education and Collective Worship.* Haywards Heath: NAHT.

NATIONAL CURRICULUM COUNCIL (1991). *Analysis of SACRE Reports, 1991.* York:NCC.

NATIONAL UNION OF TEACHERS (1989). *Education Reform Act 1988. Religious Education and Collective Worship.* Guidance and Information for Teacher Governors, Headteachers and School Representatives. London: NUT.

REGIONAL RE CENTRE (MIDLANDS) (1989). *Attainment in RE. A Handbook for Teachers.* Birmingham: Regional RE Centre (Midlands), Westhill College.

REGIONAL RE CENTRE (MIDLANDS) (1991). *Assessing, Recording and Reporting RE.* Birmingham: Regional RE Centre (Midlands), Westhill College.

RELIGIOUS EDUCATION COUNCIL OF ENGLAND AND WALES (1989a). *Handbook for Agreed Syllabus Conferences, SACREs and Schools.* The Report of a Working Party. Summer 1989. Available from: The Chairman (Dr. B. Gates), REC, St Martin's College, Bowerham, Lancaster, LA1 3JD.

RELIGIOUS EDUCATION COUNCIL OF ENGLAND AND WALES (1989b). *Religious Education. Annual Report from SACREs. Guidelines Towards the Format and Contents of the Annual Report from a Standing Advisory Council on Religious Education.* Lancaster: REC.

SECONDARY HEADS ASSOCIATION (1989). *Collective Worship.* Leicester: SHA.

TAYLOR, M. J. (1989). *Religious Education, Values and Worship.* LEA Advisers' Perspectives on Implementation of the Education Reform Act 1988. Slough: NFER/REC.

WHITE, J. (1990a). 'Fear of the godless', *Times Educational Supplement,* 29.6.90, p.62.

WHITE, J. (1990b). *Education Network Mailing No 9.* September, 1990, p.2.

Appendix 1 The Local Contexts of the Study

As an introductory part of the interview respondents were asked several questions about the local educational and religious context in order to provide background information in which to set the formation and work of the SACRE. Despite the diversity revealed, certain emerging factors and trends suggest that an overview may serve to indicate both the operational contexts for SACREs and **the state of RE in one-quarter of English LEAs.** Data can broadly be divided into two types: the profile of RE and other relevant factors.

The Profile of RE

Broadly and generally speaking the 28 LEAs in the sample could be divided, according to certain criteria, into those where the RE profile might be said to be low, medium or high. Such an assessment is impressionistic and composite, based on interviewees' responses in relation to:

- history of advisory support (status and time);
- history of the AS (e.g. recency, currency, relevance);
- INSET and evaluation (active working groups, variety of developmental work and monitoring);
- in-school provision (e.g. evidence in primary education, identifiability in Year 10 and 11 of secondary education).

On such criteria **approximately half of the LEAs could be said (some on interviewees' own admission) to have had a low profile for RE:**

for instance, one adviser, appointed during the last year, discovered that schools were often unaware of local RE guidelines dating from the early 80s, lacked primary expertise for RE and that the curricula of one or two secondary establishments had omitted RE for 10 or 15 years.

There were slightly more LEAs with a medium rather than a high RE profile. These were all supported by institutional status and resources as well as the efforts and enthusiasm of advisory staff and were usually undergirded by locally relevant and informed teacher-centred materials and a sense of local activity and interest. In addition, five LEAs in the sample had had AS which had achieved national dissemination — three in particular having been taken up by several other LEAs. Three LEAs had achieved an unwelcome national profile for RE with cases of complaint which were currently awaiting a decision of the Secretary of State (see e.g. Lodge, 1990). The considerable change in education as a whole was reflected in local approaches to RE, especially evident in new RE appointments, the transfer in some LEAs from advice to inspection, and in revision to the AS.

Title and Status of Interviewee

Overall about one-third of interviewees had reference to RE in their title. The 31 interviewees ranged from ATRE to Senior Inspector with a complete spectrum of titles, some with little or no apparent reference to RE, although this was part of their responsibility: ATRE (3), AT Primary (1), Adviser RE (5), General Adviser RE/Multicultural Education (MCE) (2), Specialist Adviser Humanities (1), General Adviser Humanities (2), Secondary Education Adviser (1), Senior Adviser Primary (1), Senior Advisory Officer (1), General Inspector RE (4), General Inspector RE/MCE (1), General Inspector Humanities (4), Senior Inspector Humanities (1), Primary (1), Co-ordinator Interfaith Centre (1), Assistant Education Officer (1), Principal Education Officer (1). At least one was also ordained.

Gender

Twenty-one of the interviewees were male (nine each in Counties and Metropolitan Boroughs, three in London Boroughs) and ten were female (four in Counties, three each in London Boroughs and Metropolitan Districts).

Time in LEA and with Direct Curriculum Responsibility for RE

With few exceptions interviewees with direct curriculum responsibility for RE (29) had been in the LEA for the same length of time as in their present post. At the time of interview length of time with RE responsibility ranged from one month to 22 years. As many as ten interviewees (in three Counties, four London Boroughs and three Metropolitan Boroughs) had been appointed to their present post since ERA. A further ten had five years or less experience in post.

Interviewees' Responsibilities and Time for RE

Analysis of responsibilities confirmed previous findings (Taylor, 1989) that relatively few RE advisers/inspectors had responsibility for RE alone, but they expected to be giving more time to RE and explicitly to setting up and and servicing the SACRE. **Among these interviewees only two ATRE had full-time responsibility for RE. In addition to RE, all other interviewees had major responsibilities with schools for at least one of the following: pastoral work, inspection, or advisory support for other curriculum areas.**

> One respondent had for three years been employed half time by the LEA and half time by a local college of higher education but was moving to a full-time RE post (80 per cent RE, 20 per cent general) from September 1990.

Several interviewees reported changes within the LEA from advisory to inspection teams; in some cases current local emphasis on inspection could vie with time for RE so that the subject link through the SACRE was sometimes welcomed. Some with mainly general school or other curricular duties in addition to RE did not have a defined percentage of time formally allocated to RE — it depended on priorities. Those with a percentage of time variously

183

estimated it as less than five per cent *'the Director told a recent meeting of SACRE I do it in my spare time'* to half time. For example:

- one General Inspector Humanities had a 70 per cent generalist role and 30 per cent Humanities which gave priority to History and Geography over RE;
- a Specialist Adviser for Humanities brief ranged from 5—18+ over Geography, History, RE, Business Education and Social Studies;
- three had joint responsibility for RE and MCE.

Although some claimed more time had been spent on RE because of SACRE and its political context, given the responsibilities of some for core areas of the National Curriculum, RE time must have been at a premium. Moreover, LEAs with RE advisers/inspectors with little time for RE did not necessarily have additional ATRE support. Two interviewees had significant roles within SACRE, but no direct responsibility for RE.

Support of Advisory Teacher(s) for RE

One-quarter of the LEAs (7) had no ATRE.

One-quarter had a part-time ATRE (ranging from 0.5 — 0.8 full-time equivalent). The ATRE was sometimes also an advisory teacher for Humanities, or in two cases was shared with CEM, other LEAs and colleges of higher education.

Just over one-quarter (8) of LEAs had one full-time ATRE. In one case the post was half funded by one of the local dioceses and the LEA was currently seeking to establish another post in this way. Some of these posts were secondments.

Four LEAs reported new ATRE appointments from September 90 or January 91; but two or three noted that expansion was not allowed because of budgeting restrictions or lack of suitable applicants.

Only two LEAs had two ATREs: in one LEA both worked cross-phase, and according to geographical divisions, one focussed on INSET, the other on methods, resources and assessment; in the other LEA one focussed on curriculum, the other ran the RE centre.

An ATRE Role in SACRE

In nine LEAs there was no involvement of ATREs in SACRE, even when there was at least one part-time ATRE.

In two LEAs where the ATRE was being appointed involvement in SACRE was uncertain.

In two LEAs ATREs were LEA members of Group D of SACRE.

In three SACREs ATREs were members of SACRE in their own right — two as teachers' union representatives(Group C) and one as a member of Group A.

Two ATREs were co-opted to SACRE.

Five ATREs attended SACRE as consultants or representatives to advise and make comments and presentations.

In three SACREs other advisory teachers (Humanities, MCE and Secondary) attended SACRE.

In three cases the ATRE was in attendance as an observer only.

And in two SACREs the ATRE ran the SACRE and was its *dogs body'* and its clerk.

Agreed Syllabuses: Dates

Overall the ASs of the quarter of LEAs sampled spanned 46 years, from 1944 - 90 (Counties 1951-87; London Boroughs 1980-90; Metropolitan Boroughs 1944-89), as did those of the LEA circular respondents as a whole. The largest number of ASs (12) dated from 1980-5, with six each from the late 80s and the 1960s, three each from the 70s and 40s and one from the 50s. Three Metropolitan LEAs in one district each had at least two syllabuses 'in use' locally; these dated from before the local government reorganization of 1974 and in two cases back to the 40s — the latter in these and another Metropolitan LEA being difficult to *'lay hands on'*. All these LEAs had currently constituted ASCs to revise the AS. Elsewhere one AS was published about the same time as ERA and two had been reviewed and published since ERA, in 1989 and 90.

Orientation of Agreed Syllabuses

The time scale represented by the AS in the LEAs sampled covers four main periods and types of AS: 1940s-50s, 1960s, mid-70s, early 80s, as follows:

1940s-50s: AS is basically related to the Old Testament, New Testament and Church History, or as one interviewee put it *'almost entirely **Biblical** with reference to saints, missionaries and heroes and with only a cautious reference to other world religions for the sixth form — grey, drab, badly printed and half-hearted'*. However, two AS for the early 80s were little changed, with only token reference to other faiths and little of relevance to young people's experiences.

1960s: one County AS, which was also in use by four Metropolitan LEAs, advocated a **thematic** age-related approach based on a Judaeo-Christian heritage. This attempted to take account of observable rather than experiential features of religions. Despite the period of immigration, no attention was paid to the inter-faith network or religions beginning to be represented locally.

Mid-70s: another AS from a County in the sample which had been widely influential and was currently in use by four other sampled LEAs (three County and one Outer London) concentrated on **processes of developing concepts, skills and**

185

attitudes rather than on a content-led objective study of religion. It emphasized belief and practice in religious traditions and the child's own quest for meaning. The AS offered a framework of aims, objectives and illustrations of basic principles. Other LEAs which adopted this AS in the early 80s sometimes added their own aims which could be confusing. The original AS was not subsequently always felt to be in harmony with local MCE policies; nor did it mention sixth-form RE.

Early 80s: with increasing recognition of a multifaith society a key issue for ASs of the 80s was the balance to be given to the study of Christianity and other world religions. A range existed.

One County LEA's ASC drew up an AS to reflect the local situation — *'there was no point in having an Agreed Syllabus from one of the London authorities which was heavily into multicultural education'*. The AS offered aims and age-related objectives and subsequently a three-volume handbook suggested thematic approaches for work schemes. It *'envisaged that the content of Schemes of Work derived from the syllabus will be drawn largely from the study of Christianity in its many forms'* though *'an exclusively Christian content could not do justice to the nature of the subject'*. The AS suggested **'an introduction'** to other world religions which could **'broaden and enrich the reflective processes and develop cross-cultural and religious knowledge, respect and understanding.'** Interestingly, two members of this ASC gave influential advice on the drafting of ERA.

By contrast, another AS of the early 80s took a deliberately **multifaith approach,** specifying the study of six world religions, and also **supporting faith nurture or adherence as such** in a school context: *'the aim is to help young people to achieve a knowledge and understanding of religious insights, beliefs and practices, so that they are able to continue in, or come to, their own beliefs and respect the right of other people to hold beliefs different from their own. Whilst it is taken for granted that Christianity features clearly, the syllabus also provides for teaching about other important faiths which are held in contemporary British society. It is no part of the responsibility of the county school to promote any particular religious standpoint.'*

Other ASs in multiethnic areas have **attempted to put world faiths on an equal par with Christianity** as part of a MCE/equal opportunities approach. One such asserted as a statement of intent that *'the major religions Hinduism, Islam, Judaism, Sikhism as well as Christianity have an equal right to the maintenance of their distinctive identities and loyalties of culture, language, religions and custom; furthermore their rich diversity should be seen as contributing to the life of the whole community.'* It aimed to provide equality of respect for individual faith believers.

Such ASs start from an empirical reflection of varied faith backgrounds in local schools whilst recognising the need to establish broad principles which can be interpreted as applicable in every school. The aim is that children from each faith background and none should be able to appreciate mainstream culture and the value of each faith. Recent ASs have continued to espouse such positive principles whilst the political context of other LEAs has allowed only bland implicit recognition of the value and contributions of faiths other than Christianity.

Agreed Syllabus Revisions

In over one-third of the sample LEAs ERA had proved a catalyst to reconsideration or review of the AS. But in addition to recent legislation there were several other **reasons** (and often in each LEA) leading to revision. These included:

age of AS or lack of a current viable AS relating to the whole LEA, especially in those authorities which had not had an AS since local government reorganization in 1974;

changes in local populations, with some localities becoming multiethnic and having representatives of world religions other than Christianity; a scripturally-based AS mentioning saints of the NE adopted 45 years ago is no longer appropriate to a multifaith West Midlands community or the educational experiences of young people; nor does it reflect schools' value statements for MCE or the educational aims of the LEA;

perceptions of **the need for more attention to be given to content in the AS,** for several reasons: to be of direct assistance to teachers, especially non-specialists in primary education who lack specific training; to clarify implicit and explicit RE and its distinctive nature; to provide for continuity and progression in a clear age-related structure; and to link with KSs, ATs and AAs in areas of the National Curriculum.

Several LEAs have recently been, or are currently actively engaged in, AS revisions (see also p.78). Local political, educational and religious contexts as well as the orientation of the extant AS make for different starting points; indeed, some ASCs appear to be revising the type of AS to which others still aspire; some LEAs and advisers are moving at a slower pace through a preparatory phase; whilst others hope that the local response will enable existing ASs to be accommodated within the spirit of ERA.

Certain **procedures** were common to revising the AS (see also pp.124-127):

setting up the ASC: some had more or less transferred the SACRE membership, usually with some additional teachers and occasionally other faith members; in one LEA, where the recent ASC had preceded the SACRE, thorough consultations were undertaken: contacts were attempted with all local places of worship, where necessary writing in languages other than English and visiting communities with interpreters in order to arrive at a representative conference;

most LEAs prospected other ASs from relevantly similar areas or where there was some prior contact to assess their applicability, whether an AS might be adopted or to what extent some ASs might be adapted;

many ASCs were linked to working parties of teachers or members of sub-groups of the ASC were divided into working groups with teachers; when established one ASC asked the local RE advisers to provide it with INSET which helped work on the AS aims, was informative on good practice for RE and set a good climate. Elsewhere an adviser was planning two residentials to inaugurate the work and one day each month for meeting, with teacher cover;

explicit budgetary support was important otherwise it could lead to suspension of work and delay, as in one LEA; yet financial provision was by no means certain; by contrast, elsewhere LEATGS money had been used to provide a co-ordinator for the ASC to administer the working groups and visit schools;

many ASC groups were said to be cordial and well intentioned and there was an impression that the work was exciting; however, wider events such as 'the Rushdie Affair' could sometimes have local repercussions: in one LEA, despite good local practice in community relations, the inspector's explanation of the need for unanimity on the AS and the previous full participation of Muslims in the ASC, as a gesture they boycotted the meeting which voted for the AS as a whole although they had previously agreed on its three separate parts. Fortunately, the ASC was quorate and the AS could be adopted;

most ASCs seemed to operate to a fairly flexible timetable often aiming at completion within a year; others were operating over a longer period and there were variations in the extent of formal consultation with the full ASC and with schools; some ASs were undergoing a pilot or trial phase with schools prior to adoption.

Opinions was divided about the form of the AS; some wanted the AS as an outline *'mapping central features'* but without prescriptive workschemes, giving teachers the flexibility to flesh out the syllabus and own it in their school context; but others appeared to want something more prescriptive *'a real working document'* which would offer practical classroom help on how to construct curriculum units.

Local Monitoring of RE

Nearly all LEAs in the sample undertook local monitoring of RE in some way, although this was unlikely to be subject specific at primary level. RE was most often included in general inspections (12 LEAs), using checklists which could include CW; quite often schools were asked for information about RE as part of their school development (7) or curriculum (2) returns; sometimes schools identified their own areas for review and RE was quite often chosen for inspection and advice. Where RE advisers or advisory teachers were involved (9) monitoring was combined with advisory support. Some saw it as part of the role of SACRE to press for inspection but SACRE's own involvement in this area was much more controversial (see pp.91-92).

Other Relevant Local Factors

Several other local factors were found to be particularly relevant to the formation and operation of SACRE. These included the local religious and ethnic composition and the significance of the voluntary sector, about which questions were asked in interview. During the study educational administrative and managerial structures and the political context also emerged as key issues.

Educational Management

LEAs have different management styles and relationships with local schools — though the nature and quality of these arrangements have been difficult to describe or evaluate. Current implementation of local management of schools (LMS) has engendered reappraisal and uncertainty about LEA—school relationships and services. The SACRE as a statutory body and RE as part of the basic but not National Curriculum form further layers interposed in the changing administrative and curriculum structure. In interview RE advisers/inspectors indicated various models of local educational management and in relation to RE, along a spectrum from fairly tight centralized direction and control to those which claimed local devolution to schools was part of established practice. Nevertheless interviewees' remarks often suggested an implicit tension in LEA-school relations between such matters as inspection and advice, direction and support. Indeed, this could be compounded by political and church pressures from the SACRE.

> For example, in one SACRE it was reported that the Labour party and Church of England representatives wished to have implemented a specified hourage for RE, whereas the LEA's approach was for schools to set policy which advisers/inspectors monitor. The LEA's central policies are not couched in 'must'/'should' language, though schools have a duty to identify RE and CW provision, even if curriculum design made this difficult.

Political Complexion

Table 10 sets out the political control of LEAs since May 1990. Labour-led LEAs predominated amongst non-respondents to the circular. Given that, and although it was not a sampling criterion, the overall interview sample (25 per cent of LEAs) was fairly representative in terms of political control. (Conservative LEAs were slightly over-represented, especially in Counties, and Labour LEAs were under-represented in London Boroughs.)

The political complexion of the local council and especially the dominant political party often had a significant influence on the SACRE, both in terms of its membership and its policies. In Group D elected members could include representatives of all three major political parties or only the dominant party. Electoral changes in local administration (which in a few cases occurred during the research in May, 1990) could have implications for the size of SACRE groups and representation of constituent bodies. The influence of local party politics was evident in Conservative, Labour and hung councils and their approaches to RE and the SACRE.

Most SACREs had a Chair from Group D, the LEA (78 per cent of 81 circular respondents giving appropriate information; 82 per cent of 28 LEAs in the interview sample). Given an analysis of political control by LEA type (see Table 10), there did not appear to be an atypical pattern of party political control

Table 10   Political control of LEAs (since May, 1990)

LEA Type	N	Political Control			
		Conser-vative	Labour	Liberal Democrat	No Overall Control
Counties					
Total	39	16	8	1	14
Circular Respondents	33	15	5	1	12
Interview Sample	12	6	2	0	4
London Boroughs					
Total	32	12	14	3	3
Circular Respondents	25	10	10	2	3
Interview Sample	6	3	1	0	2
Metropolitan Boroughs					
Total	36	2	31	0	3
Circular Respondents	30	2	26	0	2
Interview Sample	10	1	9	0	0
Total LEAs	107	30	54	4	19
Circular Respondents	88	27	42	3	16
Interview Sample	28	10	13	0	5

Source: Political Control of LEAs provided by DES Library Public Enquiry Unit

in LEAs whose SACREs were not chaired by a member of Group D. Of the 18 cases where the SACRE Chair was not from Group D half were in Labour-led and mostly Metropolitan LEAs (seven, plus one County and one London Borough). The other half were divided between Conservative LEAs (two Counties, three London Boroughs) and local authorities where there was no overall party political control (two Counties, one London Borough and one Metropolitan Borough). There was no particular association of political control of the LEA and Group A, B, C or ex-group membership of the Chair. The SACREs of five of the LEAs in the interview sample had Chairs other than from Group D: three Counties (two Group A; LEA: one Conservative, one no overall control; one Group B; LEA: no overall control); one London Borough (Group A; LEA: Labour); and one Metropolitan Borough (Group B; LEA: Labour).

The predominance of Chairs of SACRE from Group D (pp.58-59) indicated that SACRE was perceived as a political body and could be politicized in its dealing with controversial issues. For example:

- in one highly charged SACRE in an authority where a *'left-wing'* Labour group held the balance of power some of those elected members were unsympathetic to RE and had suggested a campaign of withdrawal by parents on the grounds that RE should not be part of the curriculum in a secular school;

- interviewees in both Labour and Conservative authorities, especially those where the minority ethnic population was low or only in certain areas, reported that multicultural and race relations issues were contentious and that many elected members were not in favour of RE which included religions other than Christianity. Multifaith RE could not be 'upfront' but implicit and dependent on encouragement through advisory support.

Other examples are evident throughout the report.

Religious and Ethnic Composition

There was a variable local knowledge base about local religious groups and the size of minority ethnic groups and their religious affiliations. It was rare for local surveys of minority ethnic pupils to have been undertaken. Although knowledge was not systematic, the majority of interviewees had at least a broad awareness of local religious representation and minority ethnic groups. Indeed, about one-third of RE advisers/inspectors demonstrated detailed local knowledge. In the absence of accurate national and local data and although some interviewees were unable to estimate the proportion of minority ethnic population, the sample LEAs ranged from those with almost no minority ethnic population to those with more than 25 per cent. The breakdown was estimated as follows: eight LEAs less than five per cent, eight five-ten per cent, four ten-20 per cent, six 20-25 per cent, two more than 25 per cent. Few Counties had a minority ethnic population greater than ten per cent; conversely, the majority of London Boroughs had at least 20 per cent minority ethnic population; the range was represented in Metropolitan Boroughs. Even where the minority ethnic proportion of the population was low there could be diversity of ethnic background and religious affiliation. In Counties the minority ethnic population tended to be in county towns or small industrial towns; in Metropolitan Boroughs the minority ethnic population was often grouped in certain localities. A few interviewees commented on the high proportion of pupils from minority ethnic and religious groups in certain schools even when the minority ethnic population as a whole was relatively low. The following examples illustrate the overlap of *'principal religious traditions of the area'* and minority ethnic populations.

In a few LEAs Christianity was evidently the principal religious tradition: this could include many scattered non-conformist churches, so that SACRE members were more likely to be representative of churches in the county town than of the county as a whole; in one such LEA there was also a small but strong Muslim group (two-thirds white converts), members of a Buddhist order and a Baha'i group; by contrast, a predominantly Christian Metropolitan LEA had a large local Catholic population which included Irish Catholics.

One County LEA had an overall minority ethnic population of five to ten per cent, largely in two main towns, comprised of established and new communities of Bengali Muslims, Punjabi Sikhs, Gujerati Hindus, Italian Catholics, Iranian Muslims and white Muslim converts and an Iranian Baha'i group.

In one LEA the county town comprised a growing minority ethnic population of 30 per cent (60,000 plus Hindus, mostly of Gujerati origin, 20,000 plus Muslims and 12-15,000 Sikhs) spreading into the suburbs, though there were some predominantly Asian schools; with the exception of one small town the minority ethnic population in the remainder of the county was negligible.

In one Metropolitan Borough a local survey in 1987-8 revealed that almost 27 per cent of the school population was of Asian origin (23 per cent Muslim, two per cent Sikh, one per cent Hindu). Asian pupils were in the majority in 20 per cent of schools and absent from seven per cent. The dominant Muslim group is Sunni, predominantly Barelvis or Deobandi, but there are also mosques with Saudi Arabian connections and others which are Shia in orientation.

By contrast, one inner London authority had 50 per cent pupils of minority ethnic origin, at least half of Afro-Caribbean backgrounds. Correspondingly, the Black Pentecostal Church was most active, but the principal local religious traditions also include Sikhism, Islam (Sunni and Ahmadiyya), Buddhism and Judaism.

The Voluntary Sector

In most of the LEAs in the sample the voluntary sector was of some significance. A higher proportion of primary than secondary schools were voluntary aided or controlled. Some LEAs were said to have up to 50 per cent of primary schools in the voluntary sector. But where this was significant it was more likely for LEAs to have one-quarter or even one-third of such primary establishments. At secondary level it was unusual for more that a few schools to be voluntary aided or controlled, though in Metropolitan or London Boroughs these could form up to one-quarter of the secondary school provision. Although voluntary aided or controlled Church of England schools generally predominated, at secondary level there appeared to be proportionately more Roman Catholic schools, especially in Metropolitan and London Boroughs. One Metropolitan LEA was said to have half its primary and one-third of its secondary schools in the voluntary sector. Another had two Jewish voluntary-aided schools. Elsewhere, where one new voluntary-aided school had recently been set up, it was said that voluntary aided and controlled schools were *'becoming rare specimens'*.

Some LEAs fell in as many as four dioceses, each of which could have its own AS for RE in its voluntary schools. It appeared much more common for Church of England than Catholic schools to use the LEA's rather than the diocese's AS. One County AS included a preface by the Church of England Diocesan Director of Education alongside that of the CEO. A few RE advisers/inspectors reported close working relationships with both Church of England and Roman Catholic diocesan authorities. But generally the Catholics appeared to be more distant, not always participating in the ASC or SACRE, whereas it was quite usual for the Church of England Diocesan Board of Education to be represented in Group B. It was fairly common for RE INSET, mounted by the LEA, to be open and to include staff from the voluntary sector. Although a few RE advisers/inspectors reported that they were invited to visit voluntary aided or controlled schools, they were less likely to be requested to undertake an inspection.